GOING TO COLLEGE
IN THE SIXTIES

GOING TO COLLEGE
IN THE SIXTIES

JOHN R. THELIN
Foreword by Michael A. Olivas

Johns Hopkins University Press | *Baltimore*

© 2018 Johns Hopkins University Press
All rights reserved. Published 2018
Printed in the United States of America on acid-free paper
9 8 7 6 5 4 3 2 1

Johns Hopkins University Press
2715 North Charles Street
Baltimore, Maryland 21218-4363
www.press.jhu.edu

Library of Congress Cataloging-in-Publication Data

Names: Thelin, John R., 1947– author.
Title: Going to college in the sixties / John R. Thelin ; foreword by Michael A. Olivas.
Description: Baltimore : Johns Hopkins University Press, 2018. | Includes
    bibliographical references and index.
Identifiers: LCCN 2018007460 | ISBN 9781421426815 (hardcover : alk. paper) |
    ISBN 1421426811 (hardcover : alk. paper) | ISBN 9781421426822 (electronic) |
    ISBN 142142682X (electronic)
Subjects: LCSH: Education, Higher—United States—History—20th century. |
    Universities and colleges—United States—History—20th century. | College
    students—United States—History—20th century. | Nineteen sixties.
Classification: LCC LA227.3.T54 2018 | DDC 378.00973—dc23
LC record available at https://lccn.loc.gov/2018007460

A catalog record for this book is available from the British Library.

*Special discounts are available for bulk purchases of this book. For more information,
please contact Special Sales at 410-516-6936 or specialsales@press.jhu.edu.*

Johns Hopkins University Press uses environmentally friendly book materials, including
recycled text paper that is composed of at least 30 percent post-consumer waste, whenever
possible.

For my high school and college classmates and friends

CONTENTS

The Decade of Higher Education and the Summer of Love

I was recently watching television with my teenage niece, and she noticed how riveted I was on the show, a long-running syndicated do-it-yourself show about repairing households, and on the eager carpenter who was fixing a broken and weather-beaten door. She was feigning interest and was being nice because she loves me and we had just given her a check to help her with college expenses. She said, "Uncle Michael, why are you so interested in this show and that door? If you needed a door, wouldn't you just go buy a new one?"

Well, there is no good explanation of DIY wannabes, so I told her how I had repaired an old broken desk and a revolving bookcase, and inasmuch as she had seen them in our New Mexico home, she was impressed that I had lovingly labored over the projects in college, and that I had kept them all these years later. The truth is, I like any medium where I am taught a new skill, or learn something new about an old skill, like watching car mechanics these days with all their digital diagnostic tools, so different from the days when I changed my own oil and repaired some loose car part.

Reading John R. Thelin's newest work is like watching a master storyteller tell you stories about places you've never been but want to go see for yourself after an encounter with him. I still think that his *A History of American Higher Education* is the best primer ever written on college history, and his fascinating book on intercollegiate sports, *Games Colleges Play*, is among the best in that growing genre about a field where a nodding acquaintance with criminal law and antitrust law help. Not content to rest on those Johns Hopkins University Press masterworks, he has reached into a more personal store for this volume. Actually, let me rephrase that: it is his attic he has plundered, and we are all fortunate he has done so for our collective benefit.

I have always regarded California colleges as Oz, with beautiful campuses and the great faculty and students they attract and serve, the sheer size and heft of the system, and the generous taxpayers who have erected and maintained such a magnificent achievement—although they have been less generous since the 1970s, when tax rollbacks and public penury began to take their toll. I have even known University of California, Cal State, and California Community College leaders, and have served as a legal consultant and expert witness for them when I was called upon to do so.

But John Thelin's insider knowledge of them, and his relentless search for more insider knowledge about them, have been served up in a very specific American studies fashion by his looking at them in their glory days. Of course, he is focused not just on California institutions, as his eye has been caught by public colleges elsewhere. Not so much Texas, where I have labored for thirty-five years and which gets a bit of short shrift, but he captures what I remember about going to college in the 1960s, and he has consumed more data than I would have thought possible. Each chapter focuses upon a theme (admissions, knowledge production and dissemination, student activism, the college curriculum as seen through college catalogues, athletics, and a wistful concluding reconnection with the 1960s, in his invocation of UC's Clark Kerr's chapter called the "Future of the City of Intellect" from his influential 1963 book, *The Uses of the University*). As much as I admired Kerr's book, and have used it when I have taught my higher education law course and other courses, I always felt that it (and he) were deracinated. We served together when I held my first post-PhD research position, at Howard University; I attended law school at Georgetown at night and worked by day on equity research. He chaired the advisory board of my research institute, and I would have long talks with him about his life's work in the University of California—and about apples, his passion—and I asked him once why his Carnegie Commission had never undertaken a book on Mexican Americans and college going. His disappointing answer was that "Mexican American families do not encourage their children to go to college." Never mind that in my Mexican American family, of the ten children, we count six bachelor's, four master's, two PhDs, and two law degrees.

John's eye is on the 1960s, when there was only a small but growing cadre of students of color (then called "minority students" or "disadvantaged students"), so this subject is not his focus either, but there is more than enough scholarly material about virtually all other major postsecondary issues. Given his lifelong harvesting of this field, one would expect coverage on athletics, growing new campuses and establishing governance structures, and initiating new curricular offerings.

He does not disappoint. But his review of college curriculum over time, derived from his joyous reading of old catalogues, simply blew me away. I never would have seen fifty- and sixty-year-old course catalogues as so widespread and available a resource, perhaps because in today's versions they exist in the ether of online storage.

He has a painterly eye for vivid detail, as is revealed in my favorite chapter, on the admissions process for getting into colleges, especially high-status colleges. For example, he uses personal details about the pathways traveled from hardscrabble family backgrounds to college and then illuminated careers in public service (with stints in law teaching) for President Bill Clinton and Senator Elizabeth Warren, with whom I overlapped in my early career at the University of Houston Law Center. His is not a slow drive across the landscape, but a more rapid journey with many a stopping point for those of us who are on the ride with him, as in the brief stop in Little Rock, where he compresses the complex and well-documented White resistance to African American students enrolling in what they considered was their school: "A good example was located in a medium-sized city of about 105,000—this was Central High School in Little Rock, Arkansas, which was the focus of nationally televised news coverage of local resistance to racial desegregation in September 1957." On this drive, he anchors events in small and large vignettes, from the anxious waiting for admissions results (wanting to receive the thick envelope signaling acceptance) to the quotidian preparation for the Scholastic Aptitude Test in advantaged schools. I served a term as a trustee for the College Board, so I know these various rituals, and he captures them exactly.

Creating other Charles Kuralt moments is John's narrative device, evident throughout the book, for describing the agony and thrill of sports. Readers of his previous work on intercollegiate athletics know that he can describe and situate big-time sports, particularly football and the excesses associated with its practices, but instead, he chooses two different metaphors: Chris von Saltza achieved 1960 Olympic swimming glory but then enrolled at Stanford, which in its pre–Title IX era had no women's swimming team; and a Caltech sabotage of a Rose Bowl halftime show, where nerds surreptitiously took over the halftime card-turning program to (mis)spell the home team's planned choreographed messages (and all this before *Animal House*, where such tomfoolery would have earned the students a double-secret probation).

In each such synecdoche, Thelin layers example upon example, using nuance and small strokes to paint his larger landscape. Others have attempted the same techniques—hence his surprisingly large body of nostalgic literature about college going fifty year ago—but he, like other excellent narrators, is chockful of small and precise snippets and vignettes. Over many years, I have admired many American narrators, whose work mythologized a hapless car salesman whose best years had been his high school basketball prowess, or observed midwestern life through sad Norwegian bachelors and Lutherans in Lake Woebegone. To me, Thelin is the most accomplished storyteller of college life and the observations that flow from those days. Here, he focused on the most turbulent days of college going, and with his framework, he could just as easily follow up with the intervening decades. This would allow him to comment upon affirmative action, the rise of disability accommodations and LGBTQ rights, immigration and the internationalization of higher education, sexual assault and campus crime, how student free speech rights have morphed, and the other grand themes that are more in evidence since his lodestar decade. Of course, he has done a more staid and traditional version of this narrative in his *A History of American Higher Education*, so his fans, and I surely am one, might find an unlikely series here.

My measure of a good book is how intrinsically interesting it is, how much genuine and difficult engagement there is with readers, and how well it is written. To use the obvious sports metaphor, John Thelin can run, throw, and hit, making him the MVP of this scholarly competition. As someone who has spent most of his career in Houston, living by and mostly dying by the MLB Astros, who in 2017 won their first World Series in their fifty-five years of breaking hearts, I would like to see his next installation. Like the Astros, readers will see the rise of Latinos and the careful use of sports data analytics in the following decades. And John: How about some examples of rock 'n' roll music to set out the decades? I know from my many regular interactions with John that we share a love of the music of this period, and a particular fondness for his hometown Southern California heroes, The Beach Boys. You could name it "Be True to Your School."

Michael A. Olivas
William B. Bates Distinguished Chair in Law
University of Houston Law Center

Michael A. Olivas served as interim president of the University of Houston–Downtown, was chosen president of the Association of American Law Schools, and has a regular NPR show, *The Law of Rock and Roll*.

In 2014 a longtime colleague who taught at another university told her students, "I'm the last professor you will have who went to college in the 1960s."[1] The message for me was clear: now was the time to turn my focus as a historian to writing about higher education from 1960 to 1969. Prompted by my colleague's remark, I had to confront the realization that I had been avoiding writing about campus life of the 1960s because I found most accounts to be disappointing. Journalistic coverage often blurred the world of college students with sensationalized counterculture events such as the "summer of love" and "days of rage."[2]

I too am one of those "last professors who went to college in the 1960s." Having started high school in 1961 and graduated from college in 1969, I fit the demographic profile of faculty that journalists had been tracking for several years. In 2008, for example, Patricia Cohen wrote in the *New York Times* about how the 1960s were beginning to fade as liberal professors retired. She noted that the departure of this faculty cohort was "part of a vast generational change that is likely to profoundly alter the culture at American universities and colleges over the next decade."[3] Put another way, it marked the passage of a faculty cohort from membership in the American Association of University Professors to the American Association of Retired Persons.

This shift of aging professors from the AAUP to the AARP was not the whole story—or even the main story. An alternative observation for the 2008 *New York Times* article might have been how the 1960s were beginning to *blossom* as liberal professors retired. Going to college in the 1960s is *not* fading as a topic in the public forum today. It is now poised for reasonable reconsideration, freed from the polemics that were prevalent half a century ago. For college alumni of those years, short-term memory often was shaped by fractured recollections of being subjected day after day to extreme political ideologies. Many undergraduates were lured back and forth by rhetoric promoting false hopes and exaggerated despair. The barrage of disruptive events such as a free speech demonstration in

1963 or the burning of an ROTC (Reserve Officer Training Corps) building in 1969 kept them on guard and off balance. Today, scholars and students from several age groups can join to sort out the legacies that animated colleges and universities during that decade.

This was a wrenching period for American higher education and for American politics and society. Yet among those who were in college at the time, memories today veer from sharp conflicts to thoughtful reflections. Most alumni of the era remain grateful for the opportunities they had to go to college, as higher education then was considered a privilege, not an entitlement.

"Never the center without the spread"—a classic statisticians' warning to those who look at databases. This wisdom applies to historical interpretation as well as it does to statistical analysis. A great deal of attention justifiably gravitates to the "center" events, such as those at the University of California, Berkeley. I do devote coverage to Berkeley. After all, it was an exciting, important place. I leaven that coverage by looking also at the varieties of colleges and universities across the United States.

The statistician's caution about the center versus the spread also can be the lens through which changes are tracked at a college or university over the course of a decade. Differences within a campus and its numerous student subcultures are striking and call for historical coverage. Even at a radicalized campus, volatile student demonstrations coexisted with intercollegiate athletics, fraternities and sororities, student government, and the "business as usual" of a university. A campus usually provided traditional socialization into the state's business and political establishment as well as being a source of new activist leaders. Dissident faculty were campus colleagues of professors who received federal grants in fields ranging from applied physics devoted to weapons research to political science whose counterinsurgency analyses were funded by the Central Intelligence Agency. Including historical data about colleges and groups away from the center of disruption helps me present "Berkeley in a minor key" and shapes my writing to extend to historical study of the diverse mix of college students nationwide.

Today's college students and recent alumni who read about American higher education in the 1960s often exclaim to me, "Boy! Did you have it good! Low tuition, access to outstanding public and private universities, and genuine job prospects after graduation!" I think these are good points to compare and contrast the college experience over sixty years. My initial response is that many of the optimistic and generous plans for higher education put into place around 1960 eventually fell short and fell flat. They left many college students with unexpected problems and new questions. An exciting surprise for me was that reconstructing higher education of the 1960s increased my awareness of the distinctive challenges that college students face today and will face in the future.

ACKNOWLEDGMENTS

For this book project I listened a lot before I wrote. I have relied on colleagues and friends who brought both research excellence and insights to the topic of "going to college in the sixties." Katherine Chaddock, Michael A. Olivas, Dorothy Finnegan, Maresi Nerad, Linda Eisenmann, Bill Tierney, Gerald St. Amand, Terry Birdwhistell, Ralph Crystal, and Richard Trollinger contributed thoughtful comments and memoirs. Luther Spoehr's research on Brown University's curriculum reform of the late 1960s brought history to life. I owe special thanks to Kim Nehls, executive director of the Association for the Study of Higher Education (ASHE), for having provided the opportunity for a forum on the topic at the 2014 ASHE Conference in Washington, DC.

Three of my Brown University classmates, Alan W. Blazar, Fred Berk, and Richard Crocker, have engaged me in conversations about college for over half a century, starting with our freshman year in 1965. James Axtell, Bruce Leslie, and Stanley Katz bring historical depth to our frequent discussions about higher education, past and present. Peter C. Thelin, my older brother, who entered the University of California, Berkeley, as an undergraduate in 1963, introduced me to this remarkable campus and thoughtfully helped me explore its mysteries and marvels over many years. Alan DeYoung, my faculty colleague at the University of Kentucky, provided memoirs about himself and his classmates who in 1965 were members of the first entering class at the University of California, Santa Cruz.

Sharon Thelin took time to read my manuscript and provide careful editorial advice on transitions and clarity. She reminded me to extend the scope of the book to include college life in the South as an integral part of the story of higher education in this decade.

I appreciate the research support the Educational Policy Studies Department at the University of Kentucky has given me on this project. Doctoral student Laura R. Brown served as research assistant and provided expertise on illustrations as part of her selection for the department's Martin Award for Research Excellence. Katie Cross Gibson, now a member of the editorial team at the University Press of Kentucky, read and discussed with me numerous books and artifacts dealing with "the sixties."

Time and place matter. My good fortune was to be at the University of California, Berkeley, from 1969 to 1974. Geraldine Joncich Clifford, my advisor, introduced me to her faculty colleagues who over time became my mentors and discussants. I owe much to and miss these remarkable professors, who I sadly note now are in the ranks of "the late": namely, Martin Trow, Sanford Elberg, Henry F. May, Harold L. Hodgkinson, Earl Cheit, Lawrence Levine, and Clark Kerr. Stewart Edelstein, now a distinguished college president, shared with me his perspectives about Berkeley and all higher education during the time we both were doctoral students and research assistants. Wolfgang Tatsch, an alumnus of UC Santa Cruz '69 and a master of library science graduate student at UC Berkeley, guided me to archival materials and oral history on the University of California for this era.

Since 1988 I have had the honor of being a Johns Hopkins University Press author. With this project Editorial Director Greg Britton once again has given me advice and encouragement. I especially appreciate the patient support from him and his JHUP colleagues and staff. Assistant Editor Catherine Goldstead has been especially thoughtful in working with me on all phases of the manuscript. Jacqueline Wehmueller and Juliana McCarthy were responsible for copy editing. Hilary Jacqmin and Morgan Shahan worked on various aspects of marketing and production. I also wish to thank Andre Barnett, senior production editor, and Devon Thomas, who prepared the index.

I thank numerous institutions for the opportunity to include illustrations that portray the setting, cast, and script of the higher education drama that played out between 1960 and 1970. I have adhered to doctrines of fair use, especially for illustrations that are in the public domain and more than half a century old. I wish to thank and acknowledge the following archives for courtesy and permission to use illustrations housed in their respective collections: the National Archives; the Library of Congress; the University of California, Irvine; the Eberly Family Collections Library of Pennsylvania State University Libraries; the University of Kentucky Archives; the Booth Family Center for Special Collections of the Georgetown University Library; the archives of the California Institute of Technology; Wake Forest University Archives and Special Collections; West Virginia and Regional History Center of the West Virginia University Libraries; Stanford University News Service and Chuck Painter; *Time* magazine; and Alamy.

GOING TO COLLEGE
IN THE SIXTIES

Rediscovering the 1960s in American Higher Education

Looking Backward

In October 2014, a *New York Times* article celebrated "At Berkeley, Free (Though Subdued) Speech, 50 Years Later."[1] Other commemorative articles—about college student activism, academic freedom, and campus speakers—followed. Most notable was the attention dedicated to the fiftieth anniversary of Mario Savio's speech on the steps of Sproul Hall at Berkeley. Addressing a crowd of 10,000 on December 2, 1964, Savio had urged his fellow students to "stop the university machine" and to "throw themselves on the gears" of the academic factory.[2] Twenty-first-century Americans, apparently, were rediscovering the higher education of the 1960s.

What did they rediscover? Journalistic coverage of student unrest in that earlier era is best understood as a series of postcards from the past whose vivid images do not convey the whole story of higher education fifty years ago. This book draws on media artifacts of campus protests and other sources to present a range of voices, many of which have been overlooked.[3]

A fresh history of college students, academic institutions, and American culture lets these voices fuse the past to the present. Over the last three years, the focus of articles about higher education in the 1960s has turned from commemoration to connection. A February 2017 article in the *New York Times* carried the headline "A Free Speech Battle at the Birthplace of a Movement." Its sequel proclaimed: "At Berkeley, Violence Sparks Questions about the Dedication to Openness on Campus."[4] To reinforce the collective memory of Berkeley's past and connect it to Berkeley's present, a feature article invoked that campus's activism of 1964 in framing issues of campus free speech in 2017, noting that the "Latest Battle at Berkeley [was] Free Speech versus Safety."[5] This flow of articles showed that Berkeley was back!

Resurrecting historic images of campus activism to the level of public consciousness in 2017 was neither easy nor inevitable. Many analysts who were survivors of the era worried that the legacies of higher education in the 1960s would be forgotten. In the 1980s some professors complained that undergraduates were preoccupied with grades, with being accepted into graduate professional schools, and with landing high-paying jobs.[6] Their lament about grim professionalization glossed over the fact that American college students since the seventeenth century have been concerned about getting ahead. Declaring that "a degree from Harvard was worth money in Chicago," one ambitious undergraduate in 1876 captured the priorities of many of his classmates.

Furthermore, collegiate preoccupation with business success has traditionally been accompanied by criticism within the American campus. As one student editor in *Stover at Yale* complained to a circle of classmates in 1912: "The country has changed, the function of a college has changed. . . . We are a business college purely and singly because we as a nation have only one ideal—the business ideal. Twenty years ago, we had the ideal of the lawyer, of the doctor, of the statesman, of the gentleman, of the man of letters, of the soldier. . . . Now everything has conformed to business, everything has been made to pay."[7]

Historical reminders did little to placate critical faculty and columnists who warned that American college education was on the decline. These critics claimed that college students of the 1980s who sought MBA degrees and careers in financial services or at prestigious law firms had forgotten a collegiate heritage of social conscience and political protests embraced by students two decades earlier. The articles that appeared from 2014 to 2017 suggest, however, that the college student movements of the 1960s have not faded from the nation's memory. And yet, the historic issues of higher education in the 1960s remain unresolved, especially to those who are newcomers to the topic. Anticipating a market for a book that would overcome this historical amnesia, two authors published a primer on *The '60s for Dummies*.[8]

When in 2017 the *New York Times Magazine* asked readers which decade they would most like to bring back, the 1960s was the most frequent answer.[9] Why are these issues regaining popularity? The titles of books and articles provide clues about the source of the excitement:

Years of Hope, Days of Rage
The Age of Great Dreams
Agony and Promise[10]

In 2016 the editor of the *New Yorker* anthology *The 60s: The Story of a Decade* described this decade as the most tumultuous of the twentieth century, a "time of tectonic shifts in all aspects of society—from the March on Washington and the Second Vatican Council to the Summer of Love and Woodstock."[11] One publisher proclaimed, "Say 'the Sixties' and the images start coming. Images of a time when all authority was defied and millions of young Americans thought they could change the world—either through music, drugs, and universal love or by 'putting their bodies on the line' against injustice and war."[12] In a similar vein, a 2017 book showcased oral histories whose participants were "witness to the revolution," characterized by "radicals, resisters, vets, hippies, and the year America lost its mind and found its soul."[13] In January 2018 both *Time* magazine and CNN broadcasting showcased 1968 as "the year that shaped a generation."

Books about higher education in the era invoked metaphors of combat, military campaigns, and sieges involving the war between generations, the embattled campus, and student protesters at the barricades. One undergraduate author in 1970 described the escalation of student radicalism as "push comes to shove."[14] The theme of a "campus in crisis" was used by the former president of City College of New York to introduce his 1974 book about the discontent, disruptions, confrontations, and rebellion that swept the nation's campuses as "alienated and angry students contemptuously rejected the educational Establishment, baited police and campus officials, and defied authority."[15]

Romanticizing radicalism can be risky when writing a history of higher education. Nostalgia for campus protests needs to go beyond headlines, because the events were complex and confusing. For every article today that celebrates the Free Speech Movement there are retrospectives expressing disillusionment with campus activism.[16] Publicity over campus unrest in the 1960s often subjected higher education to a case of mistaken identity. Nowhere was this better illustrated than in the 1968 book *The Academic Revolution*. Its title provided the prospect of an account of student rebellion at American colleges, whereas its authors, Harvard sociologists Christopher Jencks and David Riesman, had a different intent. Their book was not about campus protests, but about the rise to power of the faculty in the twentieth century.

Their focus made sense when they were writing the book. But Jencks and Riesman's observations about historical developments were usurped by reporting that emphasized sensationalistic events as the two sociologists' book made its way into press. No matter how important and timely their topic of the rise of the academic profession may have been, it paled alongside the news about academic rebellion. The irony was that as a book marketing strategy in 1968, *The Academic Revolution* was an unexpectedly apt title, but for reasons different from what these authors had in mind.

Campus Violence and Disruption across the Higher Education Landscape

Images of campus violence and rioting students were conspicuous parts of Americans' notion of campus activism. Today they leave us with a historical question: When and where did such landmark episodes first take place? How pervasive were they? The 2014 *New York Times* articles mentioned earlier make Berkeley in 1964 an obvious nominee. Student demonstrations at Columbia University's Hamilton Hall attracted a *New York Times* reporter's attention fifty years on, as she revisited "a

Campus riots at the University of Mississippi on October 3, 1962. (Courtesy of Library of Congress)

Registration of James Meredith at the University of Mississippi in September 1962. (Courtesy of Library of Congress)

1968 student takeover with those who were there."[17] Another likely place was the City University of New York, given its tradition of political activism back in the 1930s.

Although these campuses are plausible sites, they may lead us to look for history in all the wrong places. Consider, instead, an earlier volatile campus event that drew national headlines before Berkeley rallies in Sproul Plaza made the national news. A defining early event was the series of riots at the University of Mississippi that started on September 30, 1962, and continued for four days. They gained nationwide media coverage: hundreds of federal marshals as they arrived on campus, student mayhem, gunfire, injuries, and two fatalities, along with burned campus buildings. The governor of Mississippi sided with defiant campus demonstrators and even used halftime at the Ole Miss football game as a political podium to champion campus resistance against federal authorities. The governor's speech favored states' rights and defended racial exclusion at the flagship state university. It was cheered enthusiastically by the football crowd of university students and alumni.

The Ole Miss episode did not fit the conventional framework of the decade because the campus protesters were politically conservative.

Students, administration, alumni, and board united to oppose external initiatives to end exclusion of an African American applicant, James Meredith, on the basis of race.[18] Since student activism elsewhere usually came from the political left, it was convenient to overlook this counterintuitive and counterrevolutionary case that erupted at the University of Mississippi. Headline news at the time, it deserves to be included prominently in the story of going to college in the 1960s.

Avoiding the Pitfalls of Nostalgia

Rediscovering higher education of this decade is a good prelude to interpreting larger events. It's not an easy project. Kevin Starr, acclaimed historian of California who had written eight volumes about the state's social and political history, never finished his book on the thirty-year era beginning in the early 1960s. "It was hard to get a handle on the mixed events of the sixties and seventies," he confessed. William Grimes elaborated that "Mr. Starr's magnum opus contains a notable gap: the period from 1963 to 1990, years of turbulence and transformation that readers of the series hoped he would tackle."[19]

There's no way to opt out in a book dedicated to examining exactly this era. I will tackle this period mostly within the boundaries of higher education, but looking beyond, as well, to US society and culture more broadly. The historical record about campus protests exposes a thicket of debates among hostile factions. It starts, of course, with extreme adversaries—those who led protests and those who opposed them. However, the contentious arguments are deeply situated within the ranks of those who at one time pushed for student radicalism. For example, after reviewing numerous oral histories, one historian described the conflicts among students at Yale in 1964 as "The Class Divide."[20] As historian Stephanie Coontz has cautioned, "beware social nostalgia." "There's nothing wrong with celebrating the good things in our past," she notes, "but memories, like witnesses, do not always tell the truth, and need to be cross-examined." It means that this analysis of higher education in the 1960s will heed Coontz's advice by looking at "the trade-offs and contradictions that, however deeply buried, can be uncovered in every memory, good or bad."[21]

The heart of this book reconstructs students' experiences at different kinds of colleges and universities over the entire decade. Fortunately, we are heirs to a growing number of oral histories and memoirs by students of the era, representing diversity in gender, race, ethnicity, social class, institutional types, and region. Women were confined to the margins of the early years of campus activism, but the record and their own voices attest to their activism and ideologies. They are not silent. Women students represented a large percentage of college enrollments. Between 1967 and 1969 women's ideas and actions in matters of feminism, women's studies as an academic field, coeducation, and access to graduate and professional schools were establishing a presence.[22]

Oral histories of the Black campus movement document the activism that established Black studies within the college curriculum.[23] Not surprising is the abundance of official autobiographies and memoirs by college and university presidents of the era.[24] Less obvious, more valuable, and most welcomed are accounts by undergraduates about their experiences living and learning at college in the 1960s.[25]

Reconstructing the diversity of American higher education in the era involves paying attention to several kinds of students and institutions. "College prep" was characterized by competition and crowding as high school students sought coveted admissions offers. It included sorting and tracking in secondary schools that provided markedly different college options from one group of students to another. A demand arose for services and guides to help students and their families prepare effectively for college admissions and seek out scholarship aid.[26] Consideration of these documents introduces issues of college cost and how different kinds of families sorted out their prospects on affordability and college choice. This was an era in which, for example, there were no federal student aid programs such as Pell Grants. Even well-endowed private colleges offered relatively little in the form of scholarships and grants.

College applications and admissions pulled in opposite directions. On the one hand, selective admissions, in which a relatively small number of prestigious colleges had the luxury of choosing among numerous academically strong applicants, was a significant development.[27] In contrast, the decade starting in 1960 was an era of increased access to and even open admissions at some institutions. Analysis of college admissions also includes consideration of rejection letters and the impact of the military draft on student decision making. Equally important as college admissions was student retention. Why did students leave college? How do admissions and retention rates then compare with the situation in colleges today?

Profiles of students also allow historical analysis of different kinds of colleges and universities, leavening any tendency to be preoccupied with a handful of highly publicized campuses and to consider them as representing all colleges. How, for example, did the experiences of students at a junior college, at a small denominational college, or at a historically Black college compare to those of undergraduates at high-profile campuses marked by student activism, such as University of California, Berkeley, or Michigan, Columbia, or Harvard universities? Does historical memory of higher education in the 1960s include state universities or denominational colleges, where student memoirs indicate there was little activism?[28]

Juxtaposed against student perspectives about college was a network of organizations called the Knowledge Industry. Their leaders represented the higher education establishment whose policies and programs shaped student choices, whether college students had much awareness of

Higher education's master planner: Clark Kerr on the cover of *Time* magazine, October 17, 1960.

them or not. Clark Kerr's 1963 book *The Uses of the University* was a blueprint for the Knowledge Industry. The blueprint included the maturation of college admissions as an enterprise driven by the Scholastic Aptitude Test (SAT) and the College Entrance Examination Board.[29] Foundations overlapped with the public sector in new configurations of governance and tuition policies. The 1960 California Master Plan, for example, mediated disputes by public institutions over mission, buoyed by a no-tuition feature for in-state residents who enrolled in any of the state's public postsecondary education systems. In contrast, some states invested little to expanding access. A student's college options were determined by the happenstance of the state in which the student lived— along with marketing and recruitment from testing companies, high school counselors, and college admissions offices.

Central to the Knowledge Industry was investment in research and development. To understand how these activities and funding gained a place at universities requires looking outside the campus to such new government agencies as the National Institutes of Health and the National Science Foundation, along with the Department of Defense. Alliances between these agencies and academic scientists and administrators, combined with generous support from the United States Congress, led to the emergence of the federal research grant university.[30] The Knowledge Industry advocates were confident, especially in connecting educational systems to the national economy. This optimism peaked when Clark Kerr, president of the University of California, was featured on the cover of *Time* magazine in 1960, heralded as Master Planner.

Defining a Decade: A Confusing Chronology and Calendar

An initial puzzle facing someone writing this history is delineating what constituted the 1960s. It is useful to consider the time and location of a landmark event that is illustrative of the problem in framing the decade. On Friday, May 4, 1970, news spread across the United States that National Guard troops had opened fire on anti-war student protesters at Kent State University in Ohio. Later, journalists gave accounts of protesting students being shot by troops at Jackson State University in Mississippi. At many campuses across the United States students quickly mobilized protests to these shootings, disrupting academic business as usual. As would be expected, considering the location of campus activism in the previous decade, these protests were visible and pronounced on campuses such as the University of California, Berkeley—long a lightning rod of student protest and media coverage over political issues, including opposition to the Vietnam War and, then, the US invasion of Cambodia. In sorting through media records and other oral and written accounts of college activism demonstrations between 1964 and 1970, historians today would do well to consider that half a century ago undergraduates did not know what to expect or what was going to happen on campus from day to day.

This syndrome was accentuated by the dramatic political events and cultural changes that were both colorful and chaotic. Here was a collective memory that connected the campus to the community and to the national heritage, as exemplified in 2017 with the broadcast on PBS of Ken Burns's documentary *The Vietnam War*. As Jennifer Schuessler of the *New York Times* wrote of the semicentennial production, "Half a century after the height of the conflict might seem like an ideal moment for another look: long enough for most of the toxic political dust to have settled (and new historical sources to have emerged) but not so long that everyone who lived through it is dead."[31]

The tragic incident at Kent State University stands apart because of time and place. The demonstrations and shootings at a campus in Middle America, a politically moderate region, signaled that about seven years after initial campus demonstrations at so-called radical campuses, student protests had reached new sites. Campus unrest peaked here and then diffused nationwide before fading around 1972. Ironically for a book about higher education in the 1960s, the images associated with Berkeley and elsewhere showed that campus activism in "the sixties" did not crest nationally until the 1970s.

Historical review can bring clarity to the confusion of the recent past. Many accounts link the May 4 shootings at Kent State University and the shootings of students at Jackson State University in Mississippi with campus demonstrations against the Vietnam War. However, recent research about "the mythology of Jackson State" reminds us that "The 1970 shootings were about racist policy brutality, not the Vietnam War."[32]

Campus protests and cancelled classes represented uncharted territory for most American colleges and universities, especially in the years 1960 to 1968. An intriguing element of these events and their broadcast in national media toward the end of the decade is how much had happened on American campuses in the longer period, from 1960 to 1970. Historian Dan Horowitz, Yale '60, makes the intriguing case that he and several classmates were active in social reform groups and activities between 1957 and 1960, timing that placed them "on the cusp" of a world ready to change.[33] The resolution in this book is to give a detailed look backward from May 1970 that includes paying attention to the early years of the decade and not just to the concentration of events between 1968 and 1970.

Decades, of course, are constructs that we use to organize symbols and data—in this case to capture the spirit of a campus period. Instead of relying on the decade as the organizing principle, historian David O. Levine, for example, staked out the years between World War I and World War II as a discernible era in which to track going to college as part of America's "culture of aspiration."[34] A good example of the strengths and limits of the portraiture associated with decade-by-decade surveys of college students is Calvin B. T. Lee's 1970 book *The Campus Scene*. College life in the 1920s often is depicted as a decade of flappers, raccoon coats, college pranks, automobile road trips, and other extracurricular activities called campus hijinx.[35] College students of the 1950s are recalled as "the silent generation." Historical understanding as to what that catchphrase meant soared with novelist Philip Roth's 1987 autobiographical essay "'Joe College': Memories of a Fifties Education."[36] What, then, are the counterpart profiles that emerge from student memoirs from the 1960s?

Another prevalent oversight in campus profiles has been to pay little attention to the academic life. To correct this imbalance, analysis of curriculum herein deals with changes and continuities in academics, including innovations in teaching, fields of study, and degree programs, along with creation of new institutions. In the early 1960s students expressed dissatisfaction about universities' relative indifference to undergraduate education. Their complaints included the teaching versus research conflict in academic priorities.[37] Reform initiatives included new institutional configurations such as cluster colleges and experimental colleges.

One strategy to put news accounts into perspective is to draw on different kinds of historical sources, including the paper trail of demographics, finances, enrollments, degrees conferred, and other institutional statistics about higher education as a timeline, and to stay grounded—removing personal narrative and bias.

Vital Statistics: A Profile of American Higher Education in the 1960s

In contrast to dramatic photographs, newsreels, and accounts of student disruption, statistics about higher education in the 1960s may strike us as dull. However, these are *vital statistics* that have power to bring the evolution of American higher education to life. If presented thoughtfully, they tell an important story that explains the headline events. The center point is the profile of higher education in 1960 depicted as the culmination of changes since the end of World War II. Most memoirs of higher education in the 1960s emphasize the transformational character of the era, and our historical understanding is enhanced when we track changes over time. By 1960 higher education had grown into a part of American life. And higher education would grow even more so *after* 1960. The quantitative changes elicited qualitative changes in colleges and in students' campus experiences.

What did this mean? Following World War II student enrollment was 2.5 million, inflated by students using the GI Bill. By 1960 enrollments expanded to 3.63 million, an increase of about 45%. This was surpassed between 1960 and 1970, as enrollment soared to more than 8 million, more than doubling within that decade. The extraordinary feature of American higher education was its capacity to accommodate high school graduates when the number of eighteen–year-olds was increasing at an unprecedented rate.[38]

The surge in student enrollments was accompanied by comparable increases in the higher education ecosystem, such as the size of instructional staff, number of institutions, number of degrees conferred, and total revenues going to the nation's colleges and universities. Revenues went from about $2.4 billion in 1950 to $5.8 billion in 1960 and then surged to $21.5 billion in 1970. The nation's investment in higher education increased almost fourfold! The number of bachelor's degrees doubled, from 392,440 to 792,317.

Students and their professors in any era are central to learning and teaching. This was affirmed between 1960 and 1970. Following World War II the number of college faculty increased persistently from the postwar figure of 190,353. The academic profession continued to grow between 1960 and 1970, from 281,506 to 551,000—more than doubling in ten years. Here were the statistical data that provided the foundation for Jencks and Riesman's observations about professors and what they called the "academic revolution."

For most American families, higher education meant sending daughters and sons to college to pursue the bachelor's degree. Undergraduate education persisted as the main event. At the same time, there was a less conspicuous transformation with the increased appeal of graduate degrees. Universities conferred 74,435 master's degrees in 1960; by 1970 this number had almost tripled, to 208,291. Biggest gains were in doctoral education. In 1950 academic leaders worried there was a shortage of PhD graduates needed to staff faculty positions. Universities responded by tooling up doctoral programs so that the number of doctoral degrees conferred increased 53%, from 6,420 in 1950 to 9,829 in 1960. By 1970 the tally was just under 30,000, a fivefold increase since the end of World War II.

Where did the growing number of students matriculate? Established campuses tended to expand their enrollments. Whereas many state universities at the end of World War II typically had an enrollment of less than 10,000, by 1970 those same institutions had doubled or tripled enrollment to 20,000 or 30,000 students. Between 1960 and 1965 the number of colleges increased from 2,040 to 2,551. Most new construction took place in public colleges and universities. In 1960 the public-private mix of colleges was 35% public and 65% private; in 1970 public institutions had risen to 43% of the total. Both categories had expanded, but investment by state governments in new junior colleges, along with four-year state campuses, signaled a shift to the public sector in number of institutions and in student enrollments.

To say that college attendance was racially imbalanced is an understatement. According to the National Center for Educational Statistics, in 1960 White students represented 95% of all undergraduate enrollments. This changed a little bit in 1965, to 94%. Surprisingly, by 1969 the figure reverted to 95%. Whether looking at the statistical summaries or perusing a state university yearbook, the view is overwhelmingly White in composition. Racial diversity? It remained negligible.

The statistical record shows that American higher education between 1960 and 1980 was undergoing what Clark Kerr called the "great transformation," moving from elite to mass and universal access to formal education beyond high school—at least for White young people.[39] Some claimed that the period 1945 to 1970 represented American higher education's golden age.[40] How did this characterization mesh with expansion of American higher education?

The Changing Campus and the New City of Intellect

Reconstructing the college experience from the perspective of undergraduates requires reviewing the context of the structures that shaped American higher education at the start of the decade. By 1960 higher education leaders' speeches forecasted a new American model for an academic metropolis in which the modern university was the nerve center for economic innovation and research. Their forecasts overlooked student impact on campus, community, and culture. The new, innovative collegiate subcultures merged into the counterculture of alternative organizations, markets, music, publishing, and other ventures whose appeal took administrators, city officials, parents, and legislators by surprise. It gave the campus life of the decade a distinctive identity with a shift from student activities to student activism. Thoughtful analyses such as Theodore Roszak's 1969 book *The Making of a Counter Culture* showed that the literary, artistic, and political innovations espoused by college students were connected to American traditions whose roots extended back several decades.[41]

Yet innovations in student activities coexisted with established organizations such as sororities and fraternities. The American campus included commercialized spectator sports, but signs of dissent were visible within this environment of nationally televised games, strong fan support, and advertising. One strand that emerged was criticism of the exploitation of student athletes, including attention to the plight and rights of Black athletes.[42]

The Emergence of Higher Education as a Field of Study in the 1960s

One reason we have information today about college students half a century ago is that historic events coincided with scholarship about the college experience. In addition to Christopher Jencks and David Riesman's *The Academic Revolution,* enduring works from this period include Frederick Rudolph's *The American College and University: A History,* published in 1962, which remained influential for over thirty years. In 1962 psychologist Nevitt Sanford assembled an interdisciplinary team of social and behavioral scientists, economists, and anthropologists in his role as editor of *The American College.*[43] By 1966 current issues about colleges and universities, including federal and state legislation and campus events, gained sufficient presence to prompt Corbin Gwaltney to begin publishing a weekly newspaper, the *Chronicle of Higher Education.*[44] In 1967 the Carnegie Foundation set up the Carnegie Commission on Higher Education as a steering committee for reports on trends in higher education by political scientists, historians, anthropologists, sociologists, economists, and other scholarly experts. Several universities established graduate programs devoted to the study of higher education. Stanford

University endowed a professorship for the study of higher education. The University of California, Berkeley, sponsored the Center for Research and Development in Higher Education.

Anatomy of a Decade: Explaining College in the 1960s

Recent articles such as those mentioned at the beginning of this chapter, along with past and recent scholarship, set the stage for a new history of college in the decade. This book is grounded in the principle that historical writing gains in utility and significance when the past is connected to the present. Given the attention being paid to higher education in the twenty-first century—including over such concerns as quests for excellence and equity, college affordability, student loan indebtedness, social justice, and selective admissions—the past can serve as prologue for the present and the future. It's crucial to have informed discussions about changes in academic freedom and campus speech over time.[45] How have students navigated the complex American higher education labyrinth then and now? Taking just one example, Was college more affordable in 1965 than today?[46] As historian Luther Spoehr noted in 2016, "context and contingency" are important in understanding colleges and universities and their students.

College Prep

Crowding and Competition for Admission

College Admissions from Present to Past

Going to college in the 1960s first meant getting into college. To understand how student applicants and admissions officers operated in that era, it's useful to start with current practices as both an end point and benchmark before going back in time. At one extreme, consider Frank Bruni's 2016 report in the *New York Times* that Stanford's admissions standards were so high that no applicants had been offered admission that year. Rejected students would have to make do with other colleges such as Yale, Amherst, Pomona, Harvard, Michigan, Rice, Princeton, Berkeley, and Duke. No matter that some of these safety schools had received ten to fifteen applications for every admissions slot. They still trailed Stanford's record of twenty applicants per admissions place. More perplexing was that almost all the rejected applicants had incredible records of high school achievement measured by grades, test scores, and extracurricular activities. None, however, were deemed to be students Stanford could not live without. In the competitive game of going to college in American life, the message from Stanford was that "the future has arrived and it's the thinnest of envelopes!"[1]

High school seniors across the nation needed no further explanation. They, along with their parents and guidance counselors, all knew well the lexicon of college admissions that had evolved over many decades. Code words included the dreaded *thin envelope* that usually meant rejection. And rejection was hard to take, especially since media coverage for years had been contributing to rising expectations and competition among a favored circle of able, ambitious students. More applicants with strong academic records led to rising admissions standards, especially at the most prestigious colleges and universities. College prep students were taking on heavy academic workloads. The bittersweet twist was that psychologists and counselors reported that these high achievers often experienced low self-esteem in their quest for college admission. They shifted back and forth from calculus tests and varsity sports practices to spending spring break doing volunteer work in Guatemala. Upon returning home to high school they quickly had to focus on AP courses, internships, and other activities suggested by college counselors who promised students that these achievements would look good on *your* permanent record.

Even though the *New York Times* report turned out to be a hoax, it was sufficiently plausible to reinforce the widely held belief today that getting into a selective college allegedly is the toughest academic competition ever. College admissions can be very difficult now. What was it like to apply to college in an earlier era?

The question is pertinent because the decade starting in 1960 was the formative period of selective admissions still practiced today. The protocols, procedures, jargon, and customs, along with reliance on catalogues and filing of transcripts, test scores, and forms, were set into place and then energized by scarcity, secrecy, and selectivity in how colleges made their decisions on admissions, rejection, and what was called *wait listing*. In contrast to the admissions experiences of the 1960s, forty years earlier, in the period following World War I, selective admissions usually meant that college officials practiced deliberate exclusion on nonacademic grounds, practices often associated with quotas grounded in anti-Semitism or anti-Catholicism.[2] Students of color, if they hoped to attend, were steered toward Historically Black College and Universities. However, by 1960 the prospects of prestige associated with going to college, especially at what was called a good college, were accelerated by nationwide gains in the pool of potential applicants and emphasis on identifying a meritocracy.[3] This time the phrase *selective admissions* had come to mean that a college had more academically qualified applicants than available freshman slots.

The Flourishing of the American Public High School

A key to going to college and the resultant transformation of the college admissions process was the flourishing of the American public high school. The intensity of college admissions accelerated around 1960 in large part because public high schools had changed in their size and accessibility, combined with high school students having both more encouragement and more pressure to go to college. This confluence led to a prolonged condition of crowding and competition among students in

Class registration in McDonough Gymnasium, 1960, at Georgetown University. (Courtesy of Georgetown University Library, Booth Family Center for Special Collections, Washington, DC)

the quest for college admissions. Nationally televised public service announcements by the Advertising Council urged viewers, "Give to the college of your choice!" The advertisement featured a parade of students in high school graduation caps and gowns who were then halted by a set of locked college gates. High school seniors who were fortunate to gain admission to college faced even more crowding and long lines when they registered for courses.

The crowding that engulfed college admissions in the 1960s was not completely unexpected. Its storm warnings had started with data from elementary schools in the mid-1950s. In many metropolitan areas, public school enrollments were beyond capacity, so schools resorted to split shifts in which one cohort attended from, say, seven thirty in the morning to one o'clock in the afternoon, and a second cohort attended in the afternoon. This demographic bulge was predictable. By 1960 in both suburban and metropolitan high schools the average size of the student body increased substantially. Harvard economists Claudia Goldin and Lawrence Katz

Central High School in Little Rock, Arkansas. (Photo by Adam Jones 2012)

argued that investment in and success of secondary education was integral to the prosperity of the American economy.[4]

By 1960 the emergent stature of the high school as a pillar of American cities and towns was displayed in its architecture. It is not surprising that monumental, inspiring high school architecture can· be found in New York City, Chicago, Los Angeles, Indianapolis, and Philadelphia. Equally impressive was the high school's presence in small cities and towns. The public high school was a community showplace. A good example was Central High School, located in Little Rock, Arkansas, a·medium-sized city of about 105,000—which became the focus of nationally televised news coverage of local resistance to racial desegregation in September 1957.

The impressive high school buildings constructed between 1910 and 1960 were the educational and social settings for students in a period when enrollment nationwide increased over half a century, from 915,000 students to just under 6 million. Between 1960 and 1970 this figure increased to 8,495,000. The size of the typical American high school increased in metropolitan areas and also in rural sections, where the regional consolidated high school gained favor among school boards and local governments.[5] The typical American public high school was comprehensive in that it combined into a single institution varied missions and student constituencies. Often this comprehensive mission meant that the school was disparaged as lacking high standards in its accommodation of mass education and mediocrity. Perhaps so—but usually within each public high school there was a distinctive provision for solid academic curricula for students who aspired to go to college, as well as a range of nonacademic courses (shop, business, home economics, art, music, driver's ed) designed to train students entering the workforce after high school rather than going straight to college.

High school teachers were increasingly well educated, well paid, and respected in the local community. Typically teachers had earned bachelor's degrees combined with a teaching certificate. Many had master's degrees, a trend that increased year by year. A high school teacher's average annual salary of about $8,000 was more than most National Football League players made at that time. It compared well with the $10,000 annual salary for engineers.

Tracking and sorting of students into educational groupings, often along socioeconomic lines, meant that the academically strong college prep track coexisted alongside of but seldom intersected with the vocational and the trade curriculum. A good indicator of the disparity in life course brought about by this sorting process was that graduates of public high schools who had taken the academic track did increasingly well in every measure of educational achievement, such as national standardized test scores, college acceptance, college graduation, enrollment in graduate and professional programs, and academic honors. In short, many public high schools had become good at providing an excellent preparation for college studies in the sciences, mathematics, and liberal arts, if not for all students, at least for those who had some combination of talent and ambition, especially if these characteristics were reinforced by family support. One acknowledgment of the excellence of the college prep track was that even historically elite private college universities in the Northeast began each year to admit more of their entering classes from public high schools. This was a significant departure, because even after World War II the private prep schools had continued to enjoy a decided edge in admissions.

Increased access to college was most pronounced for high school students from White middle-class families. Students whose goal was to go to college encountered the comprehensive public high school as a fractured, potentially confusing environment in which a mass culture of student activities, clubs, social activities, and sports teams that loomed large were not necessarily academic in character. This scene contrasted, for example, with secondary schools in England and Europe, which were devoted to preparing their students for university admission. Nonetheless, the American model of enrolling all levels of students into the same comprehensive high school was academically effective because of the tracking within the school that staked out courses and cohorts of college prep studies. Bright, motivated students encountered teachers, courses, and facilities that were educationally strong and selective. Thanks to funding from major foundations along with federal grants via the 1958 National Education Act, high schools were able to participate in innovative curricula, especially in the sciences and mathematics.[6] A good example was the School Mathematics Study Group, started with funding from the National Science Foundation in 1958 in response to the USSR's Sputnik challenge and designed to reform instruction in American public schools. A think tank led by mathematics professors at Yale in partnership with colleagues at numerous leading universities, SMSG provided intense summer workshops at college campuses for high school math teachers, all of which were coordinated with original textbooks. Theirs was an approach to mathematical logic and concepts which came to be known as the "new math," starting in 1961 for selected students in an accelerated math program. Comparable experimental advanced programs sponsored by other agencies and foundations were available to high schools for chemistry, biology, physics, social studies, and foreign language instruction.

What was the impact of the numerous nationwide initiatives for accelerated high school curricula? Consider the memoir of a student, Steven Kelman, about his education in the mid-1960s at a public high school on Long Island in which the community and families had placed a strong emphasis on going to college. Kelman noted that, among his classmates and teachers, the common belief was that each year only one or two would be admitted to Harvard College, even though they thought the school's culture and teaching deserved far more acceptances. Preoccupation with getting into a good college pervaded the school—and its administration, faculty, students, and parents. Recollections of this high school, circa 1962 to 1966, were that studies were demanding. Writing in 1982, Kelman attested that most of his memories of high school involved tests and grades:

A teacher we had for two straight years in "special" (advanced placement) math made it a practice never to give partial credit for answers in math

exams where the student showed by his work that he understood the principle of the problem but made a calculation error somewhere. "Partial credit?"
she would ask the class sarcastically, with a salty Nova Scotian accent that
was a favorite for student parody. "Would they have given an engineer partial credit if he did a calculation wrong and the bridge collapsed?" . . . To this
day, I have a recurring dream (that, I understand, is relatively common
among workaholic types) in which I show up for an exam and realize that I
have forgotten to attend the classes all semester or in which I am about to
appear in a play and realize that I forgot to learn my lines. The venue of such
dreams, to this day, is high school.[7]

The American public high school's college prep course was comparable to an academic boot camp. It is surprising to recognize that Kelman
and his peers found college, even an academically selective college, to
have a relatively low-keyed atmosphere compared to the atmosphere
created by the demands of their high school teachers and courses. A
good American public school could be strict and effective in teaching
the lessons to prepare for college. The underlying questions in the back
of every college-bound student's mind were "Am I good enough? Can I
gain admission? Can I do the academic work?" At many high schools,
English teachers devoted considerable effort to having juniors and seniors learn the mechanics of writing term papers since, after all, these
papers would be the coin of the realm in college courses. Throughout
the 1960s one of the bestselling publications for college-bound high
school students was Charles W. Cooper's *The Term Paper: A Model and
a Manual*. Its format was a facsimile of a college term paper about term
papers—each page a reproduction of a typewritten page on 8½ by 11
inch bond—whose text discussed reference terms that then appeared as
footnotes, allowing students to see examples and learn the conventions
of using such Latin phrases as *ibid., loc. cit., op. cit.*, and other tools of
scholarly citation, punctuation, grammar, and presentation.

Outside class, applicants bought books that held out the promise of
providing an inside scoop, with titles such as *How to Get into the
College of Your Choice*. High school seniors who were college bound
shared a concern about having the requisite skills. A popular paperback
geared to high school students that reinforced widespread concern
about academics was *Preparing for College Study,* published in 1961.
Written by Norman A. Fedde, supervisor of the Study Skills Program at
Yale, it provided "a handbook of basic study skills for all college students as well as high school and preparatory school students." The

book's premise was that students faced an educational revolution shaped by unprecedented changes in the kinds of information, scientific discoveries, and political complexities of international events that made college courses demanding. High school students were warned that the major difference between high school and college was that in college students were not required to learn things and memorize facts. The new challenge in college was learning to handle facts, concepts, and questions. Fedde's readers were led through a succession of guides on time organization, calendar planning, note taking, methods of reading, use of the college library, academic writing, and strategies to prepare for and take various kinds of examinations. Endorsed by prominent academics, including deans of admissions, professors, and college presidents, *Preparing for College Study* became a staple for concerned and academically ambitious students nationwide. Its dominant theme was this: even students with outstanding grades would find the transition from high school to college studies demanding, and therefore disciplined, systematic preparation was called for. As such the volume played on the perennial worry of college applicants: Do I have what it takes? Will I be college material?[8]

An underappreciated characteristic of the public high school of the era was that many of its broad extracurricular offerings, although not always scholarly in nature, were beneficial to college prep students. Since many college admissions offices in the 1960s asserted an interest in balance in the student body and commitment to the well-rounded student, a public high school student who combined advanced core courses with student government leadership or president of the Classics Club, performance in the school orchestra, or a varsity sports letter enhanced his or her chances of admission to a selective college. This was especially true if a student showed genuine talent and superior performance in those selected activities in demand by directors of college orchestras and theater programs, and by varsity coaches—all of whom sought to stock their respective programs with new players and performers each year. Even academically selective institutions kept a sharp eye out for a fleet halfback, especially if he wanted to major in physics. As for a college orchestra director who was on the college admissions advisory committee, there was "always room for cello."

Bill Clinton and Elizabeth Warren are two of the best examples of how the college talent hunt embodied the sociologists' concept of "sponsored mobility" and sometimes provided exceptional opportunities for excellent student scholars who were also accomplished in extracurricular activities and whose families had a modest income. Bill Clinton graduated from Hot Springs High School in Arkansas in 1964; an outstanding student, he was also active in student government and was selected for Arkansas Boys State and then, as the state delegate to Boys Nation, traveled to Washington, DC, in the summer of 1963, where he met then president John F. Kennedy.[9] Clinton would go on to be a Rhodes Scholar, receive his JD from Yale, and be elected governor and then US senator from Arkansas, eventually serving two terms as president of the United States. Elizabeth Warren graduated from Northwest Classen High School in Oklahoma City in 1966, where her accomplishments as outstanding debater in the state led to a scholarship from George Washington University. She transferred from GW to the University of Houston, received her JD degree and became a distinguished law professor and then senator from Massachusetts. Warren and Clinton are the first in their families to go to college—and for each, a ticket for educational opportunity and social, geographic, and career mobility arrived in the form of a strong high school transcript merged with outstanding achievements in debate and student government. Warren and Clinton, however, were exceptional. The model of sponsored mobility did match high-achieving students with good colleges, but for most high school students from modest-income families, it held little realistic promise of going to college or paying for college.

In addition to college-prep courses, many high school students applying to college in the 1960s were required to take the Scholastic Aptitude Test. Administration and interpretation of SAT scores became a highly controversial and important issue for both applicants and college admissions officers making decisions about who would go where to college. Even when the SAT was a required part of the college application, no one seemed to know for certain how an applicant's score on the test factored into the admissions decision.

The Scholastic Aptitude Test

College admissions in the United States have always been characterized by local ordinances and institutional peculiarities. It could mean that a college offered its own entrance examination. Or, a college might require a particular course of secondary school study. By 1960, however, nationwide standardized testing had gained a foothold as a component in required admissions materials. Pre-college testing was dominated by rival organizations: the Scholastic Aptitude Test, widely referred to as the

SAT (pronounced ess-A-tee), and the American College Testing, known as the ACT (pronounced A-cee-tee). A rough comparison involves geography and test purpose. The SAT, introduced in 1926, was associated with admission to the private colleges of the Atlantic Coast and was hailed for its ability to identify talent at the top. In marked contrast, the ACT, developed in 1959, was used largely in the Midwest, especially by state and other public colleges and universities. Its aim was to assist college officials in their student advising and placement across a range of fields and test scores.[10]

The primacy of these tests, especially of the SAT, represented one of the most phenomenal campaigns to shape American public opinion. In a nation known for a decentralized educational system dominated by state and local control, a private nonprofit corporation, the Educational Testing Service (ETS), and its related College Entrance Examination Board had gained support and subscription from over three hundred colleges in 1960. The SAT had only incidental association or connection with public high schools. It was not part of their educational program or their curriculum. High school students, usually seniors, who wanted to apply to one or more of those CEEB-member institutions, were on their own to register and pay for an SAT session.

Three times per year the SAT was administered in sessions held usually at college campuses. The main exam lasted four hours, followed in the afternoon by achievement examinations in designated fields, plus a writing sample essay. The paradox of the SAT for high school students was that it was a high-stakes event but was promoted as low pressure. Brochures mailed to test registrants a month before the testing were understated, with sepia-tint photographs of successful students. The message was that a student should be calm, rested, and relaxed. After all, there was nothing to worry about. Reviewing and studying for the exam were explained away as neither necessary nor even helpful, because the SAT was a measure of *aptitude.*

Most high school students had been subjected year after year to numerous in-school inventories, examinations, and multiple-choice tests ranging from personality profiles to tests of mechanical skills and ability to judge spatial relations, and even some measures of intellectual strength. Their previous experience with testing, combined with their relative inexperience with the SAT, resulted in most students and their families viewing the SAT with some trepidation. The SAT consisted of two parts: verbal reasoning and quantitative. The highest score on each part was 800; the lowest, 200. Hence, a perfect score on both components meant a score of 1600. Part of college-prep lore, cutting across all schools, was the collective memory of test takers, who described a chilling and exhausting miserable experience of listening to proctors read instructions, using special pencils, watching the clock, answering multiple-choice questions, and heeding admonitions about cheating. American high school students who wanted to go to college may not have liked the SAT—but they took it. More incredible is that so many constituents came to accept the SAT scores as reliable verdicts. Sociologists talk about the phenomenon of profiling, in which a person internalizes the external records and judgments made about him or her. The SAT embodied this phenomenon. A student who did not get a high score often would explain, "After all, I do not test well." Everyone agreed that getting a high score—between 1400 and 1600—meant that someone probably was very bright and that such a score would greatly enhance prospects for admission to an outstanding college. Students and their counselors, teachers, and college admissions officers tended to think of an applicant in terms of a halo effect of the SAT score.

Even though in the 1960s there was a persistent strand of criticism that the SAT, along with many other standardized tests, tended to discriminate based on family income and race, the scores were used—along with high school transcripts and other admissions materials. The big gainers in the reliance on the SAT were bright White male students from good public high schools. Such a guy with a score of 1500, whether from Central High School in Denver or Stuyvesant High School in New York City, commanded attention from college admissions offices. This test expanded the pool and sharpened the tools in the college admissions talent hunt. The SAT scores worked best at the extreme margins. A high school student with a score of 1600 was universally regarded as academically strong. Conversely, a student with a score of 450 probably was not going to do well in college. Between these end points, however, decision making for admissions based on SAT scores was problematic and often abused.

The main problem was ascertaining its significance and validity. What did the SAT measure? What was scholastic aptitude?[11] It was a construct. Furthermore, as many Educational Testing Service test makers, officials, and college faculty and administration knew well, the major utility of an SAT score was to serve as a predictor for how a new college student would perform in the first and second semester of college studies. But even this use of the test was less reliable than a student's high school curriculum and high school grade point average as a predictor of first-year college grade point average. This concern mattered little, as all students, whether they had high, medium, or low scores, tended to come to terms with their SAT scores. When a student received from ETS the results of the SAT, the explanatory booklet included a section about "bands of confidence"—explaining ranges higher and lower that a student might achieve if he or she were to take the test again. Just as studying beforehand was purported not to have much consequence, so test takers were advised that repeating the test probably would not make a lot of difference because, after all, these tests scientifically measured aptitude. There has been some debate about whether there is racial bias on the SAT or ACT, but when faced with questions of validity, ETS typically responds by saying there is discrepancy in the way races are taught in America, so there should be discrepancies in their test scores.[12] Perhaps the discrepancy lies with an outdated view of bias as falling along racial lines rather than economic ones.

Campus Mystique and Anticipation: A Preview of College Life

At the same time that prospective students navigated the formal admissions requirements, they were tantalized by images, advertisements, and articles that reinforced college life as a coveted prize in American life. For those who were devoted to higher education and took the bait of college anticipation and admissions, the floodgates opened in early September when classes started, the campus came to life, and America went back to college. Each fall, this annual round of life became clear when many magazines, from *Esquire* to *Seventeen* along with *Playboy, Life,* and the *Saturday Evening Post* published a back-to-college issue. Monthly magazines such as *Holiday, The Atlantic Monthly, Harper's,* and *Saturday Review* regularly featured lengthy campus profiles, including color photographs. Journalist David Boroff's series of college articles in 1960 was sufficiently popular that it was promptly compiled into an anthology and published as a book, *Campus U.S.A.*[13]

The annual back-to-college mood was exciting. *Esquire*, a men's lifestyle magazine, was dedicated to conveying to its upscale readership a sense of the campus mood and pulse. Its September 1962 issue had a special fold-out section that stretched across four pages, with an illustrated, color-coded national map of campus watering holes. Its added feature was a guide to favorite places to "bug out"—a place for college students to escape campus and relax. The article also provided academic survival information, including lists of easy courses and sympathetic professors at the various campuses. Readers who wanted to learn about college had their pick of campus locations across the country, from Cambridge, Massachusetts, to Austin, Texas, from Princeton, New Jersey, to Oxford, Mississippi, from Ann Arbor, Michigan, to Boulder, Colorado, and from New Orleans, Louisiana, to Portland, Oregon. By reading *Esquire* and other magazines, a student could be in the middle of any campus and cast into college life without ever leaving high school.

Esquire featured its "Big Men on Campus" profiles of college students and recent alums who had attracted fame as journalists or as the winner of college football's Heisman Trophy. Another article imitated Machiavelli's *The Prince* to give new students detailed advice on how to seize power on campus. This issue also featured a controversial article about Vassar students and birth control, written by at that time an unknown author, Gloria Steinem. This was her first nationally published article. Steinem went on to write columns for *New York Magazine* and become an activist for feminist issues. *Esquire*'s mix of serious and humorous articles made college life familiar and at the same time mystical to readers who were outside the campus community. *Esquire* was not alone in mesmerizing US high school students (mostly boys) who were getting ready to apply to college. *Playboy* set a new standard with its annual campus guide, featuring a systematic chart with clever cartoons depicting campus student types. For one university, men were characterized as "aspiring dentists" and the women ("coeds") were "elementary education majors who loathed children."

Hollywood got into the college act with a nationally broadcast television show, *Hootenanny*. Starting in April 1963 each Saturday night during prime time, host Jack Linkletter would broadcast live from a selected campus where a packed auditorium of college students watched and cheered a lineup of folksingers. The second episode of the successful show was broadcast from Brown University in Providence, Rhode Island. The television cameras focused on the Brown banner hanging from the balcony and on Brown students dressed in crew neck sweaters, khakis, and oxford cloth shirts applauding folk singers Theodore Bikel, Judy Collins, and the Limelighters. *Hootenanny* was the top-ranked Saturday night show over the next two years. By 1963 college not only was prestigious, it was also popular.

Rounding out going to college as a popular topic in the entertainment media was the nationally broadcast Sunday night television show *College Bowl* sponsored by General Electric. Each week varsity scholars from selected colleges competed for jump ball questions, adhered to rules marked by a referee's whistle, and were even subject to rules governing

General Electric's 1963 *College Bowl* television show on NBC featuring varsity scholars from Wake Forest University. (Courtesy of Wake Forest University, Special Collections & Archives)

bonus questions and penalty points. The halftime break featured a General Electric advertisement followed by interviews and campus scenes narrated by each college's team captain. Each week the winning team received a fifteen-hundred-dollar scholarship as its trophy. A college whose team won five weeks in a row was crowned as a champion and received additional scholarships. Many of the victorious scholarly teams returned home to their campus to the cheers of crowds of students, faculty, alumni, and the college president. *College Bowl* showed that between 1959 and 1970 academics could rival athletics in competitive spirit and popular following on prime-time network television.

The symbols of college life were reinforced during the summer as college students came home from campus wearing their sweatshirts with UCLA or NORTHWESTERN in bold block letters and school colors. These same college students brought home their yearbooks—heavy volumes with such lyrical names as *The Campanile, The Illio, The Colonial Echo,*

Chaparral, and *Liber Brunensis.* The yearbooks seemed to have come out of central casting. Each had similar covers and graphics and special sections documenting the year's campus heroics ranging from the homecoming queen's coronation to varsity team pictures and championship seasons. It depicted a world by and for confident students, interrupted by a few perfunctory photographs of a dean of students in a staged scene, answering the office telephone on what must have been important business. About thirty pages were devoted to group photographs of fraternities and sororities. The yearbook images suggested that life was good on the American campus.

The informal college lore that circulated among high school students was fraught with misinformation. For example, in the Northeast, where Harvard obviously was a top choice among many prep-school students and ambitious public high school applicants, a favorite trivia question was, "Who comes after Harvard?" Since Harvard was a tough act to follow, this alphabetical quiz often made Harvey Mudd College something of a joke or, at least, an afterthought. In fact, the joke was on the smug college applicants from the Northeast, because it exposed their provinciality and ignorance. Harvey Mudd College, one of the Claremont Colleges in California, competed favorably with Caltech, Stanford, Berkeley, and the Massachusetts Institute of Technology for outstanding students in engineering, mathematics, and the sciences. Indeed, this relatively young college, founded in 1955, would become alma mater for a disproportionate number of leaders at future high-tech firms as well as computer scientists and aerospace engineers. But its merits were often lost on the insular high school students of the 1960s.

How did an aspiring, ambitious high school student without family connections process the various previews of college life on offer through these various means? A good glimpse comes from Bruce J. Friedman's 1965 novel whose protagonist, Joseph, is mulling applications and looking at brochures: "He had finished high school and sent out applications to two colleges, Columbia and Bates, the latter because he liked the name. Once, at a summer resort, he had watched a short, scrappy fellow with heavy thighs play basketball, staying all over his man, hollering out catcalls, giving his opponents no quarter. The fellow said he went to Bates and Joseph had come to think of the school as scrappy little heavy thigh college full of fast little fellows who pressed their opponents. He chose Columbia in case the out-of-town school rejected him for not being scrappy enough."

Later in the novel Friedman returned to the college application and rejection ritual, noting that, "Although Joseph did well in high school, he did not get very much in the way of college guidance. All such assistance came under the direction of a folksy old hygiene teacher named Pop Freble." The advisor usually reserved his support for the students with the highest grades and for those who showed interest in one state college that he knew well. The guidance counselor provided no information about financial aid or paying for college. When Friedman's fictional applicant, Joseph, received a cursory note from Columbia stating that "the entering class was full," he regrouped from rejection by relying on brochures and the comments of former students at his high school for inspiration and suggestions about other places to apply. Images and names were blurred. He worried that since he had told the Bates admissions office that "he had wanted to go there since childhood," the word might spread to admissions offices elsewhere, leading to his application being ignored.[14] What he probably did not know was that each college conjured associations, real and imagined—and these were the product of deliberate publicity campaigns by college admissions offices.

Creating College Images: Admissions Viewbooks, Recruitment, and Public Relations

The fusion of college admissions and public relations was part of a graphics revolution that started to bear fruit by 1960.[15] At Columbia University, for example, a 1957 *Report of the President's Committee on the Educational Future of Columbia University* included a chapter on "The University's Image and Its Projection." The report noted that some of the official public relations campaigns from the period between 1900 and 1940 were no longer appropriate: "In the past, during decades of expansion, Columbia's public relations have contributed to a misleading picture of itself. The image it has presented has sometimes been alien to its dignity, to the spirit of its main educational endeavors, and to its institutional personality as a major university." The proposed solution was to project the "true image of the university," which refuted the early image of "amorphous bigness." Whereas Columbia had once hailed itself as the "Colossus on the Hudson," the proposed new approach, especially for undergraduate admissions and recruitment, was to describe Columbia College's small size and historic identity as the "heart of the University."[16]

Comparable self-scrutiny led to new strategies at other colleges and universities. An internal report at Harvard noted, "Until very recently Harvard's official publications looked to have been designed by a Pliocene typographer whose idea of the beautiful was different from our own. Most of them still are in appearance strongly reminiscent of another epoch. Though brave new things are announced within them, they proclaim, by the grayness of their pages, that the University is stoutly resisting change. But a few official publications have turned over a new leaf and put a bold face on it." In the same spirit, a 1960 *Harvard Faculty Report* on admissions to the college reviewed admissions brochures and complimented one sample for its balance and dignity—but warned that "chilly Puritan prose" and an unwarranted reputation for seeking only "eggheads" might be causing first-rate applicants to apply elsewhere.[17] The resulting revisions in viewbooks led to the following example of magnetic recruitment prose:

> Who should come to Harvard? . . . Probably the simplest answer is the same kind of responsible, able, well-motivated student whom all colleges want. . . . It takes a certain amount of humility and venturesomeness and openness of spirit to savor Harvard to the full. The student who wants simply a "prestige college" label or four years of fun before he grows up can find these things with less work and less expense elsewhere. The student who wants to be told what to believe, what is true and good and beautiful, the student who wants the security of association with a homogeneous group sharing his particular background and prejudices, the student who needs to be nursed or prodded or taken gently by the hand and led along the safe path—these run serious risk in coming to Cambridge, although Harvard education is a potent force and extraordinary changes can take place in college.[18]

Many of the pamphlets sent to potential applicants had uninspired titles such as *The Official Bulletin of the University of California, Berkeley.* Elsewhere, however, changes in marketing and graphics were evident as college applicants received viewbooks whose titles proclaimed *This Is Amherst* or *Preface to Pomona.* The Harvard College 1963 viewbook was well stocked with photographs of Harvard Yard and an interior scene of a wood-paneled House library where students were reading on Sunday afternoon. The clincher was in the prose, such as the quietly confident statement, "Wealth, like age, does not make a college great . . . but it helps!" Easy to say when you are the wealthiest and oldest college in the nation.

College recruitment materials became increasingly calculated and sophisticated in conveying soft images of prestige and campus mystique. Colleges imitated one another in competition to convey particular kinds of messages—which led the president of Bennington College to playfully propose a brochure that captured the clichés and favored features of college self-promotion, showcasing "a small, rural, private, experimental women's college of high quality which emphasizes the development of the individual. It shares the cultural advantages of New York, Boston, and Montreal. Its hill is moderately high. From it, on a clear day, you can see, beyond the toilet paper factory, the historic Walloomsac River, flowing northward away from Williamstown, where there is a small, rural, private, experimental college of high quality for well-rounded men."[19]

Pomona College blended geography and tradition to describe itself to applicants, noting, "Whatever an atlas may show, there are those who say that the westernmost outpost of New England is Claremont, California, where one may live on Dartmouth Avenue, shop on Yale, and go to church on Harvard. . . . But an institution's heritage is not to be confused with its present. Pomona is basically a western college and a quite different place from what it would be were it located elsewhere. It is this very combination of a New England ancestry and a California environment that gives Pomona its distinctive character."[20]

If age had its promotional advantages for Harvard, Yale, and Princeton, newness created an attractive mystique for other colleges. Hampshire College in Massachusetts and the University of California campuses at Irvine, San Diego, and Santa Cruz are foremost examples, bursting onto the college scene in 1964. New colleges played their cards with attractive admissions messages. Using address files gathered at headquarters for the University of California system, University of California, Santa Cruz, officials relied on sending direct mail off to high school students with strong academic records, inviting them to be a member of the first entering class at the new University of California at Santa Cruz, as a founding member of a campus. How did college officials craft a viewbook for a campus that did not yet exist? The solution was to fuel the imagination of college-bound high school seniors using the beautiful redwood coastal site for UCSC as a magnet. Unfortunately for the admissions office, campus construction was behind schedule when recruitment materials went to press. So, the viewbook enticed applicants with the lure that a student who joined this venture could be one of the "academic pioneers who live in 20th century covered wagons." This was a clever way to say that new freshmen would be living in temporary trailers until construction of the Oxford-style residential colleges was completed. The harsh reality was softened by an artist's rendition of an aerial view of what looked like spokes of a wheel. Images eventually caught up with reality, and the residential colleges *were* distinctive. Within three years, students at the new campus had created a memorable campus culture, featured in a *Life* magazine feature story.

Reading the public relations materials could turn a college applicant into an inquisitive and critical consumer. The Santa Cruz brochures hinted that a good high school student had some leverage in the admissions marketplace because at the same time that college applicants were worrying about being accepted to the college of their choice, deans of admissions were on the lookout for students who had good grades and high SAT scores (and no felonies or psychological problems). Going to college became a game of cat and mouse, as applicants and admissions officers looked each other over. Admissions offices almost always had advantages in the deliberations, however.

Limits of College Access and College Choice: Left Outs and Left Overs

Despite gains in high school education, college preparatory courses, and inducements for students to apply to college, numerous obstacles and limits confronted the would-be college entrant.

GEOGRAPHY

A rule of thumb was that most students went to college about fifty to seventy-five miles from home. This rule has been fairly constant and still holds today. A difference is that in 1960 many students were unlikely to find a college within a fifty-mile radius of home. The situation would change gradually yet persistently, with massive construction of new campuses in the decade. Nonetheless, at the time it was problematic. It also meant that most of the undergraduates at even nationally famous colleges tended to hail from relatively near campus. In 1963, for example, Harvard's freshman class consisted of about 30% from New England, 8% from the Pacific Coast, 12% from the South, 20% from the Midwest, and about 20% from the mid-Atlantic states, and a small number of international students. In contrast, in 2017 most of the Ivy League colleges report that California and Texas have become a major source of students, along with New York and Massachusetts.

Geography worked hardships on other students in a very different manner. Colleges and universities located in densely populated states and cities did not have capacity of classrooms or dormitories to accommodate all qualified applicants. This was especially pronounced in the Northeast and mid-Atlantic area. In New Jersey, higher education was woefully underbuilt. Massachusetts had a large number of private colleges and universities, but its state universities and public colleges were inadequate to handle the Commonwealth's abundance of high school seniors who sought to go to college. The result was a distinct migration from the urban East to the rural Midwest. Dorothy Finnegan, who graduated from high school in New Jersey, wrote in her 2014 memoir: "Picture, for a minute, a kid whose Dad often during Sunday afternoon dinners shared his life-long but unrealized dream of teaching high school history. Picture a kid whose mother reminisced about winning a half scholarship to a private women's college, but had no money for the remaining tuition. From her earliest days, everyone, including the kid, assumed that she would go to college. Assured by the college counselor of admittance to the local state teachers college, the bottom fell out on the ides of March, 1965."[21]

Finnegan, known since the 1990s for her scholarly research on academic labor markets,[22] also delved into analysis of college student migration and wrote in her memoir that "in 1965 in New Jersey, the six existing state colleges had 1,200 places for new students," and that

12,000 of my fellow high school graduates sought one of those seats. The story was similar in most of the northeastern states. Although everyone knew that the number of babies born in 1947, the second year of the post-WWII Baby Boom, was the largest crop of the demographic bulge, and although my birth cohort stretched school resources from 1953 on, no one predicted that the effects of WWII, the GI Bill, and the new American post-war quest for success would translate into a much higher desire within this age grade to go to college. Northeastern public colleges were caught short—short of space, of teaching personnel, and of facilities that could welcome the bountiful harvest of student aspirants. And of course, believing in the states' system, parents and children assumed that seats would be available nearby at a reasonable cost.

The disappointment for parents and students was that the state college seats in their home state were neither readily available nor affordable, despite pledges and promises by state legislators. This critical situation meant that by 1964 concerned students sought relief by relying on "a two-year-old operation—the college clearinghouses." According to Finnegan, "five different clearinghouses east of the Mississippi matched eligible students with colleges that were hungry for a higher yield. Of course, the definition of eligible depended on the appetite of the college and grew more rigorous on a yearly basis." Finnegan described the personal side of this demographic crunch:

> Like many of my classmates at William Penn College in Oskaloosa, Iowa—at least those who came from New Jersey, Pennsylvania, New York, Connecticut, Massachusetts, New Hampshire, and Maine—I had to consult a map to find Iowa. Eighteen hundred miles from home became a miniscule distance to be able to go to college. As students, we never talked about how we got to Penn, but from interviews with fourteen classmates . . . , most of us, easterners, Methodists, Catholics, Baptists, and Jews—and a handful of Quakers—primarily found our way to this small campus on the edge of cornfields through the clearinghouses. After sending her dossier to the Chicago clearinghouse, the tipping factor to come to Penn for one fellow sociology major was the personal letters she received from the president and the deans of women and men.[23]

Art mirrored life: Joseph, the protagonist in Bruce J. Friedman's novel, left his home and high school in New York to enroll in a small private college in Kansas. Elsewhere in the Midwest, colleges such as Oberlin, Antioch, Grinnell, and Carleton experienced a groundswell of applications and, then, enrollments from students who had gone to high school in East Coast metropolitan areas.

PRICE AND COST

By standards today, the costs of a college education in the 1960s were amazingly low. Some of this apparent difference shrinks when one indexes for inflation. Furthermore, and perhaps most important, family incomes fifty to sixty years ago were far smaller, as salaries for many parents of students thinking about going to college were relatively low.

How, then, did students and their families deal with problems of paying for college in the early 1960s? Consider the case of a student applying to her or his state university that charged no tuition to in-state students. Estimated total expenses (room and board, books, fees, incidentals) for an academic year ranged from a moderate $1,113 to a high of $1,493. Indexing for inflation, this would be equivalent in 2017 dollars to $8,900 (moderate) or about $12,000 (high). By 2017 most state universities have added substantial tuition charges, rising rapidly over time, and the price of housing and other living expenses has soared such that estimated state university tuition and expenses for an undergraduate would be about $30,000 per year.

At a private college such as an Ivy League institution, in 1963 tuition was $1,760 and total expenses estimated between $2,855 and $3,220. Indexed for inflation in 2017, the figures would be about $14,100 for tuition and total expenses ranging from $22,840 to $25,760. There is no doubt that the price of college attendance today has risen inordinately, to about $55,000 to $60,000 per year for an Ivy League undergraduate.

Another way to reconstruct how students and their families fared in paying for college sixty years ago is to look at salaries and household income as a percentage of the price of going to college. In 1960 engineers and other educated professionals earned an average annual salary of about $10,000. A teacher at a public elementary school made $5,137, with high school teachers at about $8,000. A police officer's salary was $4,400. An engineer would pay $1,400 in 1960 to send one child to college at a relatively low tuition state university—about 15% of the engineer's annual gross salary. A private college was $2,800—about 30% of that same yearly income. For a teacher, a state university consumed 27% of annual salary, and the cost of sending a child to a private college consumed 55%, of yearly earnings. In comparison, today the full sticker prices of $30,000 for a state university and $55,000 for a private college consume, for a person earning an annual salary of $100,000 per year, 30% and 55%, respectively. Whether college was more affordable for a family in 1960 than today remains unclear, in part because resources for student financial aid changed dramatically after 1972.

In the 1960s college students could whittle down college expenses by working summer jobs. It was a teenage "rite of passage" to earn about $500 from June through August at such jobs as "scooping ice cream, baling hay, or stocking grocery market shelves" and learning such lessons of life as "show up on time, dress properly, and treat customers well." According to Associated Press economics writer Paul Wiseman, student decisions were markedly different in 2017 than in earlier eras because "more kids are spending summers volunteering or studying, to prepare for college and compete for slots at competitive schools."[24] Internships, summer sports camps, and travel abroad programs have gained high priority. Students today often find that what used to count as summer jobs are now filled permanently by older workers—and that estimated summer job earnings would not make much of a dent in the high prices many colleges charge for tuition and campus living, anyway.

For now, what does emerge from accounts of family life and student planning is that high school students in the 1960s had made great gains in access, but realistic college choices remained limited. Whereas today a student can readily apply to seven hundred colleges via the common application form, in the 1960s even reasonably prosperous and education-minded families followed a rule of thumb of applying to three, perhaps four, colleges—one certain for admission, a slight stretch, and then perhaps one or two dream colleges. The cost of travel to a campus far from home, combined with the limited availability of assured financial aid, tended to impose sobering limits on college aspirations.

In the 1960s students were either less able or less willing to go into debt to make college "doable" than students are today. Banks were not at all sympathetic to granting a loan for which the collateral was a student's future degree and earnings.[25] What has made a big difference for college considerations today are the great federal government student financial aid programs such as Pell Grants, which became available in 1972. Some college students in the 1960s qualified for loans as part of the National Defense Education Act of 1958. By 1965 there were limited opportunities for other federal loans, but most of these programs remained stalled due to lack of interest by banks. One important step in college admissions was for an applicant to obtain the Parents' Confidential Statement on income and finances from the College Scholarship Service. These statements were filed with the College Scholarship Service clearinghouse, not with a college's financial aid office. They provided standardized information to the colleges but provided no comparable standardized formula for awarding financial aid. How the Parents' Confidential Statement would be used in decision making by participating colleges was up to institutional discretion.

A good profile of the situation that faced many high school seniors who had strong academic records but modest income families comes from Richard Trollinger's 2017 recollection. He went to high school in the Roanoke, Virginia, area and applied to college in Spring 1967. Trollinger would graduate from nearby Emory & Henry College and later earn master's degrees from Vanderbilt and Indiana universities, and a PhD from the University of Kentucky. His academic achievement was accompanied by professional recognition, as he became nationally prominent as vice president of college relations for Centre College in Kentucky. Considering his educational and professional accomplishments, one might presume that college, for Trollinger, was both plausible and affordable. But this was not the case. What frequently gets masked from collective memory is the uncertainty surrounding paying for college for many dedicated students about half a century ago. Trollinger recalled the precarious situation he faced "about choices and money being limited for those of us who went to college in the 1960s," elaborating, "I really didn't know until three weeks before I was to enter Emory & Henry if I would have the money to attend my freshman year. The alternative, at least as I saw it, was the military. But with the Vietnam War under way, that option was not very attractive." Although some readers in 2017 might be disappointed or surprised that student memoirs are not always about high-profile campus rebellion of the late '60s, Trollinger noted that for those who attended college then, the decade also was "about the hopes and dreams of a lot of young people, myself included, who saw higher education as the gateway to the American dream."[26]

Most colleges in 1960 did not provide a great deal of grant aid to students—most offered only loans and what were called "bursar jobs." Despite assurances in college viewbooks that no student should be discouraged from applying due to concern about being able to afford college bills, few colleges had a policy of need-blind admissions in 1960. Nor did colleges guarantee that a student who was offered entry would receive a need-based financial aid package that met college costs. This situation would soon change among the Ivy League and some well-endowed universities in the late 1960s. An inside account of the Yale admissions office of 1960 included the matter-of-fact observation that admissions staff kept folders of aid recipients separated—and kept track of how much of the financial aid budget they were spending had its source in students paying full fare for college. About 30% of Ivy League college students received some financial aid, ranging from $200 to $2,800 per year. The aid was a mix of loans, work-study income, and scholarships which came to be known as "packaging." Put another way, typically about 70% of enrolled students paid full price.

The uncertain and limited student financial aid from the colleges prompted sustained initiatives by citizens and local community groups. A good example was the Dollars for Scholars program, which originated in Fall River, Massachusetts, where in 1957 Irving Fradkin, an optometrist who had sought election to the city school committee, awarded college scholarships of about $200 to each of 24 graduating high school seniors. Fradkin's neighbors donated a total of $5,000 for this purpose. The original model spread to other communities, to five hundred local chapters that awarded $600 million to 750 students over sixty years. The local project evolved into the national fund, Scholarship America, whose cumulative record was awarding $3.5 billion to 2.2 million students.[27]

RACE

Whatever problems most college applicants faced in navigating the labyrinth of admissions, they were dwarfed by the obstacles encountered by Black students who sought admission to public colleges and universities in states that practiced racial exclusion. One of the ways in which going to college in the 1960s was historically significant is that it was in this period that numerous state universities acceded, albeit slowly and reluctantly, to racial desegregation. This change put the college admissions process in the public and legal spotlight. A well-known pioneer was James Meredith, a Black applicant who was turned away from the University of Mississippi in 1962. A military veteran who had already completed two years of college and applied to Ole Miss as a transfer student, he decided to fight the university's decision with the help of the US government. The opposition and violence he faced as he succeeded in becoming the first student to integrate all-White Ole Miss were extreme and also highly publicized in the media.

Charlayne Hunter and Hamilton Holmes also ran headfirst into the dynamics of racial desegregation. Hunter and Holmes were two Black applicants to the University of Georgia and the first Black students to enter the university, in January 1961.[28] In addition to coping with the customary worries and uncertainties that most college applicants experienced, Hunter and Holmes were cast into what journalists called the role of "student heroes" who had opted to be cast into a "war" in which "battle lines were drawn." The metaphor did include physical violence, both as a threat and as a reality—but it was more accurately characterized by a long campaign involving strategies and litigation from opposing sides. Most peculiar is that the racially exclusive state universities of the South had no formal or published policy of discrimination or exclusion, yet strong customs permeated the obvious stalling tactics of both lawyers and courts who protected traditions of discrimination. Both "student heroes," Hunter and Holmes, were transfer students who had excelled in their first two years at, respectively, Wayne State University in Michigan and Morehouse College in Atlanta. Both were natives of Georgia, came from educated, professional families, and had outstanding academic transcripts from high school. They were described as "perfectly cast for the role" of college admissions trailblazers. In their biographies and interviews, they come across as committed and disciplined. Hamilton Holmes came from a family in which both his grandfather and father had worked steadily to overcome discrimination at golf courses and other public facilities, a family that was part of Atlanta's upper-middle-class Black community.

The legal and administrative obstacles were the longest part of the admissions ordeal. Once a judge ruled that the university must comply, once Hunter and Holmes enrolled and entered the student body, student riots erupted. Both Holmes and Hunter were temporarily suspended "for their own safety," but soon outright violence subsided. Their experiences illustrate that college admissions have never been wholly or even largely about academic qualifications and educational achievements.

Research by historian Peter Wallenstein shows that in the late 1960s racial desegregation took place without incident at many state universities in the segregated South.[29] However, the end of *de jure* discrimination usually resulted only in nominal enrollment of African Americans, indicating that colleges may have complied with desegregation, but they were far from achieving genuine racial integration or equity in the student culture and life within the campus. Most media attention focused on exclusion at state universities. Equally important was that the prestigious and academically strong private and independent colleges and universities in the South were slow to end racial desegregation. Historian Melissa Kean documented this syndrome with case studies of Duke, Vanderbilt, Emory, Tulane, and Rice universities, where typically some mix of boards and presidents justified their resistance to integration on the grounds that compliance would hurt their academic selectivity.[30] Ironically, the opposite held true, as the Association of American Universities—the most prestigious group of research universities—along with federal research agencies warned the laggard institutions that failure to end racial exclusion would hurt institutional chances in competition for research grants and for being offered a coveted invitation to join the national research association. At the prestigious private colleges in the Northeast there were some notable instances, especially at Yale in the mid-1960s, where a dean of admissions gave recruitment of Black students high priority—but also faced considerable opposition from the board of trustees for this initiative.

Did America's colleges and universities in the 1960s lead or follow in practices and policies of social justice? More than a decade after the

Supreme Court's 1954 *Brown v. the Board of Education* decision declaring racial segregation unconstitutional, numerous public and private institutions still were slow in ending racial discrimination in undergraduate admissions.

GENDER

American higher education in 1960 remained divided among coeducational and single-gender lines. More women than men graduated from high school in 1960, but fewer women than men went on to enroll in college. This imbalance declined gradually over the course of the decade. A significant development in the 1960s was the concerted initiative by women and their advocates to gain admission to numerous academically prestigious all-male colleges. The effort was most pronounced within the Ivy League, as chronicled by Princeton history professor and dean Nancy Weiss Malkiel in her 2016 book *Keep the Damned Women Out*.[31] Coeducation in many of the selective private colleges was not achieved until the late 1960s or early 1980s, however. One model that had been in place for half a century or more was the coordinate college, exemplified by Radcliffe College within Harvard University (until 1977), Barnard College within Columbia University (until 1981), Pembroke College in Brown University (until 1971), and Sophie Newcomb College in Tulane University (until 2005, after Hurricane Katrina).

Segregation by gender in higher education usually was associated with private or independent colleges and universities, but in fact the policies and practices also extended to numerous state colleges and universities. The University of Virginia did not admit women to the undergraduate college of arts and sciences until 1974. Texas A&M was exclusively male, as was the Citadel in South Carolina and Virginia Military Institute. Several states had pursued a separate but equal approach to gender in public higher education, including Mississippi College for Women, University of North Carolina College for Women, and Mary Washington College in Virginia. Just as cases involving racial desegregation indicated that separate was not equal, so would the question surface for gender in higher education in the late 1960s.

LEGAL EXCLUSIONS

In a state such as California, characterized by high demand for entrance to the state university and colleges, one accommodation offered was the public junior college.[32] These two-year institutions originally were under local auspices, structurally arranged as an extension of the high school system and funded through local property tax revenues. Many of them offered open admissions to local residents who were high school graduates and charged low, if any, tuition. By 1960, however, the junior colleges came to play an added role as transfer institutions to four-year colleges. The situation was such that at times in the late 1950s officials and regents of the University of California even considered converting the campuses of the University of California solely to upper-division plus graduate school offerings. The rationale was that high school graduates who proceeded on to their local community college and completed an approved two-year academic curriculum could then transfer to the university for their junior and senior years, receiving the university bachelor's degree. Making this articulation model mandatory, however, was squelched by President Clark Kerr, who realized that the model would cost the university revenues from per capita state subsidy enrollments and also would mortally wound the university campus varsity sports teams and other traditional activities of the four-year university experience.

The resolution was that a substantial number of students who enrolled at junior colleges did indeed transfer to the university. A 1981 study by the California Postsecondary Education Commission indicated that the junior college transfer students did better in grade point average during their junior and senior years at the university than did students who had entered as freshmen.[33] Despite such achievements by their former students, the junior colleges persisted as an inexpensive, geographically convenient option for students with a wide range of high school records—often as a safety valve or institution of last resort.

THE PARADOX AND PLIGHT OF THE PREP SCHOOLS

Students who attended private boarding schools (also known as college preparatory or prep schools) enjoyed real as well as symbolic advantages in college admissions. A paradox of the 1960s was that although these advantages remained strong, they also declined over the decade, reflecting the rise in size and strength of academic programs in US public high schools. Furthermore, admissions offices' reliance on SAT scores meant that a high SAT score from a secondary school unknown to admissions officers might trump a reference letter from a college counselor at a prep school that had long enjoyed a feeder relationship with a college.

The term *prep school* usually connoted a small number of prestigious and academically strong boarding schools, probably between twenty and thirty with name recognition. Porter Sargent's 1960s *Handbook of Private Schools*, however, suggests a more diverse, complex profile. Despite the schools' substantial tuition, boards and headmasters often were hard-pressed to compete with public high schools in providing laboratories, libraries, and credentialed teachers. Furthermore, many private schools filled a niche by providing affluent parents a place for their children who might be disciplinary problems or indifferent students. Headmasters and college counselors faced pressure from parents who were paying tuition and had high expectations that the school would assure their child's admission to acceptable colleges. The decision day by which headmasters were judged was how their students fared in the college sweepstakes competition. One answer is that the top prep schools have always enjoyed great success in admissions to the Ivy League colleges, but at the same time, their success subsided in the 1960s. By the early 1970s the *Harvard Crimson* featured an article titled "Prep Schools Sing the Blues." Top students from top prep schools, of course, fared well in college admissions. Less clear by the mid-1960s is why a dean of admissions would necessarily choose an applicant who was in the middle or lower third of his class at a prestigious school over a high-achieving applicant from a public high school. This trend continued and confirmed what was documented in 1960 by Harvard College's institutional research, which found that top students who were graduates of public high schools won a disproportionate number of academic honors at Harvard and occupied a growing proportion of the entering freshman class year after year.[34]

Inside the Admissions Office

Innovations in college viewbook graphics represented the external face of a comparable transformation within a college admissions office. For years at many colleges, admissions was a perfunctory office, often one in which the director also served as registrar. In the 1960s this official character changed, as the director became a dean of admissions whose role emphasized recruitment and selection, especially at ambitious and prestigious institutions.[35] Whether drawn from the faculty or initiated in through the administrative ranks, the dean of admissions became influential inside and outside the college. Assisted by a staff of recent college graduates (many of whom had stayed on to work for their alma mater), the dean of admissions sought to attract an abundance of applicants who fulfilled simultaneous goals of quantity and quality. The applicant pool had to be sufficiently large to allow sorting, with the ultimate goal of enrolling the target figure that filled dormitories and lecture halls with academically able students within whose ranks were students having a range of other characteristics and talents that made a campus community work well—all in accordance with the image and mission of the college itself.

In campus interviews, correspondence, and the tone of viewbooks and admissions brochures, a college admissions office promoted a personal touch in the consideration of each applicant as an individual. Ultimately, however, all information, from transcripts to reference letters and test scores, had to be systematically coded and distilled so that staff members, along with faculty and alumni on the admissions review board, could make succinct ratings and rankings and compare students across the breadth of the applicant pool. Keeping track of these permutations, especially if the number of applications was growing, led some admissions offices to make use of what they called "computing machines" for data processing. The machines allowed systematic updates on rankings and ratings of students in various categories. These early forays in using technology for ongoing data analysis are simplistic and primitive by our standards in the twenty-first century, but were cutting edge at the time, and indicative of increasing reliance on quantitative records to make qualitative decisions. Despite such technological innovation, stacks of manila envelopes and file cabinets stuffed with application materials made admissions offices crowded and hectic places to work while keeping track of a prodigious number of paper records.

When a college succeeded in attracting a sufficient number of good applicants to allow it the luxury of choice, each applicant's folder had to be evaluated—sifted and sorted—in terms of the entire entering class. The task was not merely to review each application. An admissions staff also had to devise a valid way to rate the confidence they had in a student's secondary school, to make systematic sense of reference letters, and to decide how much weight to give to scores on the SAT or the ACT. Fine-tuning also included safety valves, to allow the admissions staff to give reconsideration to an interesting candidate whose dossier risked being overlooked due to some question that warranted additional investigation. This process meant that a college ultimately could admit or reject any applicant it wished without having to explain its decision.

Relatively unknown to many students and their parents was the fact that at a competitive college, an individual applicant was not always compared to the whole population of applicants. Rather, if a student passed the first cut of academic review, she or he most likely then would be placed in a category based on some defining characteristic. It could be merit, with such specialties as biology, history, journalism, or varsity swimming. If a student claimed a particular talent, the crucial deliberation by the college officials along with coaches and program directors was whether this student would continue to participate in this field or activity once enrolled and, if so, was it likely they would contribute at a high level—one that would bring honor to the college?

According to this algorithm of review, probably the most demanding category was the well-rounded student. A central debate within each selective college was whether the goal was to attract a well-rounded student or to achieve a well-rounded class. Colleges wanted reasonable assurance that an admitted student could survive academically and excel in their selected and designated activities. It was an internal numbers game. If a theater arts director was allotted five admissions slots each year for future thespians, the director had to choose well and wisely among the fifteen academically strong applicants who reported drama as a major pursuit. This calculus played out across numerous specialties and activities. Furthermore, allocation of coveted admissions slots also included non-merit groupings, such as children of alumni (known as "legacies"), relatives of donors, and children of famous figures from politics, business, and numerous other fields. A dean of admissions worked with staff to try to compile a numerical ranking of all applicants. If this was not feasible, the staff tried to place each applicant in some tier indicating relative strength and appeal.

To complicate the matrix, a college admissions office might incorporate some measure of concern for geographic diversity and gender balance (if a coeducational campus), plus keep one eye on the scale of how much financial aid an admitted applicant would be offered. These layers of decisions and comparisons coexisted with outreach activities in which admissions staff attended college nights at various high schools or conducted interviews for applicants who visited the campus. Most attention by journalists focused on the anxiety of applicants who waited to receive letters from various colleges in April. Yet for the dean of admissions, a crucial event was the sequel, in which a college waited to see which applicants accepted the college's offer and agreed to enroll in the freshman class for the autumn semester. In quantitative terms, this meant measuring and parsing the admissions yield. If a college sent out one thousand offers of admissions, what number said "Yes!"? And then, were the higher-ranked applicants accepting the college's offer—or were they going elsewhere?

The high-stakes dimension of the decision making was that some colleges attracted a large number of excellent applicants—a favorable sign. Yet they might find that they chronically lost their top applicants to rival institutions. Each of those students was a lost source of prestige and professional bragging rights. In fact, one of the most closely guarded secrets within any college admissions office in the 1960s was the precise breakdowns on what were called "cross applications." For example, where did the pool of students who applied both to Stanford University and to Occidental College choose to go? How did Vassar fare in head-to-head competition with Wellesley? What was the box score in comparing Northwestern University with the University of Chicago in undergraduate admissions? Did Duke rise or fall in competing with nearby University of North Carolina or with Vanderbilt and Tulane?

Across the entire universe of colleges and universities in the United States, this scenario tended to describe the crowding and competition primarily at attractive institutions. Some colleges, usually large state universities, relied on a formula of high school grades and test scores to determine whether a student was admissible. In some states, a student who had graduated from an accredited high school in the state and had taken certain courses was offered entry to a state college or university. An institution could even use non-merit factors, such as date of application,·to make decisions as to who would be admitted and who would be turned away—comparable to selling tickets for a flight or a movie. Some selectivity was a function of a college's relative commitment to creating a residential campus; those institutions that made such a commitment had to limit enrollment according to the availability of dormitories. However, college officials at a college or university that made no promises about on-campus housing, and at any commuter school, could expand the entering class as much or as little as they wished, leaving admitted students to fend for themselves on housing, parking, and other support services.

Feature articles that provided readers with insider accounts of the annual round of work surrounding admissions decisions at selective colleges tended to emphasize the angle that making admissions decisions among a talented pool was no easy job. This notion was reinforced in a report by the Harvard faculty about the dilemmas of selective admissions: "No one who has ever participated in the April meetings of the Admissions committee could fail to appreciate the difficulty of keeping balance, or even in mind, all the particular arguments which can be brought to bear on the acceptance or rejection of any boy, be he from

New York City, Roxbury, or a Dakota farming town, from Phillips Exeter or Blue Earth High School."[36]

No matter how difficult selective admissions deliberations were, they were surpassed by the headaches facing deans of admissions at hundreds of invisible colleges. According to Alexander Astin and Calvin B. T. Lee, these institutions were "private, often church-affiliated institutions with relatively open admissions policies and enrollments under 2,500 that comprise one-third of the four-year colleges in the U.S. and enroll almost 500,000 students."[37] Another important category was what Alden B. Dunham called the "colleges of the forgotten Americans"—state colleges that enrolled a high percentage of students who were the first in their families to go to college. Many of them were regional comprehensive campuses that provided a solid education, yet in contrast to the flagship state universities or the Ivy League institutions had relatively little recruitment leverage in areas such as prestige, publicity, or financial aid.[38] Many scrambled to enroll an adequate number of students who had acceptable academic credentials and who could afford to pay even modest tuition.

The Curious Consumerism of College Admissions

How hard was it to get into college? Making comparisons with selective admissions today is difficult, but there are some case studies to use in assessing the combined impact of the graphics revolution of college publicity and the annually increasing number of well-prepared college applicants. In October 1964 *Newsweek* featured a story titled "Brown Grows the Ivy." Just as the *Hootenanny* television show in 1963 brought increased attention to Brown University and other campuses selected as broadcast sites, so did the *Newsweek* article boost Brown's reputation among college applicants. The article noted that Brown had received ten applicants for every first-year slot. The profile of high grade point averages, high SAT scores, and class valedictorians led *Newsweek* to exclaim that "it was like having a baseball team with all the line up having .300 batting averages."[39] The *Newsweek* article about Brown also gave readers some clues about the changing landscape of college admissions across the United States. Ten applicants per admission slot in 1964 certainly cannot match Stanford's profile today of twenty applicants per slot. But it dramatizes the point that the number and quality of college applicants nationwide were on the rise in 1964 and would continue the rest of the decade.

Going to college in the early 1960s usually meant limited choices, for reasons of finance and availability. In many states applicants did not have a lot of available colleges. State universities such as the University of Massachusetts and Rutgers in New Jersey each had a total enrollment of about 6,000 each. These institutions could admit only a fraction of the state's academically qualified high school seniors who wanted to go to college. The double jeopardy was that private colleges on the East Coast imposed geographic quotas in their work at crafting a class. As sociologists Christopher Jencks and David Riesman wrote in 1968, the coded complaint among deans of admissions in the Ivy League was, "We're getting too many kids from New York." This complaint buttresses observations made in student memoirs from the mid-1960s.

College admissions deans openly discussed their concern that applicants might start a bidding war among colleges from whom they had received offers of entry including financial aid. The college deans and presidents strongly opposed such acts, yet college officials from various consortia often shared information among themselves and reached agreements on what was known as the "overlap group." For example, every year the eight presidents within the Ivy Group met at the University Club in New York City to discuss both institutional competition and cooperation for what they considered to be the most talented male high school graduating seniors. As *Newsweek* quoted one Ivy League college president in 1964, "We have a splendid time. Then we go home and try to steal away each other's prospective freshman class."[40] Decades later, the overlap group was subject to a 1989 antitrust suit by the US Treasury Department in a controversial case involving charges of price fixing in need-based financial aid. Sixty years ago, however, there was no such external criticism. Public opinion deferred to colleges' right to collaboration and self-determination, which meant there was little concern for student consumer protection, even if the images and information students received were comparable to empty calories.

In retrospect, American higher education admissions between 1960 and 1969 appear as a mosaic of college categories in which enrollment was shaped substantially by self-selection in matching students and institutions according to some defining affiliation, such as religion, race, family legacy, or geographic proximity. For example, Catholics and numerous Protestant denominations had their associated colleges, Blacks theirs, and women theirs. And, within each state, the public colleges and universities had their own customs and tracking in which the historic flagship campus tended to attract a relatively affluent group, including children of alumni and state legislators. The result was an uneven mix of sponsored mobility that was beneficial to a talented few coexisting with a broad contest for upward mobility, all played out in a caste system across hundreds of institutions.

In the early 1960s there were a few signs of innovation that substantially expanded or diversified student recruitment. The Ford Foundation provided funding in 1963 for selected prestigious colleges to participate in what came to be called a Tom Sawyer Program, intended to fund admission of young men who were academic risks yet showed other characteristics worth consideration as signaling the potential for success and leadership in college and adult life. Using Mark Twain literary metaphors, this grant-funded project seeking out a Tom Sawyer included no comparable strategies to admit a Jim or a Becky Thatcher—an oversight indicative of the relative lack of attention given to race and gender in admissions recruitment in the era.

Recruitment and admission of African American students would gain momentum in the late 1960s, especially in the wake of the assassination of the Reverend Dr. Martin Luther King, Jr. Prior to that, however, results were meager. The dean of admissions at Princeton, Alden Dunham, was strongly committed to recruiting African American men, even though he faced substantial resistance from some groups on his campus. Despite Dunham's commitment, success was hard fought and gains were small, as freshmen enrollment of African Americans went from five in 1960 to eighteen in 1963 out of an entering class of about a thousand.

Allowing women to enroll in historically all-male colleges showed signs of gaining momentum in the late 1960s and early 1970s. But awareness of and concern for numerous underrepresented groups, including Latinos and Asian Americans, was not high on the academic agenda of the decade.[41] One significant development that started to come into practice in the late 1960s involved the connections and commitments associated with admissions and student financial aid. The ultimate arrangement, achieved by only a few fortunate and well-endowed institutions by 1970, was the double-pronged pledge to applicants of need-blind admissions followed by need-based financial aid.

On balance, students had made greater gains in access than they had in acquiring increases in college choice or college affordability. These prospects indicated that the diverse, sprawling array of what was called postsecondary education provided students with access that often meant accommodation without great options or financial assistance. Although applicants received growing stacks of promotional materials and recruitment brochures, college consumerism of the 1960s was curious in that it tended to favor the colleges rather than the students in terms of recruitment and selection. Colleges took on little risk and made minimal explanations about their rankings and ratings of applicants. In contrast, student choices were usually limited and applicants had little information about how decisions were made on admissions or awarding of student financial aid. Competition and crowding among an expanded applicant pool shaped the prospects and percentages facing high school graduates starting fifteen years after the end of World War II. Going to college in the 1960s was a partially stacked deck that favored the house of the admissions office. As historian Marcia Synnott observed, college admissions, especially for the prestigious private and public colleges and universities, created a "half-opened door" for a new and large generation of college applicants.[42]

The Knowledge Industry
The Higher Education Establishment

Confidence and Coordination: The Optimistic Belief in Systems

Most undergraduates and their families in the 1960s understandably were preoccupied with the demands of enrolling for courses, paying tuition bills, moving into dormitories, attending orientation sessions, going to class, and participating in campus activities. Out of their view, American colleges and universities during that decade were being built, funded, shaped, and steered by a new generation of prominent leaders who were in charge of overlapping initiatives and organizations. Turning attention in this chapter to leadership and structures of higher education may at first seem a puzzling side trip that diverts from the focus on a history of undergraduates who were going to college in this era. Although the two disparate groups, students and academic leaders, usually were disconnected, they were interdependent. By the mid-1960s their separate orbits converged. And, sometimes they collided, with consequences for all of American culture and higher education by the end of the decade.

Tom Wolfe gained fame for his 1987 novel *The Bonfire of the Vanities*, about a power elite of business executives, lawyers, financiers, investors, and politicians who immodestly referred to themselves as the Masters of the Universe. Their counterparts for higher education between 1960 and 1970 aptly could be called the Masters of the University. These academic leaders transformed the policies and programs of higher education and were effective in accommodating massive expansion of student enrollments and the growth of higher education as an enterprise. Eventually they overestimated some of their influence while they overlooked or ignored other institutional and cultural currents that undermined their agenda. By mid-decade these blind spots among many university presidents led to a curious mix of organizational success combined with unexpected problems and unpleasant surprises. This combination would ultimately have implications, even repercussions, among undergraduates in their college experience and in how students viewed what came to be called the higher education establishment.

The confidence and optimism of these higher education leaders included a belief in the efficacy of systems and master planning. It was an extension of the 1920s Carnegie Foundation for the Advancement of Teaching leadership gospel that promoted an emphasis on standards and standardization.[1] The totality of higher education and its auxiliary moving parts came to be known as the Knowledge Industry. Those involved in it liked the association with the business model of the post–World War II economy, especially when a familiar adage was that "what was good for General Motors was good for the country." The Knowledge Economy was measured in such categories as research dollars, conferral of degrees, production of patents and papers, and manpower planning. The result was that higher education was proudly characterized as the late twentieth-century successor to the railroads and then the automobile factories.[2]

Even though the planners and leaders of higher education at the time invoked and also saw themselves as experts who were part of a managerial revolution characterized by industrial organization charts and factory production, they first had to tend to the messy task of getting legislative approval for their plans to broker coherent, coordinated institutions. The task of creating systems in the late 1950s and early 1960s brings to mind medieval rather than modern motifs, reminiscent of a politically chaotic thirteenth- and fourteenth-century Europe where dukes, barons, sheriffs, and bishops battled in turf wars, all accentuated by the lack of strong, centralized national governments. Their strategies and maneuvers suggested a twentieth-century version of the Italian city-state rivalries illustrated by Florentine politics, as narrated by Niccolò Machiavelli in *The Prince*. This interpretation is not mere hyperbole or conjecture; *Time* magazine writers celebrated President Clark Kerr of the University of California as "the Machiavellian Quaker" in his administrative style in institutional and statewide politics.[3]

The same spirit of local rivalries was true of higher education in the United States as skirmishes over higher education jurisdictions underscored the importance of state and local academic fiefdoms and provided the reminder that the idea as well as the reality of a national ministry in higher education was uncertain and unfulfilled. Charters to colleges and universities were granted at the level of the state, where politics and funding were both intense and important. Hostile takeovers, raids, alliances by marriage, and annexation were the order of the day in state, local, and regional campaigns over the control of campuses. There was relatively limited centralized federal control with more customary power accruing to states, regions, and local groups along with the academic fiefdoms within universities themselves.

Creating and Controlling the Campus

A conventional way to handle growth of enrollment and programs was to expand the size of a campus. Indeed, by 1960 several major state universities (including the University of North Carolina, University of Texas, Ohio State University, Michigan State University, University of Michigan, University of California, Berkeley, and the University of Wisconsin) accommodated enrollments of between 21,000 and 30,000 students. The University of Minnesota in this era grew to over 60,000. Enrollment growth was accompanied by increased complexity within a campus, marked by a proliferation of new entities such as research centers and institutes. Each new unit brought along new administrative positions, support staff, and offices for budgets, record keeping, and data collection.

Planning the new American campus made university presidents into celebrities. The cast, including William Friday of the University of North Carolina and John Hanna of Michigan State University, expanded the traditional land grant mission to encompass a wide range of academic services and expertise that was characterized by partnership with and funding from federal agencies, private foundations, and the new orbit of heads of state and governments from other nations, especially in Asia. Robben Fleming led the University of Wisconsin and, later, the University of Michigan to enhanced international stature. Samuel Gould was the diplomat and broker who in his roles as chancellor and president of the State University of New York brought political coherence to an extended network of more than sixty campuses. Presidents Milton S. Eisenhower of Johns Hopkins University, Grayson Kirk of Columbia University, and James Perkins of Cornell personified the presidents who oversaw a complex array of programs and personnel which required continual negotiations and lobbying with external constituencies ranging from donors to senators and foundations. Foremost in the public spotlight was the University of California's President Clark Kerr, featured on the cover of *Time* magazine's October 17, 1960 issue.[4]

Form and function in higher education planning were linked. The higher education boom extended to feature campus architects as iconic public figures. Most prominent was William Pereira, selected by the

The new American campus of the 1960s: UC Irvine architèct William Pereira, Chancellor Daniel Aldrich, and Charles S. Thompson survey the Master Plan.
(Courtesy of the University of California, Irvine)

University of California regents to design the new campus at Irvine, including a new city on land that had been part of a large ranch. The September 6, 1963, cover of *Time* magazine hailed the campus as "Vistas for the Future." The biographical profile of "The Man with the Plan" conveyed an image that suggested James Bond had left Her Majesty's Royal Service for the intrigue of the bold new field of campus design:

> The black and grey Bentley snaked south out of Los Angeles along the Santa Ana Freeway, shook free of the traffic, and began to climb fast on a mountain road through the open country. At the wheel was a shapely brunette .beauty—secretary, assistant and part-time chauffeur to the man in the back seat listening to Mantovani on a built-in-stereophonic tape recorder. The car stopped on the mountaintop, where a friend was waiting; the man got out, a trim 6 feet with heavy-lidded blue eyes and an actor's dash. The wind riffled his wavy, iron-grey hair as he gazed out over Irvine Ranch, the miles and miles of grazing land and citrus groves rolling down to the Pacific.[5]

When Pereira took on the commission to oversee the design of both the University of California campus and the neighboring city of Irvine, he drew from what had been called, because of his Transamerica Pyramid in San Francisco and urban planning for Brasilia, his brutalist architecture and science fiction vision. *Time* magazine writers praised his role in shaping the new University of California campus, noting, "The handsome man who can play such a godlike game is neither conqueror nor commissar, but one of a new breed of artisans rising in the world, the regional planner. . . . The regional planner orchestrates vast areas of wilderness with cities, villages, farms and forests to serve the needs of men." The campus had become a showplace for American architecture and design.

Although the campus was the basic building block of the Knowledge Industry, it was supplemented and supplanted by new institutional structures. The emphasis on a single campus gave way in several states to creating a multicampus university system. New branch campuses matured to coexist with the historic main campus. When a state adopted a state university system model, the public needed to be made aware of name changes, and a readjustment had to be made about what the term *university* meant. Whereas *the University of North Carolina* in sports and publicity implicitly meant the historic campus at Chapel Hill, the new university structure meant that the University of North Carolina was now a system of numerous campuses for which Chapel Hill was the home of both the historic campus and the massive system-wide headquarters. The same held for the University of Texas, which no longer consisted only of the historic Austin campus.

Consolidating several campuses into a single university system also required diplomatic negotiations, including concessions and compromises. Institutional prestige often was at stake, played out in many states with historic rivalries between the state's flagship university and the rival land grant universities, each of which had acquired over time its own base of alumni and legislative support along with extension services and outposts. In one state the head of the system was the chancellor, with each member campus having its own president. The opposite held true elsewhere. At the University of California, the system-wide leader was the president, with each campus having a chancellor. Public events such as ribbon-cutting ceremonies hinted at tensions over jurisdiction between the system and the campus. Franklin Murphy, the popular, successful chancellor of the young University of California, Los Angeles (UCLA), campus, was responsible for the growth of its medical center and academic ascent. Little wonder that he was not happy to have to share the podium and praise with the system-wide university president, Clark Kerr. On a multicampus system, gravitation toward centralized governance competed with campus quest for self-determination and decentralization within the system. Within each state, legislators and academic leaders hashed out compacts on campus autonomy and limits on system-wide regulations.

Lobbying the state legislature was another consideration in moving to system-wide governance. Each campus had a keen sense of its political capital earned over many years in gaining legislative support for construction, addition of new programs, and other measures crucial to campus growth and success. A trade-off in joining a system is that a campus leader often forfeited the opportunity to be a free agent in lobbying and fund-raising. It meant having to defer to the system-wide administration, which had set its own list of priorities and which often demanded to be the main, even exclusive, lobbying agent for all campuses in the system. A campus that had once been freestanding now had to pass system-wide review to establish that its proposed new academic program was not duplicating or interfering with a comparable program offered by another campus in the system.

A downside in this rationalization of decision making toward a systems model was that it clashed with the historical fact that for the American public, loyalty and tradition meant attachment to a campus, not to a system-wide headquarters. A university system's offices enrolled no students, conferred no degrees, taught no courses, and sponsored no student activities. The system's offices usually were located within large, impersonal buildings apart from all the features of a campus—here, perhaps, was academia's department of motor vehicles in that the bureaucracy was useful and necessary. The headquarters for the new, large systems often were seen as an academic equivalent of the Pentagon in Washington, DC. Their architecture and office spaces were overwhelming and powerful but neither endearing nor memorable. A system-wide president had a great deal of persuading to do to bring coherence to the new structural arrangement.

State plans to accommodate growing college enrollments emphasized creating new institutions and expanding old ones.[6] One pioneer was the state of New York with its two large systems. The State University of New York, known as SUNY, was created in 1948 and underwent expansion in the early 1960s. The SUNY system annexed numerous previously private campuses as part of a complex tier structure that ranged from community colleges to doctoral-granting campuses and special health field sites. By 1967 SUNY's undergraduate enrollment was over 139,000. SUNY personified the success story of political and planning efforts as it became the largest comprehensive public university system in the nation, characterized as "sixty-four campuses—one university."[7]

About the same time, the CUNY system took shape. The governor and state legislature agreed in 1961 to aid the historic municipal system by combining the city's four existing four-year colleges (City, Hunter, Brooklyn, and Queens) and three community colleges (Staten Island, Bronx, and Manhattan) under the aegis of a single entity, the City University of New York. New York State would provide funding to expand the new entity, just as dozens of other states had in these years. However, state support was tied to a demand that CUNY impose tuition on all of its students—as Governor Nelson Rockefeller had done at SUNY in 1962. A long-range planning report for CUNY articulated three major goals: to build or acquire more community and four-year colleges, to expand enrollment by creating a more flexible admissions policy, and to maintain free tuition for full-time four-year college students. By 1964 CUNY undergraduate enrollment was 49,000 students.

Combining Accessibility and Affordability

Variations on the theme in creating statewide higher education systems can be found in Texas, Louisiana, North Carolina, Wisconsin, Minnesota, and Massachusetts, to name just a partial roster. A defining element of deliberations over these state systems was the general belief, shared by governors and legislators and applauded by students and their parents, that public colleges and universities should be affordable for students who were state residents. This was not universally true, as the political economy and tax traditions of some states still viewed attending college, including the state university, as calling for a user's fee. Low-tax states, for example, frequently had relatively high tuition charges. To another extreme, California and New York led the way with their commitment to no tuition or low tuition at state institutions.

Low or no tuition in state colleges became the standard invoked by higher education advocates, although it always raised serious policy discussions with private or independent colleges within the state, which claimed that such largesse created an imbalanced academic market, including what they called a tuition gap. Furthermore, leaders of state university systems could be presumptuous in leaving out independent colleges and universities when counting assets to their state. How much sense did it make for SUNY and CUNY to talk about statewide planning in New York, which also was home to such truly great universities as Columbia and Cornell? No matter how great the University of California might be, the state of California was comparably well served by contributions to education and economy made by Stanford, Caltech, the University of Southern California, the Claremont Colleges, Occidental College, and the University of the Pacific.

In New England states a strong historic tradition of great private colleges and universities made statewide planning incomplete without private universities. Just within Boston alone, the contributions of the Massachusetts Institute of Technology, Harvard, Northeastern, Tufts, Boston University, and Boston College underscored the importance of private as well as public institutions as essential to the common good.[8] Systematic studies of the undergraduate origins of PhD recipients in the sciences documented that a disproportionate number had been students at private liberal arts colleges. One way that several state legislatures acknowledged the contribution of independent private colleges and universities to the state's educational and economic well-being was creation of state-funded awards in the form of portable scholarships usually called Tuition Assistance Grants (TAG), which eligible state residents applying to college could have credited to their tuition charges at any accredited college, public or private, within the state.

Despite such differences, the general mood at the start of the 1960s was that state governments and other partners were working to make higher education increasingly available and affordable to high school students.

Master Plans for Higher Education

Gaining cooperation and approval for creating and staffing a state university system was difficult in itself. Yet in some states, accomplishing this task was followed by a more complicated feat: constructing and then selling the notion of statewide coordination across several academic systems.[9] The case of California was especially significant because it was pioneering, took place in a large, prosperous state, and came to be portrayed in the national media as the leader for the United States—and for the world. The capstone legislation in 1960 was the Donahoe Higher Education Act, named in honor of state legislator Dorothy M. Donahoe, who died shortly before legislation was signed into law.[10] The California Master Plan, as noted earlier, led to publicity in such national publications as *Time* magazine.[11] It was a source of state pride, one that set forth a blueprint intended to guide the years 1960 to 1975 and to ensure that mass education did not degenerate into mob education.

The victory pronouncements and public relations photography sessions glossed over what had in fact been a contentious quarrel across institutions statewide. A summary profile of the agreement is that public postsecondary education in the state would fit under the umbrella of what was called a coordinating council. Eventually this council would take the name and form of the California Postsecondary Education Commission, whose main components were the University of California, the California State University (Cal State) and state colleges, and the junior colleges. Each segment had a distinctive mission and a general admissions constituency. The categories were in large part indicative of power and prestige. The University of California system had six campuses in 1960, namely, Berkeley, UCLA, Riverside, San Francisco, Davis, and Santa Barbara. On the drawing board at the time of the Master Plan approval were three new campuses, each located on spectacular sites overlooking the Pacific Ocean—San Diego, Irvine, and Santa Cruz—all of which were open by 1965. The University of California would draw its undergraduates from the top 8% of high school graduating seniors. It also would be the eminent, and the only public, institution in the state allowed to confer the PhD.

California's State University and colleges system, which ultimately would be the largest in terms of four-year campuses and enrollments, had seventeen campuses in 1960 and would confer bachelor's and master's degrees. New campuses were authorized at Fullerton (1957), Hayward (1957), Stanislaus (1957), San Fernando Valley (1958), Sonoma (1960), San Bernardino (1960), and Dominguez Hills (1960). In 1961 the California State Colleges (CSC) was established as a system with a board of trustees and a chancellor by the Donahoe Act, which assigned different functions to the University of California, the California State Colleges, and the California community colleges. The primary function of the state colleges was broadened to include undergraduate and graduate instruction in the liberal arts and sciences, in applied fields, and in the professions; doctoral degrees are authorized if offered jointly with the University of California.

Public junior colleges provided courses of study leading to the two-year associate degree and were designated as transfer institutions to the numerous four-year campuses. Sixty-five junior colleges were operating within the state of California in 1960. This number would increase rapidly over the decade, eventually topping one hundred junior colleges within the state. Most significant is that in California and other states that opted in to junior college construction, the public two-year colleges eventually would enroll more college students than any other sector. In other words, starting in 1960, public two-year colleges would be the largest growth segment in higher education and would become the institutional home of a vast majority of college freshmen and sophomores, even though these schools were not the traditional popular image of a college campus.

The California Master Plan also included the state's numerous and highly regarded independent colleges and universities in its planning and deliberations.[12] "All's well that ends well" might have been an appropriate and welcomed verdict when the Master Plan was approved. It took years to resolve tensions and intersegmental disagreements over jurisdiction, funding, and student recruitment. The paradox of planning was that the gains in coordination and coherence still were bewildering to the uninitiated. Furthermore, whether in the state of North Carolina or in the states of New York or California, the master plans worked imperfectly. Articulation agreements promoting transfer for students seldom operated as smoothly as had been hoped. Legislators and system architects tended to look over and above the internecine rivalries and inefficiencies. For undergraduates, the box score was that tuition was low—in California, nonexistent. But the labyrinth of potential choices was overwhelming.

As many states took the lead in edging toward mass higher education, the gains in access were remarkable and worthy of applause, but once students were enrolled within a system or within a campus, regulations and restrictions proved to be more than mere nuisances. In short, the Master Plan movement was a political and educational success in accomplishing expansion and reducing local fiefdoms. Moving closer to the experience of the typical undergraduate student, whether at SUNY Buffalo, North Carolina State University, or Long Beach City College, however, it's clear that internal problems remain unresolved.

Why the shortfalls? First, the perspective of politicians was understandably on facilitating funding and construction. And they had done their part. They largely left to the higher education experts the fine-tuning needed to fulfill promises and visions. Second, the conceptual blueprints of the master planners ran ahead of their information systems. From budgets to enrollments and beyond, data were not readily available or analyzable, so it was difficult, perhaps impossible, to monitor institutional responsiveness adequately. What was clear in the numerous master plans was that state government was the leader in terms of innovations, accommodations, and funding for the expansion of higher education in the 1960s. The question surfaces, then, what was the role of the federal government in the decade of master planning?

The Federal Government

When considering the politics and programs in the United States in the decades following World War II, numerous important examples surface in which the federal government played an expanded and growing role. Starting in 1957, for example, the construction of the interstate highway system comes to mind. For higher education, however, the federal government's role in the 1960s is uneven, complex, and even surprising because it was counterintuitive. One recurrent mischaracterization of the federal government portrays it as a monolithic unified force in higher education issues, a portrayal captured in good-natured references to "the Feds." In fact, for the 1960s the federal government's role in higher education was fragmented and often uncoordinated, even inconsistent and contradictory. Its role in education, including higher education, often involved a large amount of funding, but the programs in which the funds could be spent were limited. In the 1960s there was no US cabinet position of secretary of education. Nationwide data on a range of indicators such as enrollments, degrees conferred, revenues, and expenditures were inconsistent because no federal higher education agency existed to collect them.

Most surprising is the absence of large-scale federal programs for student financial aid. Despite the 1947 Truman Commission Report dealing with higher education in a democracy, including issues of affordability and access, these issues received little federal attention and even less funding. Notwithstanding the popularity and success of the GI Bill of 1944 in providing generous scholarships to veterans who enrolled in accredited colleges, Congress never got around to grafting the GI Bill student scholarship model onto the domestic or peacetime economy as a program available to all US students who sought to go to college. By the late 1950s numerous federal projects in infrastructure, health, military, and defense were up and running. By 1964 there was a federal focus on civil rights and racial discrimination, especially with the Civil Rights Act—a focus that ultimately extended indirectly or secondarily to some dimensions of higher education. But the US government did not focus directly on higher education, despite passage of the federal Higher Education Act of 1965. The act's authorization language indicates a strong federal presence: the law was intended "to strengthen the educational resources of our colleges and universities and to provide financial assistance for students in postsecondary and higher education."[13] Its intention was to give federal money to universities, create scholarships, give low-interest loans for students, and establish a National Teachers Corps. On closer inspection, searches for evidence of concrete program funding and implementation turn up meager results. A bipartisan coalition in Congress worked diligently to set up an attractive federally underwritten student loan plan that offered low interest rates. Yet, year after year, representatives from the banking industry showed little interest in participating, even though the congressional terms on underwriting the student loans were incredibly favorable to the banks in terms of minimizing their risks.[14] The Higher Education Act of 1965 could be seen as the Magna Carta of federal support for higher education, but it would not be fulfilled and funded until later, especially with the 1972 reauthorization.[15]

The area where the federal government's impact was swift and great was in its role as a source of support via its various agencies for sponsored research and development. Federal support in this arena led to the flourishing of what came to be called the federal grant university, one of the most dramatic and consequential developments in the history of American higher education.

RESEARCH AND DEVELOPMENT: THE FEDERAL GRANT UNIVERSITY

The United States had invested in research and development since the late nineteenth century, but there were no imperatives that the investments be centered in academic institutions or that they would be funded by the federal government. Indeed, wealthy patrons such as Andrew Carnegie thought universities presented too many distractions to serious research. Among federal civil servants, the favored model was the free-standing federal agency or commission, as exemplified by the US Geologic Survey. By 1960, however, the source of funding and the place of research came together to help consolidate the federal grant university, typically a prominent university with highly skilled personnel, substantial laboratories and research facilities, and a track record derived from industrial contracts, World War II projects, and positioning in specific, high-profile fields. The institutions in this favored circle also would match well with the priorities in research spending held by various federal agencies. In 1963, for example, this confluence of funding and institution profile resulted in six universities receiving 57% of total federal agency research expenditures. Expanding the scope further, twenty universities accounted for just under 80% of federal research grants. Ratings and rankings were based on data about research grant dollars, scholarly publications, and international awards. A snapshot of the rankings of the twenty universities receiving the most research grant dollars reported by the National Science Foundation in 1968 indicates the victors in the research competition associated with the new category of the federal grant university (dollar amounts from 1968 can be increased tenfold to get approximate equivalents in 2017 dollars):[16]

Massachusetts Institute of Technology	$79,776,000
Stanford University	$41,407,000
Harvard University	$39,177,000
University of Michigan	$37,754,000
University of California, Los Angeles	$36,534,000
Columbia University	$34,693,000
University of California, Berkeley	$34,031,000
University of Wisconsin–Madison	$30,993,000
University of Illinois, Urbana-Champaign	$29,804,000
University of Washington, Seattle	$27,940,000
University of Chicago	$26,956,000
University of Minnesota	$26,378,000
New York University	$24,318,000
University of California, San Diego	$23,996,000
Cornell University	$23,306,000
Johns Hopkins University	$22,201,000
Yale University	$19,637,000
University of Pennsylvania	$18,414,000
Ohio State University	$16,398,000
Duke University	$16,226,000

The specialization and intensity were underscored by the fact that since 1950, federal allocations for research had expanded consistently and generously. This generalization broke down into important specifics as to kinds of topics, fields, and institutions which would be competitive in this relatively new sweepstakes. The National Institutes of Health (NIH) represented 37% of all federal research funding, including to universities. This amount and percentage would increase persistently, with the result of catapulting those universities with an academic medical center into prominence, especially as new bio- hybrid partnerships (biochemistry, bioengineering, and biophysics) pulled away from traditional arts and sciences departments such as biology, physics, and chemistry as objects of research patronage. Looking at the roster of the top twenty universities in 1968 in terms of grant recipients, it is clear that the primacy of research related to medical and health fields was just starting to take place. Within the next decade Johns Hopkins University, with its strong programs in engineering, medicine, and public health specialties such as tropical diseases, would surge to the top of the rankings.

The NIH was followed by the Department of Defense at 32%, the young National Science Foundation at 11%, the Atomic Energy Commission at 8%, the Department of Agriculture showing 6%, and the National Aeronautics and Space Administration, 3%, with the remaining 1% distributed among disparate federal agencies. Not until the mid-1960s would Congress authorize creation of the National Endowment for the Humanities, a good and symbolic gesture in terms of expanding important fields. In dollars allocated, however, NEH was still distant from the so-called durable goods and hard sciences of medicine, physics, engineering, applied biology, and agriculture.

The federal funding disparity between favored fields in the sciences and the humanities would at first blush seem to be far removed from undergraduates going to college. This was true, but was modified by the codicil that ambitious universities seeking grants and inclusion in the select ranks of Federal Grant Universities shifted according to the bait offered by federal agencies' requests for proposals, commonly called RFPs. Directly and indirectly the chase after RFPs altered campuses' approach to allocation of resources for teaching. For universities that had committed heavily to PhD programs, the prospect of federal research grants indelibly altered the script of what was emphasized and funded—and what was not. Eventually these decisions at a small number of prestigious universities and in a select number of fields would shape priorities of the academic profession and also teaching and learning in the undergraduate curriculum.

State Systems: Consolidation, Control, and Coordination

Clark Kerr's *The Uses of the University* was first delivered as the Godkin Lectures at Harvard University in 1963. Both the message and the messenger captured the spotlight of higher education planning nationwide.

It was unheard of for the president of a state university on the Pacific Coast to command such attention from an historic, private New England university. Kerr's talks and writings were central to transforming the geography and landscape of the future of American higher education.

The interesting wrinkle was that Kerr's University of California, ranging from its historic Berkeley campus to its newer additions such as UCLA, was home to both research innovation and the extension of undergraduate education to an unprecedented number and percentage of high school graduates. Quality and quantity—excellence and accommodation—now were combined in the model of what Clark Kerr called the modern multiversity. The concept was exhilarating, impressive, and influential. In some respects it was democratic, in that it spread the wealth of prestige toward the Midwest and the Pacific Coast, diluting some of the hegemony of the Northeast and mid-Atlantic universities.

In contrast, however, henceforth prestige in American higher education often would drift toward advanced programs, funded research grants, doctoral degrees, and national research awards. Competition among top universities was portrayed as the "frantic race to remain contemporary."[17] Prestige associated with growth in research and development often meant, directly or indirectly, diminishing focus on the quality and content of undergraduate education. The balancing act of American higher education starting in 1960 is that colleges and universities nationwide showed increased interest in enrolling undergraduates. Yet some institutions, especially those in the category of research universities, looked in the opposite direction as they paid inordinate attention to PhD programs and faculty research, which were often far removed from the concern of effective teaching and learning for students pursuing a bachelor's degree. This disparity, often glossed over and explained away by higher education architects in the early 1960s, would come back to haunt a generation of university presidents, provosts, and deans between 1964 and 1970.

Redefining the Role of Major Foundations

By 1960 private foundations had relinquished their role as a major external influence on higher education for the pragmatic reason that the new presence of the federal government provided a lot of money as incentives to colleges and universities. At the same time, many of the once affluent foundations had spent down their endowments and out of necessity now devoted their staff efforts to consulting on projects—to bring in money rather than to give it away. An important exception was the relatively young Ford Foundation. It was foremost among foundations in the 1960s in providing encouragements and prods (and funding) to colleges and universities on numerous initiatives, intended to mold the offerings and priorities of colleges and universities. A Ford project might be a pilot project in which, for example, five prestigious universities agreed to use Ford Foundation funding to rethink what the master of business administration degree and curriculum ought to be. Other major initiatives included critical examination of Historically Black Colleges and Universities in the South and agricultural research exchanges between land grant universities in the United States and nations and universities in South America or Africa. Yet these projects funded by private foundations ultimately lacked the funding power of federal agencies that had an interest in international projects.

Even though the major foundations lost ground in actual dollars for higher education funding, they assumed an important role as a partner with the federal government, with international projects and governments, and with universities. Many biographies of prominent government and academic leaders of the 1960s note that a president who left campus office subsequently assumed a leadership role at the Carnegie Foundation or the Brookings Institution, perhaps an intermediate step on the way to appointment as a member of the cabinet of the president of the United States or to head up a federal agency. When President Dwight D. Eisenhower was leaving the White House in 1960 he noted the importance of the military-industrial complex. Given the role of foundations and universities in the network, this term might have been expanded to be the military-industrial-educational complex.

Universities, International Relations, and Program Development

The prestige and power of the Knowledge Industry in the 1960s extended to establishing new international educational alliances. Illustrative of this confident expansion was the motto "The world is our campus!" The genesis of such initiatives lay in federal exchange programs such as the Fulbright Scholarships as well as agency initiatives associated with the post–World War II Marshall Plan for economic and political recovery in Europe. Two concurrent developments gave research universities a new presence beyond campus, state, and even national borders. First was the increasing expertise of professors in a range of specialties that had potential appeal to international constituencies. Second was the push and pull as research universities were sought by external groups and simultaneously sought new sources of funding. National governments, especially in what was called the Third World, from time to time viewed universities as attractive partners. Furthermore, US government agencies such as the Association for International Development and some private think tanks were viewed both at home and abroad as instruments the United States could use in the Cold War to promote US-style expertise as an integral part of democracy and what was termed *nation building*. Also, the Central Intelligence Agency looked to prestigious American campuses as a place to recruit talent. Political scientists, economists, and other scholarly specialists who had knowledge of and experience in developing countries could be consultants and program officers in these partnerships among the United States, a host foreign nation, and the academy.[18] Cooperating nations and their governments included countries in Africa, Asia, Europe, Central America, and South America.

This confluence of talent across academics, business, and government led to a super-meritocracy hailed as "the best and the brightest."[19] This circle, also known as the whiz kids, included those who served in the cabinet of President John F. Kennedy and then with President Lyndon B. Johnson. Foremost within a select group called the Wise Men was McGeorge Bundy. Bundy was bright, from a patrician Boston family. His notion of rebellion against tradition was attending Yale rather than Harvard. Later he served in the US Army as an intelligence officer in World War II, was a member of high-level federal discussion groups, and in 1953 became the youngest dean of arts and sciences at Harvard, even though he had no graduate degree. He connected academic leadership with public political life in 1961 when the new president, John F. Kennedy—a Harvard alumnus and a fellow Bostonian—appointed him as national security advisor. According to public profiles, Bundy "played a crucial role in all of the major foreign policy and defense decisions of the Kennedy administration and was retained by Lyndon B. Johnson for part of his tenure. Bundy was involved in the Bay of Pigs Invasion, the Cuban Missile Crisis, and the Viet War." In 1964 he served as chair of the 303 Committee, which was responsible for coordinating government covert operations. Drawing on the research of Kai Bird in his 1999 book about brothers McGeorge and William Bundy, *The Color of Truth* along with Mark Danner's April 4, 1999, review the same year in the *New York Times* titled "Members of the Club," the inference from documents is that McGeorge Bundy's service as a member of the presidential cabinet was characterized by support for US involvement in Vietnam. In 1965, for example, he was in favor of sending large numbers of ground troops as well as bombing North Vietnam. Furthermore, he maintained these positions over several years despite the declining prospects for the United States to win this war.[20] Bundy personified the scholar as policy expert and political insider in Washington, DC, and among numerous foundations and agencies. His influence and reputation peaked around 1965–66, after which his priorities and policies met with disapproval, especially from campus-based anti-war groups. After leaving government service he was named president of the Ford Foundation in 1967.

During the same years that McGeorge Bundy combined academic expertise with political influence in Washington, DC, another prominent example of a higher education alliance with government at home and abroad in public policies and programs was the Michigan State University Vietnam Advisory Group, known as MSUG. MSUG included Michigan State professors along with their president, John Hanna, who had been on leave to serve as assistant secretary of defense for President Dwight D. Eisenhower. The president of South Vietnam offered to pay MSUG to establish technical education programs in Saigon, including graduate studies for selected officials in alliance with the country's National Institute of Administration. The group also provided language training and advanced courses and field studies at the university's East Lansing campus, with sessions for students to visit federal agencies in Washington, DC, and police departments in cities such as Chicago and Detroit. The US State Department approved, using the project as a showcase for providing American-style technical training in public administration and police administration to make a higher education program part of foreign policy in 1956.[21]

Elsewhere, initiatives such as the Green Revolution allowed American university academics in agronomy and plant biology to introduce US models of scientific agriculture and economic production and training to developing nations.[22] Ultimately these attractive projects that brought prestige and money to universities also brought problems. Academic senates on the home campuses in the United States raised justifiable questions about academic standards in the new international programs when compared to graduate degree requirements elsewhere in the university. One concern was at least the appearance of possible overlap with federal agencies whose agenda might be advocacy or propaganda rather than academics. Another was that universities were glossing over essentials of academic freedom, including sharing of research findings, subjecting research projects to peer review, and accountability for funding. Such ventures led some concerned faculty at the host university to read closely the technical reports and annual summaries, leading to motions in faculty meetings to expose university relations and in some cases demand cutting program ties.

Most troubling was the question as to whether a cooperating host foreign government was controlling the applied research agenda, with power to cut off funding to a university for political reasons. Typically, a president or head of a foreign government was maintained in power by the United States; some became dictators, perhaps tolerated by the State Department because the department viewed the dictator as a potential counter to indigenous communist party leaders and movements in that country. In 1962, for example, the president of South Vietnam—one such president—abruptly ended the MSUG project in part because he objected to university demands for adherence to protocols of academic freedom. Also, cultural differences between the civil servants from South Vietnam who enrolled in the MSUG graduate courses led to instructional problems and disappointing results in terms of graduation rates and curriculum content. All these factors imploded at Michigan State University by 1966—a reversal of fortunes from its 1956 grand hopes and generous funding that had been highlighted by press conferences and public ceremonies. The meteoric rise of academics in international affairs and national policy such as McGeorge Bundy, along with the inaugural publicity associated with the MSUG program, suggested a high point of professors and politics—and MSUG also demonstrated how abruptly such influence could erode.

Universities' international projects faced a spotlight of public scrutiny in student demonstrations starting in the mid-1960s, when their appearance of alliance with, for example, dictatorships, or even cooperation with the CIA in foreign policy, raised essential questions about violations of academic freedom, lack of public accountability, and appropriateness of academic institutional involvement. One recurrent allegation by radical student groups was that the university-based international programs were illustrative of inappropriate and ineffective attempts at cultural imperialism.

Associations and Alliances outside the Campus

Colleges and universities joined national associations and alliances that provided services to member institutions in activities ranging from political lobbying to developing special interest public relations. Although colleges persisted as the essential institution, American higher education now included a network of organizations operating outside the campus.

THE WASHINGTON, DC, ASSOCIATIONS

Colleges and universities gradually recognized the potential benefits of collective action, including lobbying in Washington, DC. Since about 1890 the federally designated land grant institutions led the way in banding together to press for federal support. By 1960 the foremost national groups included the American Council on Education, which · was an association of college and university presidents, and the Association of American Universities, comprised of about sixty-two outstanding research universities. Given the high regard in which colleges and universities, especially research universities, were held by Congress and by the American public in the early 1960s, these groups and their member institutions became increasingly confident that they would break new ground. Research presidents looked forward to congressional appropriations with few strings attached and providing direct funding to colleges and universities.[23]

What went awry by the late 1960s was a declining confidence by Congress in the ability of universities to keep order on their own campuses. In addition, a growing and well-organized student advocacy movement, including lobbying and other activities, eventually elevated student financial aid as an agenda item for Congress, whether higher education officials and associations endorsed this focus or not. Eventually the advocacy movement would lead to the legislation creating the Basic Educational Opportunity Grants (later renamed Pell Grants), the Supplemental Educational Opportunity Grants, and other major student aid programs that were given directly to students and were portable to accredited colleges. The political implication was that many of the pillars of the higher education establishment had been scooped by upstart, mobilized, and effective student lobbying groups.

THE EDUCATIONAL TESTING SERVICE AND THE NATIONAL
MERIT SCHOLARSHIP CORPORATION

The Scholastic Aptitude Test was a formidable and usually unpleasant part of the student experience. Stepping aside from the student experience, important to note is the organizational and policy prominence the Educational Testing Service had gained by the early 1960s, including gaining exclusive rights as vendors of the required test for admission to some state university systems, among them the large and prestigious

University of California. The prominence of the ETS was indicated in part by their headquarters in New Jersey, whose bucolic features included a duck pond. Its academic image was consolidated by being located adjacent to the Princeton University campus. It attracted a top-flight staff of researchers in the social and behavioral sciences who were experts in test development and learning. In terms of services and influence, the ETS helped in the development of numerous academic and professional field tests beyond the SAT, including the Medical College Admission Test (MCAT), the Graduate Record Examination (GRE), and the Law School Admission Test (LSAT). Numerous other educational screening and sorting groups sought the expertise of the ETS. The result was an American hybrid—a private nonprofit organization that operated much like a commercial enterprise. At the same time, the ETS became a proxy for national testing largely by default, since the US government claimed no jurisdiction in this area.[24]

A good example of ETS presence in shaping American educational practices was its connection with the prestigious National Merit Scholars Program established in 1955. Even though the name of these awards made it sound as if they were bestowed by a national body, perhaps a federal agency, the program was in fact set up by a private nonprofit corporation in Evanston, Illinois, which had no official "national" status other than a copyrighted organizational name, the National Merit Scholarship Corporation.

The National Merit Scholarship Corporation relied on student results on the Preliminary Scholastic Aptitude Test (PSAT) that high school students could take, after paying a fee to the ETS, in their junior year of high school. The scores, although no one was clear what exactly they measured, were used to cull about 1% of test takers at the top, who then were invited to proceed through stages of applications, submitting transcripts and other materials for committee review. A college or university sought prestige by announcing that it had, for example, enrolled two hundred and fifty National Merit Scholarship finalists for the academic year 1963–64. Often what that meant was that the host university had merely taken its own scholarship monies and dedicated them to providing non-need-based funding to encourage and entice National Merit finalists to enroll at *their* school. The resultant question was whether the university was buying talent. Offering funds was a competitive strategy frequently used for attracting and enrolling outstanding graduate students, but it was less typical in undergraduate admissions and recruitment. Offering funds in the National Merit situation was a spurious symbol of academic attraction and university public relations which often was not critically examined. Its attractiveness to presidents and provosts was that it provided instant *gilt* by association as a university marketing tool, built on the dubious foundation of a single score on the PSAT designed by the ETS.

COLLEGE AND UNIVERSITY TRUSTEES AND BOARDS

Even though academic institutions invoked customs and heritage of shared governance, in the United States, ultimate power and authority was and always had been vested in the board of trustees. A perennial feature is that trustees seldom sought to run an institution and almost always preferred a strong president—an administrator hired and fired by the board. One comprehensive profile of university trustees published in 1969 indicated that the vast majority were business executives, served on the board of their alma mater, favored hierarchical decision making, and wanted faculty governance confined exclusively to some academic matters. Trustees were predominantly White, affluent, and Protestant. There was miniscule representation of Jews in their ranks. Thirteen percent were Catholic, but the overwhelming majority of these served as trustees at Catholic colleges and universities.[25] In other words, the composition of college boards reflected an American tradition of accommodating a range of interest groups—but as separate *but equal* institutions.

At state universities, most trustees were appointed by the governor, so that affiliation was as much political as it was educational or academic. This distinction would prove to be crucial in those cases during the late 1960s when, for example, a governor went head-to-head with a state university president over institutional direction, where trustee allegiance tended to go to the appointing governor. The collective profile of trustees suggests homogeneity, but homogeneity did not always ensure consensus or polite agreement. The Board of Regents of the University of California, an especially powerful group of talented men and women, had power over contracts, policies, construction, and hiring of university presidents. Despite this collective influence, being a university regent was described as "being a member of a large, unhappy family," as their arguments at meetings sometimes led to lawsuits within their ranks.[26]

A Profile of Presidents

A strong presidency working in tandem with a business-oriented board of trustees evolved as the staple of American higher education by 1960.

This configuration was not especially new, but it did proliferate. Given the interlocking network of campus systems, coordinating councils, legislatures, foundations, testing organizations, national associations, federal agencies, and Congress, there is little doubt that the role of campus or system-wide president brought particular demands and opportunities. Who were the university presidents of the 1960s and what were their characteristics and values?

University presidents were overwhelmingly White males in mid-career, most of whom had come up through the faculty ranks, with service as a dean or provost. A growing number had held academic and leadership roles in professional schools such as law, engineering, business, and academic medical centers. The increasing prestige and power of academic medical centers was due to the transformation of the health sciences and medicine in terms of enrollments, federal grants, and expansion of programs and curriculum. An important added component of the presidential resume was experience in serving on boards for federal agencies, involvement in foundations, success in private fundraising, and an ability to listen to and get along with board members from the corporate leadership ranks. A good example is the biographical profile of a president of Cornell University:

> James A. Perkins became Cornell University's seventh president in July 1963. Previous to that he was vice president of the Carnegie Corporation of New York and of the Carnegie Foundation for the Advancement of Teaching. From 1945 to 1950 he was vice president of Swarthmore College, his alma mater, and during World War II he served in the Office of Price Administration and in the Foreign Economic Administration. He received his doctorate in political science from Princeton in 1937, where he later became assistant professor and assistant director of the School of Public and International Affairs.
>
> Mr. Perkins serves on a number of governmental and educational advisory bodies. In March 1965, he was named chairman of President Lyndon B. Johnson's newly created General Advisory committee on Foreign Assistance Programs. A member of President Johnson's advisory panel on foreign policy, he was also a member of the President's special committee on nuclear weapons. He is chairman of the New York State Regents Advisory committee and a trustee of the RAND Corporation.[27]

The presidents of the 1960s contrasted markedly with the heroic leadership and public demeanor of the legendary college and university presidents from around 1890 to 1910. The new president of 1960 was highly respected, reasonably well paid, and probably served on numerous boards for both business and nonprofit groups such as foundations and museums. By our standards today, presidential salaries were modest. Clark Kerr, for example, recalls that when he was named chancellor of the Berkeley campus, his salary was essentially his prior faculty salary with a 30% bump. What the university presidents of that era did enjoy was deference and courtesy. Their speeches, book-jacket photographs, and magazine covers exuded the demeanor of senior statesmen and seasoned diplomats who were not ruffled when facing big issues.

In figuring out how to lead a multiversity or a multicampus system, the preferred style was that of the mediator. The code was that a modern university president ought not mimic the style of captains of erudition or captains of industry of the late nineteenth century, known to be ruthless and insensitive. University presidents of the 1960s had to accept the organizational fact of life that some deans and vice presidents and perhaps some coaches held great fiefdoms, and dealing with them required finesse and persuasion. For a president to capriciously joust publicly with the dean of the medical college was not wise. In external relations, the president needed to use persuasion, data, and compromise to achieve goals. The ideal style of the modern university president was that of calm and moderation, with a reliance on staff and data for informed decision making. Maintaining balance and order, placating outliers while advancing a mission or agenda, was the endgame. Flamboyance and authoritarian brashness were out of vogue.

Some of this emphasis on mediation as a leadership style was a self-deprecating appearance and illusion, as the new breed of university president really was intent on gaining, not sharing, internal and external authority. The president of Cornell told a Princeton University audience in 1963 that ultimately it was only a strong president who could balance internal constituencies of faculty and students with the growing external relations with government agencies, Congress, and international organizations. He noted, "But someone must be concerned with the institution as a whole, the activities it supports, the public face it presents, and the private concerns with which it is occupied. This job cannot be divided among disparate elements of the university. So it is the administrator—the president and others with managerial responsibility, cooperating with faculty and student leaders—who must be concerned both with the apparatus of the university and with the idea it represents." Perkins concluded that the modern university president "must not fear power or be afraid to exercise it."[28]

The logic of the modern university president tended to conclude that shared governance, inside and outside the campus, was destined to diminish. Within a university, students should be studying and professors should be spared institutional decision-making burdens so they could devote themselves to teaching and research. Outside the campus and the university system, legislators and governors were as a matter of course not really qualified to adjudicate academic matters. Furthermore, a president and the board had a responsibility to keep political intrusion or interference at bay. It was the president and his lieutenants of academic managers who were best suited to institutional leadership in the new postsecondary education environment. For several years the logic and justification for this presidential case was accepted by numerous external constituencies.

In addition to James Perkins of Cornell as a visible, successful academic leader and spokesman, William Friday of North Carolina gained statewide and national respect for bringing national recognition to the South. Friday's diplomacy and good relations with governors and the state legislature led to collaboration among the land grant institutions: North Carolina State University in Raleigh, the historic flagship campus at Chapel Hill, and a number of newer, smaller campuses. Friday was central to the success of the highly praised Research Triangle, which involved collaboration between the two major public universities and Duke University in Durham. Another celebrated public figure was Sam Gould, head of the State University of New York. One university president deserving detailed mention in this group was Howard R. Bowen, who was inaugurated as president of the University of Iowa in December 1964. He was an important figure because his policies countered some of the conventional wisdom about the efficacy of university growth:

> The next several years are almost certain to be critical ones in the history of the university. I expect the student body of the University of Iowa, now 14,500, to grow to 25,000 or more in the next decade. And I expect the appropriate activities and functions of the university to change and expand—especially in the direction of relatively more advanced study, and more research and scholarship. Rapid growth opens the opportunity for equally rapid progress. It will require the appointment of new faculty, the construction of new buildings, the reshaping of educational and research programs. If these things are done well, growth can become an instrument of qualitative progress. On the other hand, there are dangers in growth. There is one danger so great that I

wish to make it the central topic of my address. This is the danger of the submergence of the individual. I propose that in all our plans, we fix our attention on the goal of preserving and promoting individuality.

Bowen advocated for paying close attention to student housing, campus activities, and appropriate human scale, and for resisting the lure of preoccupation with prestige and national rankings. He concluded, "I hope we shall seek individuality for the university itself, as well as for the persons who are part of it. If we are true to ourselves, we need never worry about our prestige."[29]

Howard Bowen's priorities went against the grain of most of his fellow university-builders, a split in philosophies that would become glaringly evident over the next five years. Bowen was not a firebrand but, rather, a calm speaker who was a distinguished economist and professor whose experience included serving on the Federal Reserve and as dean of the University of Illinois Business School. He brought to the presidency the added perspective of having spent time at distinguished liberal arts colleges— as a professor at Williams College and, later, as president of Grinnell College in Iowa. He also made essential contributions to the serious study of higher education with his research on investment in learning and the benefits to society of a college-educated citizenry.[30]

Even though Bowen was respected in academic circles and had experience on Wall Street and with federal agencies and international corporations, his emphasis on societal conscience and proper institutional mission placed him on the margins of the academic orthodoxy among research universities of the decade.[31] Few universities or their presidents or boards followed his example or heeded his warnings and recommendations—but there were exceptions. Liberal arts colleges, which did not pursue federal research grants on a significant scale, still tended to give priority to undergraduate education on a residential campus. Junior colleges and state colleges struggled with overcrowding, yet by custom and statute they struggled with problems of educating large numbers of undergraduates and had little incentive or allowance to enter the sponsored-research sweepstakes. Among state universities, one interesting deliberate counter to Clark Kerr's vision of the multiversity was the College of William and Mary in Virginia, which used its regional accreditation report to project its identity as the miniversity.[32] This college was committed to an older style of teaching and learning, where research was marbled into faculty work with undergraduates and graduate studies were added harmoniously, all within the setting of a residential campus. Some private universities took pains to advance their model of what sociologists Christopher Jencks and David Riesman called the university college. Such a college was committed to maintaining an undergraduate liberal arts college within the research university structure.[33]

These exceptions did not derail the powerful model in which pursuit of growth and prestige was the norm for ambitious, aspiring university presidents in the mid-1960s. They often enjoyed an advantage in their role as proponents of the research university systems model, perhaps leading to overconfidence where they could count on governors and state legislators who were alumni—creating affiliations and alliances from campus to capitol. Generations of prosperous alumni also had come to occupy business leadership roles as chief executive officers, all leading to a network of diverse organizations and mutual interests which had been persuaded that investment in higher education was good for state and national economic development.

POLITICS AND THE PERILS OF PRESIDENTS AND PLANNING

Despite the impressive academic and professional pedigrees that defined the new university presidents, they still sometimes had to consider the limits of their own leadership preparation and style. Although many had served on corporate boards, few had been business CEOs. Most of their work was done within circles of cosmopolitan influential individuals. On April 20, 1964, for example, in a talk to the Associated Press in New York City, President Johnson observed, "This is the kind of a distinguished gathering that reminds me of a meeting in the Cabinet Room the other day. Around the Cabinet table sat three Harvard men, two Yale men, Dean Rusk, and three other Rhodes Scholars—and one graduate of the Southwest Texas State Teachers College." (LBJ was a graduate of Southwest Texas State Teachers College, now known as Texas State University.) Most university presidents had little experience and even less success in electoral politics. A contrast in cultures between the professional presidents and elected politicians—presidents, members of Congress, governors—represented markedly different ways of negotiation and decision making.

Also missing in the professional socialization of the new generation of academic leaders was familiarity with and connection to student life, especially that of undergraduates. By the mid-1960s the presidents and their staff had little experience or patience in dealing with student concerns about instruction and residential life. They had even less familiarity with or toleration for student dissent that started to percolate at a growing number of campuses. News clips and videos of college and university presidents of that era addressing groups of students asking questions about or protesting campus policies show presidents who were flustered and flabbergasted. They were incredulous that they were not necessarily beloved or heeded and then had difficulty dealing with uncertainty and spontaneity from what was presumed to be an obedient, agreeable constituency. Here was an Achilles' heel that would unravel many presidencies.

The repercussion was that governors, legislators, business executives, and taxpayers who traditionally gave great deference to university presidents in their state also were upset by what they perceived to be a lack of leadership in the inability to maintain student decorum and order on the campus. This assessment of the situation would be central to Governor Ronald Reagan's decision to strongly recommend that Clark Kerr be fired as president of the University of California in 1967. Concerns about this issue were followed by new scrutiny of higher education spending related to the economy. Public support for higher education expansion and funding was most generous when the state and national economies were flourishing. This was the case in 1960, but by 1966 federal spending on the Vietnam War and other priorities cut into support for maintaining, much less increasing, higher education's percentage of the financial pie.

Had university presidents lost control of spending as well as having lost control of the campus and of student conduct? Some politicians believed this to be the case, as taxpayers and state legislators began raising questions about the funding models and expectations that had been put into place by 1960. The prospect of charging no or low tuition at state universities while facing several years of increased enrollments became a source of worry for two reasons. First, these policies of low price had not fully succeeded in expanding access across all family income levels. Second, governors and some legislators concluded that such low charges probably were unsustainable for the state government over many years.

In California, the state that was the paramount model for generous funding and no tuition, there were signs of concern by 1967. State Senator George Deukmejian of Long Beach represented a new conservative state leadership cadre. In addressing citizen groups throughout Southern California, he endorsed then Governor Ronald Reagan's new equal education plan that "called for the adoption of modest tuitions of

$250 per year by the university and $80 per year in the state colleges. It included grants or loans to those who could not afford the modest tuition."[34] He noted that half the students enrolled in the University of California and the California State Colleges came from relatively affluent families of more than $10,000 income annually (indexed for inflation, about $100,000 in 2017), whereas only about 12% came from modest-income families earning $6,000 a year or less (about $60,000 in 2017 dollars). Imposing tuition combined with tax reform was the prescription for making public higher education sustainable and accessible. Ironically, these observations about the unintended consequences of a zero-tuition policy working counter to widespread access would later be invoked by higher education reformers from the left.

State support of public higher education was tapering and even declining, but surely the powerful federal grant universities had a diversified funding model to spare them financial difficulties around 1969? After all, by definition, these were universities whose annual operating budgets were probably funded between 25% and 50% by revenues from grants provided by federal agencies. Although the 1960s were considered the peak decade for federal research support to universities, the annual increases had started to slow by 1968. This trend gained momentum so that the decade starting in 1970 would be considered the nadir of post–World War II federal grant funding. A university that had grown accustomed to substantial federal grant funding was susceptible to forgetting the distinction between soft money (grant income determined on a project basis) and hard money (recurring, permanent line-item funding).

The fiscal vulnerability of research universities became evident when provosts and deans discovered that to be competitive for federal grants, a campus had to spend its own resources for construction of laboratories and other facilities, along with covering other research expenses typically not allowed by federal reimbursement. Maintaining the large research enterprise meant transferring tuition dollars from undergraduate programs. The federal grant universities received another storm warning by 1969 with signs that the academic labor market for their recently completed PhD recipients was becoming saturated, as each subsequent year there were fewer tenure-track faculty positions advertised.[35] To continue enrolling new doctoral students was expensive if they were going to be awarded research fellowships, and more new doctoral students eventually added to the glut of the PhD academic labor market.

Meanwhile, outside the circle of top federal grant universities, each year an increasing number of universities mimicked the prestige model by adding their own new master's degree and PhD programs. The aspiring newcomers usually did not have sufficient success in landing external grants to make their new doctoral programs self-supporting, and the predictable dysfunction of that budgetary strategy was to further alienate undergraduates, who had started to raise questions about large class size and other shortfalls in the undergraduate curriculum. By 1969 almost all colleges and universities were starting to feel a financial pinch that was not going to go away.

Differences in a Decade: Ten Years of Unexpected Changes and Problems

The changes within a decade in the prestige and popularity of university presidents at prestigious research universities was dramatic and unexpected. In 1960 American colleges and universities were news—more specifically, good news connecting state pride with optimism that the nation's higher education institutions and systems could combine quantity and quality as they grew and prospered in tandem with the state and national economies. What a difference a decade makes! By 1969 national and local headlines emphasized higher education's fall from grace, a descent, a loss of a gyroscope, and a decline in public and government trust. Presidents and boards were on edge as they faced the prospect of student sit-ins and office takeovers as part of the new job description. The best observation illustrating how the situation had come full circle was made by Clark Kerr in 1967 when the Board of Regents of the University of California dismissed him from office. Kerr remarked to reporters about his tenure as president of the University of California that he left this job as he came into it, namely, "fired with enthusiasm."[36]

The construction crane was a dominant symbol of higher education due to the unprecedented investment in new buildings, including completely new colleges. Bigger, however, was not necessarily better, as changes in campus architecture between 1960 and 1969 reinforce the theme of disappointments along with declining optimism. Whereas the proposed new college and university construction projects early in the decade were celebrated as models of heroic modern architecture combined with the art and science of regional planning, years of campus construction boom left a legacy of lackluster buildings. On many university campuses there was little sustained commitment to coherent master planning, contrary to the high expectations that had been fostered around 1963 with the *Time* magazine story about the modern campus planning of architect William Pereira. What one increasingly found on campuses by the end of the decade, especially as institutional budgets started to tighten, was reliance on a tall, drab, reinforced-concrete office tower that brought to mind a Moscow apartment building rather than a brave new world of inspired futuristic design. These lackluster buildings stood in stark contrast to the brick-and-ivy buildings of previous millennia. The buildings also turned out to be expensive, because when they were planned, in the mid-1960s, energy for heating and cooling was cheap—but it did not stay that way. Offices in the new generation of academic structures were hermetically sealed. Faculty and staff could not open windows in the controlled-temperature structures. For vice presidents of business affairs, such office towers became an expensive headache as energy bills started to soar. Above all, the new ivory towers were uninspiring to students, faculty, and staff, and to alumni and donors.

Campus architecture of the 1960s. (Courtesy of the University of Kentucky Archives)

Campus computers of the 1960s: the IBM 7950 Harvest. (Courtesy of NSA)

One partial explanation for the dismal design on many campuses was that in the 1960s many states required public colleges and universities to accept low bids on proposed campus architecture proposals. The result was that the new campus construction of the decade leaned toward quantity more than quality. On many campuses, a sign of prestige was to have an office in a historic building that had been renovated. Meanwhile, those who relied on the new high-rise office buildings endured problems with elevators not working and electrical blackouts. Symptomatic of this architectural syndrome was the University of California, Berkeley, where the new concrete Evans Hall office tower was a source of universal contempt and aptly nicknamed Fort Evans. One observation on these trends was that the colleges and universities had drifted from "classical dreams to concrete realities."[37]

Higher education, the Knowledge Industry, was indeed what business analysts called a growth industry all the way from 1960 through 1969 when analyzed by the indicators of inputs and outputs along with annual increases in student enrollment and construction of new buildings, including complete new campuses. A real and symbolic sign of this evolution into an industry was increasing reliance on (and confidence in) punch cards and computer systems. Computer-generated data and other statistical indicators tended to mask the growing pains and internal tensions that characterized this sustained expansion. The external events of state and national politics fueled the fall from great expectations to a loss of confidence for American higher education. It's essential to look closely at the lives, thoughts, and actions of college students in this era as students responded to the master plans and academic priorities of college and university leaders.

Student Activities and Activism

Collegiate Culture to Counterculture

Best Class Yet: A Profile of College Students in the 1960s

One ritual of college each year from 1960 to 1969 took place when a dean welcomed freshman students and their parents with the good news and good-natured observation that this entering group was indeed "the best class yet." And the observation was true on two counts: both admissions standards and academic selectivity rose in this period at most colleges nationwide. Measured by high school grade point averages, Scholastic Aptitude Test scores, and other indices of sorting and selecting, the academic profile of entering college students got better and better. Even as selectivity increased, enrollments surged at most campuses, stretching services and facilities to maximum occupancy and usage. Dormitories were crowded, as the housing staff often relied on extra bunk beds to put three or four students into rooms designed to accommodate two.

Once parents headed home and the new students were left on their own at campus, the dean's message and tone changed abruptly. At the freshman class opening convocation of the academic year, the dean's earlier praise was replaced by his equally strict warning and prediction. Time and again student memoirs attest to some variation of the academic dean's convocation remarks in which each freshman is told, "Shake hands with the classmate on your left. Shake hands with the classmate on your right. One of you will not be here for graduation in four years." This harsh, even perplexing, administrative observation persisted even though one just might think that increasingly strong academic preparation among students would lead to better academic records in college courses, leading more freshmen to stay and fewer to leave.

College officials did not show much concern about student attrition. Indeed, some professors took perverse delight in telling students in class, "Just because we accepted you doesn't mean we have to keep you." One

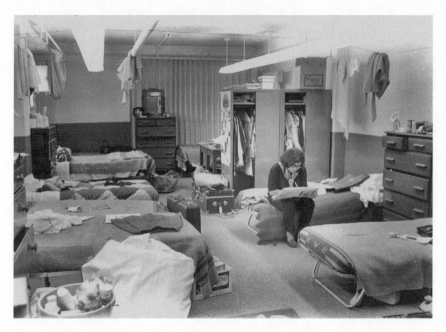

Crowded dormitories: "emergency staging" (the university's term for temporary housing) in the basement of Cross Hall at Pennsylvania State University. (Used with permission from the Eberly Family Special Collection Library, Penn State University Libraries)

could even argue that a high dropout rate showed outsiders that a college was rigorous—that dropouts were a source of perverse institutional pride comparable to weeding out weak military recruits at boot camp. So, even though academic preparation and records of new students improved every year, attrition rates, or what was called washing out and flunking out, remained high. Many large state universities arranged for extra busses to transport departing students back home after midterm examination grades were posted in October. Students may not have liked these harsh verdicts but they accepted them. Getting in and then quickly and unpleasantly getting out had become institutionalized and ritualized in the round of campus life for a substantial percentage of freshmen.

Campus support services for undergraduates were lean or nonexistent. Sparse were career planning, psychological services like counseling, international programs, and other standard features of college life today. Student affairs administrators were cast in the role of enforcers and overseers rather than professional helpers. Every campus had its "mean dean" who scrutinized misbehaviors.[1] Dropping out for financial reasons was accepted as a fact of academic life both by students and by campus administrators.

College students at most institutions in the 1960s were homogeneous—almost all were between the ages of seventeen and twenty-two. Enrolling as a full-time student was the norm. The phrase *nontraditional student* was not used until the mid-1970s. The small number of part-time, older students were referred to as "those taking classes," a designation signaling that they probably had little integration into campus life. Colleges were stingy on allowing transfer credits from other institutions. Shared religious affiliation was another source of homogeneity. Numerous colleges, private and public, remained gender exclusive, either all men or all women. As a result, diversity within most colleges was minimal.

Regulations and Rules

College students have always created their own worlds within the campus, and they have imaginatively done so within the structure of official constraints.[2] Rule books of the era were short in length but strict in message. Students joked that these booklets could be compressed to a single command: "Don't!" For many, perhaps most, colleges, the norm was in loco parentis. This meant curfews, parietal rules, and restrictions on conduct and calendars. Dress codes were in force—such as wearing a coat and tie to dinner for men and skirts or dresses for women. At Vassar, a campus legend held that one young woman obeyed the rule that students wear evening gloves and pearls at a tea but made a dramatic statement about conformity to the letter of the law by wearing nothing else.[3] Rules were strictest at campus dormitories, and especially in sororities. Enforcement at fraternity houses and off-campus apartments was less likely, unless there was some crisis or injury. It is possible to track how the regulations started to break down over the decade with a pattern edging gradually but persistently from overt compliance to signs of evasion and disregard. These transgressions were not so much resistance or rejection as an orchestrated contest in which students confirmed the adage that one could break laws so long as one obeyed the customs of student life.

In stark contrast to the remarks of the controlling dean of students, here was another university's welcoming remark by a campus official, what *Time* magazine reporters called a "fairly chilly official statement: 'We assume you are adults. We won't check up on you to see that you are in a given place at a given time. We won't make sure you ask questions if you need answers, and we won't make sure you seek outside help if you need it. Come to think of it, we won't do much of anything for you. We assume you can take care of yourselves.'"[4] This bold manifesto of a laissez-faire approach to undergraduate conduct was, in fact, overstated and not at all descriptive of campus administration of student affairs nationwide, even at the most liberated of institutions. College officials ultimately had legal responsibility for student conduct whether they could control it or not.

Steven Kelman's diary for his freshman year at Harvard in fall 1966 noted that graduate students serving as house advisors clearly warned undergraduate students that the residential rules were firm and strictly enforced. Young men wanting to have women as guests at their dormitories, and especially in their rooms, were subject to sign-ins and sign-outs that were checked systematically. Buying alcohol if under twenty-one years of age was a serious offense and carried an added penalty if the purchaser was caught using a fake ID card. In sum, colleges did not tolerate certain kinds of misconduct and were especially vigilant on offenses such as destruction of college property and failing to obey campus officers and academic officials. Drunken and disorderly conduct may have had little if anything to do with radical politics, but it frequently led to a student being suspended or expelled. One bit of pragmatic advice residence hall advisors gave to new students was to distinguish between city police and campus police. The former were tough and loved to arrest a student, whereas the latter were the students' protectors and friends—up to a point. With the important exception of urban campuses, security guards at most colleges were benign and supportive, often not sworn in or registered as police officers who could bear firearms. This situation changed dramatically toward the end of the decade, however, after a succession of serious episodes of violence and vandalism, when a modern campus security office became comparable to a municipal police force. In this new arrangement, university officials and mayors had to negotiate formal agreements about town versus gown jurisdiction on arresting students.[5]

Student memoirs from different kinds of institutions reinforce Steven Kelman's account of strict codes of conduct. It was not unusual for an undergraduate student to have a car on campus. At the same time, having a car was neither necessary nor taken for granted. Most colleges and universities forbade freshmen from having a car unless there was some extenuating individual circumstance. Some colleges offered their student body a referendum on whether to allow alcohol on campus or to allow students to have cars—they could have one but not both. These restrictions were not insurmountable; many students simply did not report to the dean of students or the director of parking services that they had a car, and they rented a private garage or parking space, all beyond view of the dean. In contrast to residential campuses, commuter schools, including junior colleges, did not have such issues about parking and permits.

Boys Will Be Boys

Time and time again, across regions and campuses, there was an institutional indulgence in college boys' predictable boorish behavior. Men and their organizations were subject to less enforcement than women and theirs. At campuses where fraternities were entrenched, attempted enforcement often led to a controversy with the administration over control. Could a college revoke a fraternity's charter for severe misconduct? Did affiliation with a national fraternity organization restrict local campus officials' control? Some college presidents and their boards dealt with accumulated headaches by banning local chapters of national fraternities. Another administrative strategy was to allow fraternities to exist but to prohibit them from occupying off-campus residence houses. Between 1960 and 1969 fraternities endured at campuses where they were long established, but many fraternities experienced a decline in interest by freshman students who chose not to rush. On balance, the changing relative power of fraternities attested both to innovation in student priorities and persistence of traditions. Where fraternities did show weakness by the end of the decade was in their declining ability to win elections and control campus-wide student government.

As for sorting and tracking, even when a student was offered a bid to join a fraternity that set him and his fellow frat brothers apart from the rest of the student body, the pecking order of each fraternity (or sorority) was harsh, as each staked out a distinctive character. Every campus had its fraternity known as the "Animal House."

The male tenor in student life, however, extended beyond fraternities and the Greek system. When presidents and deans spoke to external audiences about students, frequently they used the pronoun "he"—seldom "she"—and the possessive "his" to describe the student populace. Campus organizations and activities, including varsity sports, remained exclusively male. Admission into some advanced programs, such as law and medicine, formally and informally favored male applicants. Most campuses had a prestigious cadre who might be called "Little Men." These were late adolescents who dressed and acted beyond their years, already reading the *Wall Street Journal* and *Business Week* and positioning themselves for contacts and clubs that they believed would lead to executive careers.

The military had a sizeable impact on men as college students in the 1960s. First, many land grant colleges interpreted "A&M" to extend from "Agriculture and Mechanics" to include an *M* that meant "military." Nowhere would this idea be taken up more fully than at Texas A&M, which had graduated more commissioned army officers than West Point. Elsewhere the military influence extended to numerous other land grant campuses that required from one to four years of service and mandated participation by all male students unless there was some formal approved excuse. The second military influence came from the armed services draft and the Vietnam War. Whatever advantages and indulgences men enjoyed in college activities and campus traditions, by 1964 they had to register with the United States Selective Service and keep their local draft board informed about their academic standing. Men as college students soon became familiar with the glossary of codes, including 1-Y as a student deferment, 4-F designated unfit for service usually due to some physical condition, and 1-A indicating eligible for military service. Draft boards typically granted 1-Y status for a year, renewable for a maximum of four years. Furthermore, a student's 1-Y status ended when a student completed a bachelor's degree or dropped out of college. The military draft made studying at college to obtain at least minimally acceptable course grades and good conduct consequential.

Women and the Struggle for First-Class Citizenship in the Academic Community

With coeducation came ritualized relationships on campus between men and women, which were frequently depicted and reinforced in the media as well as within the collegiate culture. A good example of gender and college stereotypes broadcast to popular audiences was the 1960 Hollywood movie *Where the Boys Are,* dealing with spring break at Florida beaches, dating, proms, engagements, pinning ceremonies, and the interdependence of fraternities and sororities in the collegiate Greek system. The fanciful film did capture some elements of truths about social relations of the era. The movie title was infectious and enduring, as each year women who were newspaper editors at Smith College and Mount Holyoke College published candid profiles of college men at New England colleges aptly titled "Where the Boys Are." According to the books' editors, Amherst College was "Marlboro Country," with students who were "Cowboy Cool." Wesleyan University's profile featured a football player on a motorcycle and the caption "Wes and the Linemen." For one men's college, a coed from Smith or Mount Holyoke was asked to consider whether, as a corporate wife, she could "keep house on a vice president's salary?"[6] Even within the academically rigorous Seven Sisters colleges, then, women as college students in the 1960s were expected to seek husbands and be good spouses, and nothing more.

These stereotypes were reinforced in another Hollywood movie from 1960, *Tall Story*. Jane Fonda portrayed a first-year woman student, or coed, who is waiting in line to register for courses at the fictional Custer College (filmed at Occidental College in Los Angeles). Standing behind basketball player and campus hero Tony Perkins, Jane Fonda overhears his conversation with the faculty advisor. After Perkins finishes and moves on, Jane Fonda immediately tells the academic advisor, "I'll take the courses he's taking!" Although the message was leavened with humor, movies and magazines dramatized that even with access to college, women were not necessarily fully respected as equals in campus life and professional prospects.

In campus residence halls for women, regulations were strict and elaborate, with little tolerance for misbehavior. Curfew and lockouts were enforced. A coed living in a campus dormitory who was absent overnight, for example, without signed permission slips for a road trip, quickly had explaining to do to the house mother and the dean of women. Wearing curlers, pajamas, and even pants in the lobby and common areas was prohibited and penalized. One woman from the class of 1969 recalled, "The one essential piece of wardrobe of every woman student was a trench-coat, which served as camouflage over shorts or pajamas when attending early class, but especially sitting for exams. In an age when jeans—and gradually bell-bottoms—had become *de rigueur* for our age grade, we were required to wear skirts to class and to the dining hall through my years."[7] Few student health centers or infirmaries prescribed birth control pills; doing so was controversial and long prohibited nearly everywhere until a few landmark incidents at a small number of colleges. The most publicized controversial incident was at Brown University in September 1965, when the medical doctor who was director of health

Hollywood goes to college: 1960 publicity still of college students portrayed by Anthony Perkins and Jane Fonda in *Tall Story*. (Courtesy of Alamy)

services for Brown University and Pembroke College acknowledged to the press that he had prescribed birth control pills for "a very, very small" number of girls (perhaps as many as five) in his official capacity. The girls were over 21 years of age and were intending to be married. He emphasized that he had had lengthy consultations in each case, because "I want to feel I'm contributing to a solid relationship and not to unmitigated promiscuity."[8] Whether by custom or regulation, an undergraduate woman who became pregnant typically dropped out of college.

How did gender relations play out in the "bold new deal" of student protest groups which was gaining momentum starting around 1963? Women were not treated as equals or as leaders in the early years of the student reform movements. Some accounts indicate that at radical group meetings there was blatant sexism, with (male) leaders expecting women members to take notes, make coffee, stuff envelopes, and run errands. Reform leaders referred to these tasks as women's work. Lynne Hollander Savio recalled, "Looking back, there was only one woman in the leadership for a dozen males. But our consciousness was not raised yet."[9] In the lengthy documentary *Berkeley in the Sixties,* one of the featured interviewees in 1991 was Jackie Goldberg, who comes across as informed, articulate, principled, and sharing good-natured insights about the Free Speech Movement. Later, she was elected to the California State Assembly, served on school boards in the Los Angeles area, and was a longtime advocate for civil rights and social justice. And yet in interviews in 2014, she acknowledged that she and other women, who from the start were active in student protest politics, were not taken seriously in the Berkeley planning sessions.

Whatever concerns the Free Speech Movement and the Students for a Democratic Society may have had regarding political races or social justice, there is little evidence these concerns extended to gender respect or equity. Starting around 1967 what eventually came to be known as the women's movement was a growing accumulation of initiatives whose members collaborated to work for women's studies as an academic department and to usher in feminism as a strand of activism and analysis fused with related issues. Despite institutional and cultural obstacles, the women's movement persisted.[10] Women between 1963 and 1969 made up about 48% of undergraduate enrollments nationwide, and they consistently showed strong records in grade point average and in receiving academic honors such as election to Phi Beta Kappa or selection for the campus-wide coeducational College Bowl teams of "varsity scholars." Given women's strong academic grade point averages, statistics showing many women dropping out without having a bachelor's degree are puzzling. There was a further disconnect for women in the realm of admission to graduate school and programs for advanced professional degrees. Regardless of a woman's academic achievements and contributions to campus leadership and activities, she was not eligible for a Rhodes Scholarship.

Initiatives by women to gain admission to and academic citizenship in prestigious all-male colleges, especially in the Ivy League, gained momentum in the late 1960s and faced equally intense opposition characterized by slogans like "Keep the damned women out!"[11] Even more daunting for women's integration and success was the lack of planning for women to be included fully in the workforce, especially in professions that would benefit from educated expertise. Explanations ranged from outright sexism and gender discrimination to more subtle trends such as young women being counseled out of taking mathematics courses even though they were doing well in math. An unnecessarily narrowed undergraduate curriculum limited women's choices for graduate schools, because an applicant lacking calculus was ineligible for more than half of a university's advanced programs. By the late 1960s the number of women pursuing and completing advanced degrees steadily increased. By the early 1970s women held a large percentage of graduate school positions in selected fields such as English, modern languages, history, biology, library science, and education. Yet they lagged far behind elsewhere, in fields such as engineering, physics, chemistry, business, and law. At Harvard Law School, 1971 marked the first year that more than 10% of the cohort of *One L*s was female.[12]

The limits of opportunities for women in coeducational campuses strengthened the case for women's colleges. The argument was that a woman student at a woman's college had more chance of being student body president or editor of the student newspaper or being taken seriously in a class discussion than a woman enrolled at a coeducational campus.[13] What was evident was that women were not included in the mainstream of student radicalism. Indeed, gains women made as members of the campus were not substantial. The campus-based women's movement was possible only because of the persistence of dedicated women in the late 1960s who acted in the face of indifference and hostility by various groups. These obstacles eventually strengthened the women's effort. Academic women from a variety of roles cooperated in numerous reforms that by the mid-1970s would start to show results.[14]

Structures and Strictures: Patterns of Student Subcultures

College students of the 1950s have been characterized as the silent generation, many of whom would be recruits into the corporate world. No doubt there were significant exceptions to that mold. There were signs that this collective identity persisted into the 1960s. Yet the puzzle facing

Campus coeds, 1967. (Courtesy of Chuck Painter/Stanford News Service)

historians of higher education is how to reconcile this persistence with the well-documented student reforms and rebellions of the late 1960s. An intriguing clue comes from the profile for undergraduates at Pennsylvania State University.

In 1966 the president of the undergraduate student body at Penn State asserted that the typical student at his campus

is passive, conscientious, law abiding, responsible and [socially] ultraconservative. He is content to study, date, and perform the rituals of existence. . . . The term system has reduced his extracurricular activities and has increased his concentration on his books. Yet these years are best remembered as the era of student activism, a time when youth rebelled—sometimes violently—against established authority. The extensive attention captured by this rebellion often obscured the reality that at Penn State and most other institutions, most students took no part in protest marches, sit-ins, flag burnings, building occupations or other activities favored by campus dissidents. The importance of the student activist movement should not be measured by the relatively small number of participants. Although only a few students were outspoken in their opposition to established policies, these few effectively changed the relationship between administrators and all students. As administrators and students came to realize, the passive majority often embraced the goals, if not the methods, of the activist minority.[15]

This is an intriguing hypothesis to keep in mind in sorting out nuances and complexities across and within colleges and universities over the decade.

The diversity of American higher education in regions and institutional types reinforces the importance of trying to keep in view what was taking place in student cultures at a range of colleges. At many small private colleges, often characterized by college officials and by parents as safe colleges, alumni from the 1960s recall "Villagers, Weejuns, and welcome"—shorthand for a campus set in a picturesque small town where students wore traditional college fashions and became part of a cohesive campus community. Women recalled spending hours collaborating with new roommates to plan the dorm room decor. These campuses were idyllic and sheltered. As one student recalled in 1964, "In another world, far from the tranquility of this tiny college town, war waged in Vietnam. Students protested across the country: they raised their voices—and fists. Drugs and the sexual revolution embraced the young. But in this cozy small town, all was well for the College's girls."[16]

Elsewhere existed a markedly different kind of campus life and student attitude. According to Dorothy Finnegan, some "high school graduates from the metropolitan Atlantic Coast . . . were forced to find college vacancies in an unexpected place, namely, at William Penn College in Iowa. The influx of refugee students from the East financially saved the college and at the same time diversified and energized campus life. By every measure the class that entered in fall 1965 engaged in activities and academics. The varsity sports teams went from lackluster to conference championships." As another William Penn student observed, "Almost every classmate reminisced about faculty and staff members who helped to forge their adult life. They also spoke of their personal development through the college—some due to the attention from the faculty, some due to the organizations that we led, and some due to the diversity of our classmates. The college was small enough that it was impossible not to get to know people who came from different backgrounds." Although adjustment to a small campus in rural Iowa took time, "as we grew to care about the college and each other, we also felt that the college cared about us."[17]

Often left out of the college saga are the voices of undergraduates at new commuter state colleges. To begin to remedy this lacuna it's important to incorporate the accounts of students from California State University, Northridge (CSUN), called Valley State, in the San Fernando Valley. By 1968 students were sufficiently concerned about problems within the campus and at the state and national levels that they established a chapter of the Students for a Democratic Society (SDS), which published a mimeographed newsletter, *Outcry*, in which the peace symbol was embedded in the letter O. Another group of reform-minded students started a newspaper called *Open City* which caused a splash with a cover story titled "Why Valley State Revolted." Student memoirs include numerous admiring mentions of one English professor, Dr. Richard Abcarian, who worked with students to take "an active role throughout the last of the 1960s, supporting several key protest movements that occurred on campus, including those against U.S. involvement in Vietnam and in favor of the establishment of the Chicano Studies and Pan African Studies departments at CSUN." The archives of related memoranda, clippings, posters, news releases, and other documents note such events as the state of emergency declaration by the acting university president on January 9, 1969, which led to a ban of all demonstrations, assemblies, and rallies—along with arrests of student demonstrators, who served jail time for violating the order.[18] A few months earlier, in November 1968, members of the Black Student Union were joined by SDS members in a march on the administration building to protest the shoving of an African American student athlete by an assistant football coach. Protesting students took over the fifth floor of the administration building, leading the president to call in the Los Angeles Police Department, a move that resulted in campus violence and the arrest of twenty-four students, of whom nineteen were convicted and received prison terms of between one year and twenty-five years.[19] This case study confirms that by the end of the decade, campus crises and unrest had spread to many different kinds of campuses.

THE ROOTS OF STUDENT DISCONTENT

External politics (such as resistance to the military and the Vietnam War or concerns about free speech or civil rights and racial discrimination) inspired student reform movements, but one of the original sources of strong student dissent, one that marked a major change in student conduct with administrators, goes back to competition and crowding as part of campus life. Those two sets of bunk beds crammed into a small dormitory room, for example. New students seldom complained, because they had never been to college before and probably thought they were fortunate at least to have obtained campus housing, unlike many of their classmates, who were scrambling to find off-campus apartments.

By 1961 semester course enrollments, typically processed in the gymnasium, were in such high demand that students often camped overnight to ensure a good place in line and to increase their odds of getting into courses they sought (and sometimes needed to fulfill graduation requirements). Computers relying on punch cards processed course enrollment data. Students grew tired of standing in line in crowded lecture halls. They displayed their frustration by wearing computer cards as a badge, proclaiming, "Do not fold, bend, mutilate, or staple," and with the companion slogan announcing, "I am *not* a number." These collective actions bore witness against what was called the "impersonality of the multiversity" and its growing bureaucracy, symbolized by the reliance on IBM technology.[20]

Administrative Angst

The general attitude of presidents and provosts toward undergraduates was one of benign paternalism that provided for some latitude regarding certain kinds of student misbehavior. After a big football victory, for example, it was acceptable for students to riot and block off traffic, so long as this ritualized vigor did not result in all-out mayhem or threaten the authority of the administration and board. Administrative tolerance was operative for very different activities, with some selective allowance for innovation and reform in the activities associated with campus life and organizations. Not far beneath the surface of administrative benevolence was a saturation point beyond which predictable administrative control was activated. There was little tolerance for dissent about substantive issues of campus life. In short, deans and presidents did not want problems. Aspiring presidents and their ambitious colleges and universities faced increasing demands for valuable external relations generally—and for fund-raising, political favor, and government grants specifically. The insular life of students held only partial and often diminishing priority for them. Starting around 1963, little by little there emerged signs of increasing flash points for, and reminders and remonstrance from, administrators, all of which would culminate in fireworks and upheaval in 1968 and 1969. Here is the infamous statement a university president, Clark Kerr, made to an external group of corporate executives, board members, and prospective donors: "One of the most distressful tasks of a university president is to pretend that the protest and outrage of each new generation of undergraduates is really fresh and meaningful. In fact, it is one of the most predictable controversies that we know—the participants go through a ritual of hackneyed complaints almost as ancient as academe, believing that what is said is radical and new."[21]

The angry reaction by discontented students to President Clark Kerr's public statement was immediate and widespread. A fact of life is that most events of life are repetitive and familiar, even for those in learned professions. Imagine a lawyer telling clients that drafting yet another will or real estate document is boring. A medical doctor might pine for pathbreaking discoveries in esoteric surgeries, but such discoveries, of course, are rare. Why should university presidents be exempt? Most professionals conduct ritualized ceremonies and events as a customary professional obligation. Furthermore, Kerr's public pronouncement glossed over the reality that some of the student concerns were warranted, their scale and scope unprecedented.

Students criticizing the impersonality of the university—neglect of and indifference to undergraduate programs, crowding in class registration and living quarters, huge lecture classes, and bureaucratic indifference—stood on legitimate grounds. When college and university officials ceased to take students' reasonable concerns seriously, brushing them aside as predictable minor problems without substantive solutions, the door was opened for the persistence of student concerns and in turn an escalation and extension to other issues and matters. Then students' concerns traveled far afield from academic and educational services, eventually touching on a succession of political matters such as civil rights, racial equity, free speech, political organization, investment policies, inclusion of students in campus governance, gender issues and women's studies, and, ultimately, protests against the Vietnam War. Presidents such as Clark Kerr along with their administrative lieutenants would pay dearly for their early weary dismissal of organized student concerns. Some presidents opted to stand strong against campus unrest, adopting a law-and-order public persona, as recalled in one presidential memoir, *The Year of the Monkey*.[22] But administrative denial and defiance seldom worked effectively.

A generation of university leaders were caught off guard and were in disbelief about the harsh student criticisms in part because until the mid-1960s most college presidents saw themselves as respected, even beloved, by students. Taken to extreme, however, student protests escalated into violence. At Columbia University and elsewhere, student protesters took delight in barricading the presidential office, then sitting with feet propped up on the president's desk, smoking cigars and indulging in other excesses that had little to do with meaningful campus reforms and caused student protests to lose a great deal of support from the public and even from fellow students. Office takeovers turned public sympathy away from students.

The traditional organization of formal and sponsored student activities was resilient and lent itself to the gradual addition of these new student demands and interests. Some universities had in place a historic base of student organizations with autonomy and activism—namely, incorporated student associations or student unions. Foremost would be the example of ASUC and ASUCLA, acronyms for, respectively, the Associated Students of the University of California and the Associated Students of the University of California, Los Angeles. Each of these campus organizations had its own revenue sources, was registered as a lobbying group in state politics, hired its own lobbyist to represent student interests, rented office space and other facilities, and had a payroll for its employees and staff. Such a student association might, for example, be the corporate home of a student newspaper. At one time, some associated student organizations ran co-op bookstores and numerous campus shops, provided art studios, recreational facilities, and game rooms for student use, and even paid the salaries of college varsity athletic coaches.

College students of the early 1960s also had new opportunities to extend their horizons and concerns beyond traditional campus life. Student campus coalitions were partners with community groups in pressing city councils and local government for fair housing agreements. Students participated in voter registration drives in the South. Students had the opportunity to visit and study policies and programs in South Africa. Recent college graduates could choose to serve in the newly formed Peace Corps and VISTA (Volunteers in Service to America, now known as AmeriCorps). Civic, condoned, and unpretentious, these activities provided effective training grounds for organized efforts and leadership in social reform initiatives. Ultimately student participants would bring what they learned—ideas as well as strategies—to their own campus's organizations and activities.

Even if administrators were indifferent toward students and control of students, at most American colleges and universities, whether large or small, private or public, campus life blossomed in its array of student-based extracurricular activities. Theater and other performing arts, music groups, literary magazines, special interest clubs, radio stations—recreational and leisure groups abounded. Campus life included inviting and publicizing guest speakers, sponsoring a concert series or a film society. Another interesting complexity of the American campus was its enrichment by unofficial organizations that technically were off campus but were, in fact, functional and integral in student life. The YMCA located near many colleges and universities provided a welcoming site for guest speakers, special events, and discussion groups. Hillel International, Newman Centers, the Wesley Foundation, and other organizations with dedicated houses added to the array of places that welcomed student congregation and innovation.

Although most accounts of college students in the decade observed that American undergraduates tended to be apolitical, synapses existed to connect students effectively to the traditional ideas and membership pools of politics, especially state politics. Some fraternities, especially at flagship state universities, were attractive because they were regarded by rush candidates and pledges as an initiation into a future state political leadership cadre. Certainly this route into future authority was exclusive and limited diversity, as it tended to perpetuate selective initiation into state politics. At the same time it was testimony to the influential power of some student organizations both during college and in the adult life that followed. So, a question was whether the existent student organization umbrella had some capacity to extend to newcomers and new interests, and the answer to that question was yes.

At universities associated with energetic and even radical student protests, it is clear that the existing student organizational structures helped make the protesting groups and events possible. The 1963–64 Free Speech Movement at Berkeley stands as a foremost example. The crux of controversy was the university administration's announcement that tables holding political leaflets and materials were banned from a campus area traditionally set aside to accommodate them. The administration may have been most concerned about radical leftist groups. But in its zeal, the administration overlooked the fact that the Berkeley campus, by tradition and organization, had long allowed *all* registered political interest groups to set up tables with pamphlets. The administration may have momentarily squelched student groups on the radical left. But their prohibition of tables also meant that, to be consistent and thorough, they had to exclude an entire spectrum of political affiliations. Young Americans for Freedom and Young Republicans were equally upset as the Communist Youth League in being told to shut down and move on. And, thus, student groups usually at odds with one other pulled together, at least for the moment.

The university administration had become a common foe to all student political groups—and to the overarching Associated Students. Historical continuity can easily be detected between the archetypal conformist conservative student activities and the new breed of student radicalism. Even the extreme campus marches of the Far Left of 1964 still adhered to a code of responsibility and respect; the men marching wore sports coats, ties, and dress shirts, had trimmed hair and neat beards. They were *earnest*. It appeared that the dynamics of a student culture could fuse traditional conduct with concern for new issues through peaceful means and orderly public demonstrations, all in accord with the American grain of civic activism. But the character and appearance of protest would change abruptly about four years later, with activism marked by violent confrontation.

Regional and Institutional Differences: Students at Campuses in the South

Since primary attention about student unrest in the 1960s understandably dwells on accounts from Berkeley, Columbia, Harvard, and Michigan, other institutions and regions are characterized as being involved too little and too late. Indeed, the colleges and universities of the South figure prominently in this characterization. However, an accumulation of excellent historical case studies, including books and journal articles since 2007, make a strong case for amending this portrayal.[23] The colleges and universities of the South are an illuminating focus also because the region brought into proximity Black and White students in a complex mix of aggression, cooperation, and neutrality on such issues as civil rights. Indeed, organized student concern over civil rights would be the defining legacy of southern colleges. Organizers of the movement included student leaders and organizations at South Carolina State University in Orangeburg, and the famous sit-ins in Greensboro, North Carolina, by students organized from North Carolina Agricultural and Technical University.

The word *organized* is an important descriptor because these early efforts were highly disciplined, with a savvy awareness of how counterproductive violence and disorder would be in making effective stances and conveying messages about racial desegregation and access in restaurants, hospitals, schools, and other public places. Less recognized until recently is that the student groups at the Historically Black Colleges and Universities extended their organized initiatives and protests to a range of other issues, including demands for curricular improvements and for more equitable funding for their institutions. Another important historical note is that even though the HBCU students in the South were among the first to raise questions about and awareness of racial equity and social justice, by the mid- and late 1960s, national student organizations such as Students for a Democratic Society stopped paying attention to them, opting instead to focus on other styles and sites of student activism.

Student activism at Historically Black Colleges and Universities in the 1960s: the February One (1960) monument and sculpture stands on North Carolina Agricultural and Technical State University's campus and is dedicated to the actions taken by the Greensboro Four, which helped spark the civil rights movement in the South. (Photo by Cewatkin 2002)

For students at traditionally White institutions, many of which still were racially exclusive in the 1960s, student activism took two divergent forms. The highly publicized student opposition to racial desegregation and enrollment of African American students at the University of Alabama in 1957 and to the 1962 enrollment of James Meredith at the University of Mississippi demonstrated student concern about race relations—opposition, that is. What often has been overlooked is that in the late 1960s numerous southern colleges and universities were the source of organized student reform, especially in anti–Vietnam War initiatives. One possible reason these efforts have tended to be overlooked by historians and other analysts is the South's regional culture, in which reform rather than rebellion was the watchword.

An excellent example of this overlooked participation took place at North Carolina State University. Participants and analysts agree that the student culture was decidedly conservative. This was not surprising in a historically White land grant institution in the segregated South. A critical distinction is that students were not so much politically conservative in national party affiliations or voting as they were basically apolitical—as were many, perhaps most, American college students of the 1960s. Most important, what one finds is a remarkable mobilization of student leaders and groups within the campus during the 1969–70 academic year. It included the appearance, persistence, and triumph of grassroots student leadership that eventually gained widespread campus support and held sway in campaigns and votes against candidates from established, traditional constituencies such as the Greek fraternities and sororities. Furthermore, the student reform groups at North Carolina State University were ahead of the faculty and its representative bodies and succeeded in influencing the president to endorse anti-war resolutions. Attending an institution located in the state capital, North Carolina State University students were well positioned to reach the media and the state legislators and governor.

One NC State student, Cathy Sterling, ran an organized, imaginative campaign to become the first woman elected president of the student body, an achievement that few women on the more radical campuses could claim. Once elected, she persisted in mobilizing and bringing together disparate groups within a heretofore quiet and largely disinterested campus. Cathy Sterling's leadership as elected student body president took place at a relatively overlooked campus that was not radical and was out of the national media mainstream. North Carolina

State University made no claim to be a Harvard or Berkeley or Columbia in its student activism and militancy. Indeed, some of the success of the students was achieved because they consciously avoided the more violent, volatile actions and tactics of students in the national spotlight. As one NC State University student activist recalled, expressing quiet pride without apology, "We didn't fire a shot, we didn't burn a building."[24] Both participants and historians readily acknowledge that the strong student reform initiative ended soon, in part due to the time of year. The initiative began in May 1970 in response to the Kent State shootings and was soon followed by the end of the academic year, with students resuming summer activities and obligations. (The conclusion of the academic year contributed to the winding down of student activities on campus and was a national phenomenon, hardly particular to the college students of the South.) In 1969 there were comparable student marches and cancellations of classes throughout the South, including at Duke, the University of North Carolina, and the University of Kentucky, to name a few. The University of Kentucky was noteworthy in that it departed from the decorum and discipline at North Carolina State. Burning an ROTC building, jeering at the new university president, and disrupting the talk of the governor showed at least for a moment a more rebellious side of southern discomfort.

Minority Voices and the Participation of Students of Color

Even though civil rights were an early and high priority of campus activism in the 1960s, efforts tended to be focused on voter registration and other community activities, especially in the states of the South. By 1966–67 a new and growing campus concern was on Black students in terms of admission to and inclusion in the campus. Volatile external events such as the Watts riots in Los Angeles and police confrontations in Newark and Detroit kindled this emphasis. Ultimately it led to self-scrutiny on the composition of the student body where at historically White colleges, even with desegregation, minority groups such as Blacks and Latinos were woefully underrepresented. The student organization umbrella was extended to include the Black Student Union or La Raza and other representative bodies. Student demonstrations within the campus eventually pressed college and university admissions offices to amend their recruitment strategies and admissions policies to make at least some progress toward racial and ethnic diversity. Each underrepresented group organized its demands for academic change, such as adding courses, programs, and formal departments in, for example, Black Studies or Chicano Studies.[25]

A high-water mark of public attention and controversial media coverage about the plight of minority students took place at Cornell University in late April 1969 when a student group occupied Willard Straight Hall. According to a student memoir, Cornell University was immersed in controversy and conflict:

> Within hours, police deputies from Rochester, Syracuse and across New York state massed in downtown Ithaca. "Had they gotten the command to do so, they would have gone and taken the Straight [Hall] back and arrested people, or who knows what would have happened. It could have made Kent State and Jackson State look like the teddy bear's picnic. It would have been just absolutely terrible." . . .
>
> Although physical disaster was averted, deep psychological scars burned into the minds of many on campus. Four decades later, feelings in some quarters are still raw. The university as a bastion of reasoned argument, thoughtful debate and academic freedom seemed to be under siege. Relationships among faculty members were destroyed. Students were torn. An atmosphere of pervasive fear and anxiety gripped the campus and the nation. The AAS [Afro-American Society] students were not punished, outraging some faculty members, students, and alumni.[26]

The volatile and conspicuous incident did lead to reforms, as Cornell University gave added acknowledgment, facilities, and resources to the Afro-American Society. Along with such gains, the occupation of Straight Hall was embedded into the university's collective memory, creating a schism that drained energy from numerous constituents. Institutional change extracted a heavy price on all groups, especially for the university in its future external relations, as the images of students bearing guns on campus was etched into the public's imagination.

Analyzing Activism: Probing the Mystery of Outside Agitators and External Groups

One of the fast and facile ways in which a disgruntled university official or a governor or state legislator could try to defuse and dismiss a student activist group was to tell the press that, after all, the group was organized by outside agitators. Implicit in this claim was that real college students were not involved in such hostile, disruptive movements.

There was some truth to this. Documentaries and memoirs about the Free Speech Movement at Berkeley, circa 1963 through 1966, illustrate that the cast of leaders includes numerous young adults who were not enrolled at the University of California or who had only a tenuous campus affiliation. This revelation is rebutted in part, however, by the further revelation that several of the leaders had been UC students or were recent alumni, or perhaps were recent graduates of colleges elsewhere. Each campus made its own accommodation for nonstudents. It was, for example, less likely that a nonstudent would hold a campus leadership role at Harvard, Yale, or Princeton than at a more fluid, larger state university and community such as Berkeley.

There's no doubt that many of the campus leaders had academic and intellectual roots that shaped their ideas and ideals in the movement. Mario Savio at Berkeley was an outstanding student in philosophy and physics. Bettina Aptheker, the daughter of Marxist historian Herbert Aptheker (a relationship that years later would be controversial), was a highly visible political activist and scholar. The campus was fertile ground for discussion and for forming alliances and groups. David Horowitz, who was the first editor of *Ramparts,* the new radical left magazine started in 1967, had been a graduate student at the University of California, Berkeley, but had left his formal studies to concentrate on writing and editing.[27] Yet the most influential controversial political groups nationwide were not campus specific. Students for a Democratic Society originated at the University of Michigan but soon transformed itself into a nerve center and clearinghouse, with speakers such as Tom Hayden, who followed the circuit of campus speeches, seldom staying long or involved at any one college or university. These groups were examples of what has been called horizontal history—cutting across the higher education landscape.[28]

Student editors of campus newspapers often saw themselves or were depicted as bold outsiders, pacesetters in new ideas and shaping student opinion toward anti-war and leftist movements. Steven Kelman carefully matched the chronology of the *Harvard Crimson* editorial positions against events. His conclusion was that the *Crimson* writers and editors were less like trailblazers and more like chameleons—holding back and then becoming a champion of an extreme cause once it became safe to do so.[29]

Elsewhere, student newspapers were the source of innovative commentary. At Yale, for example, starting in 1968 Garry Trudeau wrote a cartoon series satirizing local and national politics and social trends. Called *Bull Tales,* it depicted thinly veiled campus figures and was so appealing that by 1970 it had been syndicated in newspapers nation-wide with a new title, *Doonesbury*. The series had a long track record of success that included receiving a Pulitzer Prize for its political commentaries.

One view of the collegiate culture was that it was sufficiently estab-lished, strong, and appealing that it transformed novitiates (members of the entering first-year class). In the late 1960s, however, a different model started to kick in as new students brought with them from their high school years fashions, values, tastes in music, art, and literature, and drug use, along with behaviors that were bold and new—and shaped the collegiate world into which they entered. Media and journalistic coverage would speak and write less about a collegiate culture and more about a youth culture that might include but was not limited to the campus.

From the Marketplace of Ideas to the Marketplace of Ideologies

With the established student organization structure accommodating a large and growing number of interests, the campus culture became home and host to layers of issues and related groups. A progression included anti-business, anti-war, civil rights, Black Power, support for lettuce work-ers, La Raza, women's rights, and gay rights. A question was whether sup-port of one necessarily meant support for another. Alliances were seldom coherent or complete. Slogans with false dichotomies abounded, as college students were scolded, "If you're not part of the solution, you're part of the problem." Another variation was, "If you're not with us, you're against us." Furthermore, maintaining commitment to a political move-ment that had few institutions or enduring organizations was tiring and quickly lost its appeal to college students and young alumni. In con-trast, numerous events and media productions increasingly held out to college students the lure of cultural and lifestyle alternatives to what was depicted as mainstream American life. These cultural trends could be pursued quite apart from political activism.

College students joined social and political causes in the 1960s. Furthermore, many students came to see themselves as alienated from society. For example, one self-descriptive slogan that emerged in the mid-1960s was "Although we as college students were the most privileged group, we came to see ourselves as the most oppressed group." Invert-ing the conventional perspective revealed a world turned upside down. By 1968 at some campuses the clustering of causes and concerns, all centered on student alienation, led to a vague blurring, as suggested in omnibus grievances such as the following, undergirding a call for a campus strike:

STRIKE FOR THE EIGHT DEMANDS STRIKE BECAUSE YOU HATE COPS STRIKE BECAUSE YOUR ROOMATE WAS CLUBBED STRIKE TO STOP EXPANSION STRIKE TO SEIZE CONTROL OF YOUR LIFE STRIKE TO BECOME MORE HUMAN STRIKE BECAUSE THERE'S NO POETRY IN YOUR LECTURES STRIKE BECAUSE CLASSES ARE A BORE STRIKE FOR POWER STRIKE TO MAKE YOURSELF FREE STRIKE TO ABOLISH ROTC STRIKE BECAUSE THEY ARE TRYING TO SQUEEZE THE LIFE OUT OF YOU STRIKE[30]

Such public outbursts signaled an end to rational discussion, public discourse, and coherent social or political organization. Students increasingly shifted from focusing on electoral politics and demonstrations to being preoccupied with the cultural changes and choices increasingly available by the late 1960s.

Collegiate Culture to the Counterculture

Whether the American campus was the source or recipient of new ideas and aesthetics, it became a staging site. Often overlooked was the role of the faculty and their classroom teaching as an incubator. Elsewhere, opportunists took advantage of the changing times. Former Harvard psychologist Timothy Leary, having been kicked out of the academic profession, became an advocate and polemicist for psychedelics and drug use, including LSD. One of his messages was for student movements to turn away from systematic political discussions and toward cultural and spiritual mantras, often finding homes in communes and communities far removed from a campus. This general drift is evident in the 1990 documentary *Berkeley in the Sixties*. One distinctive part of the American campus in the 1960s was the flourishing of new popular art forms, ranging from several diverse strands of rock 'n' roll innovations to periodicals such as *Ramparts, Mother Jones*, and the Free Press Newspapers available in several cities. What's not readily evident is the role of the campus and college students in these undeniable trends and innovations. College students would be unwarranted in taking full responsibility for founding and producing these forms. Besides, if a college student did heed Leary's call to "Turn on, tune in, and drop out," she or he was going to be dropping out of college and perhaps, society. It was hard to be a hippy and still attend lectures, write papers, take exams, and complete a degree.

Often, within the counterculture, college students were consumers as readers, listeners, and attendees who contributed to changes in American life. It was an incredible era for rock 'n' roll, whether as a musician or a listener. Historian Theodore Roszak published a thoughtful analysis of the varied literary, intellectual, political, and cultural strands that created a distinctive social fabric in his 1969 book, *The Making of a Counter Culture,* in which he provided "reflections on the technocratic society and its youthful opposition."[31] A year later, another book, *The Greening of America,* struck a chord with its categories of consciousness, abbreviated as CON I, CON II, and CON III to distinguish the evolution from agricultural to industrial and, finally, to modern liberated modes and values. The author, Yale Law Professor Charles Reich, gained widespread attention with his "Reflections about U.S. society & its new generation":

> There is a revolution under way—not like revolutions of the past. This is the revolution of the new generation. It has originated with the individual & with culture, & if it succeeds it will change the political structure only as its final act. It will not require violence to succeed & it cannot be successfully resisted by violence. It is now spreading rapidly, & already our laws, institutions, & social structure are changing in consequence. Its ultimate creation could be a higher reason, a more human community, & a new & liberated individual. It is a transformation that seems both necessary & inevitable, & in time it may turn out to include not only youth but the entire American people. . . . This means a new way of living—almost a new man. This is what the new generation has been searching for, & what it has started to achieve. Industrialism produced a new man, too—one adapted to the demands of the machine. In contrast, today's emerging consciousness seeks a new knowledge of what it means to be human, in order that the machine, having been built, may now be turned to human ends: CON III.[32]

Critics pointed out (and even the author acknowledged) that his optimistic predictions did not come true and that the ensuing years really were the un-greening of America. For many observant and opportunistic college students of the era, the aim was not so much to change the system as to master it. A predictable by-product was that the counterculture became an audience and a market for a formidable counterculture capitalism, despite ideology and slogans about anti-materialism. Stores such as Tower Records and producers such as MGM made great profits from LPs, singles, and other music products whose lyrics deplored capitalism while sales receipts endorsed it.

Town and gown relations were transformed as new kinds of shops and services sprouted in campus communities, including restaurants, photocopy shops, head shops for drug paraphernalia, record stores, clothing outlets, and shops featuring independent artisans and craftsmen who catered to a student market that was drastically different from those who frequented campus villages earlier in the decade. Not the least significant change was in the performing arts, with rock concerts and summer festivals gaining attention of promoters and ticket buyers alike. Music's diversification was driven by the appreciation of college student audiences for sitars and tambours from India along with the British "invasion" of The Rolling Stones and The Beatles—and indigenous American popular music stretching from Motown to the Californian Beach Boys. Recreation and enjoyment trumped serious politics in altering American cultural choices.

Sorting out Legacies of Activism on Student Activities and Organizations

The high-profile events and demonstrations of the student protest movement had little endurance or institutionalization by 1970, despite projections that they would change the American political system. For example, the so-called Princeton Plan, in which university officials permitted undergraduates to be excused from academic obligations so they could participate in election campaigns, disappeared by 1974 for lack of student interest. Opposition to the Vietnam War probably was the most unifying focus of student unrest. It also was the source of the greatest conflict across American society. For all the movement's mobilization, anti-war protests emanating from colleges and universities in the 1960s did little to change national elections or federal policies. Raising consciousness against the war was accompanied by equally strong commitment by pro-war citizens and candidates well into the 1970s. The cultural energies and forms of the counterculture did persist and spread over the next decade but, contrary to the priorities of 1960s student radicalism, it would be the women's movement and gender equity that flourished in the 1970s as the foremost social and political concerns.

What happened to the vocal and visible leaders of the student movement? Surveying the cast and characters from 1963 to 1970 reveals a high degree of burnout and dropout from center stage. In some cases, the turnover and transformations were extreme: many strident revolutionaries had a change of heart and an accompanying change of rhetoric. Sociologist David Horowitz, who played a pioneering role in founding *Ramparts* magazine, illustrated perhaps the most dramatic shift. His messianic pronouncements for upending capitalism and the corporate university subsided as he eventually became disenchanted with and distrustful of the Far Left. His changes of mind and heart eventually would lead him to the political right as a leading figure in neoconservative circles. By 2017, according to David Streitfeld's profile in the *New York Times,* "David, after a political odyssey that took him from the extreme left to the extreme right, has a surprise last act that puts him once again in the thick of insurrection. His radical views on immigration, race, education, the duplicity of the media and the treachery of liberals have abruptly made their way to the center of power. If the Trump administration has an intellectual godfather it's David Horowitz."[33] At least in this case, the ideas and causes that were strong in 1967 turned out to be relative and transient. Twists and turns in the patterns of various student activists, of course, varied. Horowitz's biography indicated that the inspiring messages of movement leaders directed at college students could be fleeting, sometimes with a hit-and-run quality even for and perhaps especially for the spokespeople and advocates themselves who came of age in the turbulent 1960s.

What effect did students have on academe, society, culture, politics? At best, students' participation in the campus activism and political movements of the decade may have contributed to increased awareness of civic engagement, community organization, and political involvement. The focus of the contribution becomes blurred, however, as suggested by the peace movement, which for one student might connote a deliberate political involvement constituting support for a candidate for office or a ballot referendum, perhaps tied to ending the war. Yet for another student it may have meant acquiring a philosophical or spiritual sense, as in the state of inner peace, or flashing the peace sign as a show of comradery. Bumper stickers in college neighborhoods proclaimed "Envision World Peace." Hip humorists played off this with their own version, "Envision Whirled Peas." What had originated as serious, principled politics eventually stretched across a wide range of involvement, ideas, and images. Opposition to the war at its most pronounced included students who resisted and defied the military draft, opting for conscientious objector status, facing conviction and jail time, or leaving the United

States to apply for citizenship in Canada or elsewhere. College men nearing graduation often chose to enroll in officer training school programs as an alternative to being drafted to serve as a soldier or sailor.

Questions about seriousness of purpose and radical reform, although difficult to answer, were worth asking, because movement leaders relied on messianic polemics to ensure participants conformed and made a political commitment very like a religious conversion. Steven Kelman, class of 1970 at Harvard, wondered about fellow Harvard students who participated in the university strike in spring 1969. What did their participation mean in terms of commitment and long-term change? Did student strikers, for example, risk their preordained future by forfeiting the chance to finish their bachelor's degree? Should a student show loyalty to the reform cause by paying a price such as not going to law school or not entering an MBA program—both signs of political conversion in which "the establishment" was rejected? The questions surface because leaders in the movement were not modest about self-congratulations and self-importance as they frequently claimed that this cause was revolutionary or would change the world or exhilarating hyperbole.

One area where college and university officials did respond to the tumultuous student protests was in reforming the organization and professional staffing of student life and campus activities. Starting around 1970 there emerged at most colleges a proliferation of new student services and a transformation of the student affairs profession into a helping profession at all junctures of a student's college experience. Freshman orientation programs became kind and friendly, even concerned with helping students to find themselves. A student union building added offices and professional staff for career planning, academic advising, course tutoring, and psychological wellness. Academic governance changed at many colleges and universities where students gained formal recognition with designated slots as members of the board of trustees. College admissions underwent substantial reforms, with new priority placed on diversity in recruitment and need-based financial aid for underrepresented groups.

The student activism conflicts that startled established colleges and universities also led to two innovations. First was what has been called a managerial revolution, in which boards of trustees and presidents realized that institutional decisions required more and better information, whether in student affairs or in fund-raising or admissions. Second, since so many higher education leaders ranging from presidents to professors had been caught off guard by student protests and activism, there was a groundswell of commitment to research on the college experience—student learning and values and a host of other ongoing higher education issues.[34] In 1959 these applied research efforts were marginal; by 1970 they were central.

Media coverage focused on prestigious colleges and universities as the forum for radical change, but the institution to which most groups would look to accommodate a new generation of students was relatively low profile—namely, the public junior college. This expectation would be fulfilled in part as the public junior college emerged by 1969 as the place where the most newcomers to higher education would enroll. That enrollment achievement, however, was not a substantive probe; it did not uncover the impact of the community college on its students. As sociologists Jerome Karabel and Steven Brint observed, here was the academic site for a "diverted dream."[35] For starters, the per capita funding for a community college student lagged far behind the amount state governments appropriated for undergraduates at the state flagship universities. Sociologist Burton R. Clark identified a syndrome in which students with lackluster academic records who were admitted to a public junior college encountered what was called the cooling-out function, in which academic advisors encouraged them to lower their goals and expectations, to take remedial courses, and, eventually, to drop out. This pattern was in stark contrast to providing academic support and tutoring that would help them to stay enrolled and eventually succeed in academic work.[36] Even though most research on college students indicated that a residential campus tended to make great differences in student learning and the college experience, most public community colleges remained bare-boned in terms of dormitories and features usually associated with a four-year residential campus.[37]

One consequence of the dramatic events associated with student activities and student activism was that colleges and universities lost a great deal of public confidence and legislative support by the end of the 1960s. Federal agencies' funding for academic research and development had started to decline, causing problems and questions for what had been the most prestigious and prosperous feature of major universities since World War II. Campus administrations were left in disarray by months, even years, of student unrest. Demographic changes meant that the number of high school graduates who considered going to college was starting to taper off, creating new concerns about future enrollments.

Additional sobering and unexpected news that started to surface around 1970 was that most colleges and universities were financially weak, as economist Earl F. Cheit's research pointed to what he would call "the new depression" in American higher education.[38] In sum, the legacy of the decade was that American colleges were overextended, exhausted, and uncertain in their mission and direction. Colleges and universities had lost self-confidence along with public support. Even though many academic structures and institutional forms had endured the unexpected series of internal and external crises, most campuses were left battered and bruised and facing fundamental questions. The controversies and conflicts that had taken place unexpectedly left them with unfinished business.

Colleges and Curriculum

Continuity and Change in Academics

Students and Their Challenges to Teaching and Learning

Curricular reforms were at the start, if not always at the heart, of the student movement of the 1960s. Media coverage, focused mainly on campus political activism against the Vietnam War, tended to miss grassroots activism for academic changes. Undergraduates pushed for curricular reforms starting early in the 1960s by showing their dissatisfaction with large lecture classes and complaining that teaching was neglected in favor of research.[1] Over time, students' initiatives in changing courses of study gained momentum, expanding to gain supporters among the faculty and exert influence on academic programs nationwide.

The conventional wisdom in higher education has been that changing a college curriculum was comparable to moving a graveyard.[2] This colorful characterization misses the mark in describing how curricular changes took place in the 1960s, however, because academic reformers adopted approaches that were less onerous and more creative than moving a graveyard. Foremost was building a new college and curriculum from scratch. Another strategy was for students to burrow in and around the existing academic caskets and course catalogue gravestones, more like gophers and moles than a moving company. The popularity of the subterranean motif among undergraduates over the decade was marked by a proliferation of publications dealing with academic survival, such as *The Underground Guide to the College of Your Choice*, whose irresistible lure to students was its immodest claim to be "The only handbook that tells you what's *really* happening at every major college and university in the U.S.A."[3]

Creating New Kinds of Colleges from the Top Down

Reforming undergraduate education in the 1960s from the top down drew from a long heritage of initiatives in which college and university

Large lecture halls and the impersonality of the 1960s classroom: Professor McDowell teaching class in Chemistry Building auditorium, West Virginia University. (Courtesy of West Virginia and Regional History Center, West Virginia University Libraries)

administrators took on the role of visionaries to stake out their model villages whose catalogue and mission they believed undergraduates ought to encounter and experience at a campus and as a college education. This recurrent impulse was defined by what Gerald Grant and David Riesman described as "the perpetual dream."[4] Several liberal arts institutions had already gained academic respect and prestige for their efforts, such as Reed, Antioch, and Swarthmore, who had achieved status as what sociologist Burton Clark called "the distinctive college."[5] The model for this innovation was for a charismatic leader (usually the president) to create new institutions or else intervene at a crucial point in an existing institution's saga. At Antioch College in rural Ohio, for example, the successful formula was to combine a progressive work-study program with deliberate recruitment of outstanding students from the Northeast and Middle Atlantic regions. The transformational president of Swarthmore relied on an impressive honors program to energize a liberal arts college. Reed College in Portland, Oregon, attracted serious, bright students with its approach to liberal education that included a freshman year humanities core, a senior thesis, no varsity sports, and a commitment to providing a sound alternative to what the college's founders considered to be characteristic of private colleges on the East Coast. Elsewhere this tradition of change had included bold new ventures such as Bennington College in Vermont, Bard College in the Hudson Valley of New York, and Black Mountain College in North Carolina.[6]

The reform logic after World War II was that in the age of the research university, an attractive strategy to reduce the tension between research and teaching was to try to create a distinctive college within the university structure, what was called the University College—for example, Columbia College and Barnard College were liberal arts colleges within Columbia University.[7] The same characterization held for Harvard College within Harvard University, and for the College at the University of Chicago. In 1956 the University of California transformed its citrus research station in Riverside into what was proposed to be an exemplary small residential undergraduate campus. The resultant UC Riverside was hailed at one time as a state college that was an "Amherst of the West." Another announcement compared it to an "Oberlin of the public sector." Eventually, however, the Riverside faculty lobbied to add graduate programs and research facilities, features that meant abandoning the public liberal arts college model and turning the campus into a more typical medium-sized research university.[8] A more daring agenda in the 1960s was to move the structure and spirit of undergraduate education completely outside the established university and focus on creating a new experimental college, an academic genre that included Hampshire College in Massachusetts, Ramapo College and Stockton State College in New Jersey, New College in Florida, and UC Santa Cruz.[9]

Driving the reform impulse toward creating new colleges was the recognition by some academic leaders that mere expansion of the typical large university model would cease to be effective. The concerns of this scattered band of reform-minded presidents and professors came in a range of tones. Foremost was the concern that something was wrong, or imbalanced, in the shape of most colleges and universities, at least in regard to the appropriate, effective education of undergraduates. These disciples may not have agreed on what a college should be, but they knew what they wished to discard or avoid among standard academic practices. The recurrent theme was to break the lockstep of a set curriculum and pedagogical structure, along with critically examining the credentials monopoly. It also included initiatives to provide alternatives for the role of a professor, especially an antidote to the publish-or-perish hallmark of research that had inordinate appeal at some institutions. The theme of breaking out of the established model prevailed throughout the 1960s and surfaced as a dominant emphasis in the 1971 Newman Report on the Condition of Higher Education.[10]

A slightly different inflection was that although American higher education was, indeed, remarkable, it could be better. Here the aim was not so much to repair damage as to make a fresh start. It conjured images from Puritans who, arriving in the New World, were soon committed to building a school upon a hill.[11] The new alchemy of higher education of the early 1960s was to make the university seem smaller as it grew larger. So, although most expansion of higher education within existing campuses or in constructing new ones tended to perpetuate the standard model of large lecture classes and a complicated elective system characterized as the "cafeteria model" or an "academic smorgasbord," there were persistent signs of innovation and concern. In most cases there was a life cycle of intense initial enthusiasm followed by disorientation and a search for order. After a few years, many experimental colleges gravitated toward a conventional academic model, meanwhile shedding many of their unique practices and forms.

An early example of the impulse to create drastically different colleges came about in Sarasota, Florida, in 1960. A group of donors, a church foundation, and renegade reformers (who were either alumni or administrators at established colleges) set out to jump-start the creation of an academically strong private liberal arts college in the South. Housed in what had once been a luxury resort hotel, New College opened for its first one hundred students in 1964. According to Gerald Grant and David Riesman, the college's trustees and administrators insisted on recruiting academically top students from the start, and tried to do so by using college funds to "buy" applicants who had been designated as National Merit Scholars. The college eventually reached an enrollment of about five hundred and persisted in its commitment to liberal education. By 1974, however, financial problems, combined with an increasingly competitive market for colleges in attracting students, led New College to negotiate a deal to become a public institution, annexed as a distinctive part of the University of South Florida. Some years later this public-private identity would be redefined, with New College leaving its University of South Florida connection and being recognized as the state of Florida's freestanding public honors college.[12]

Even though experimental colleges were all about students and undergraduate studies, the point of view both in planning documents and memoirs leans heavily toward control by adults who had definite, set ideas about what students should be provided with. Only later, after new colleges were operating, does the historical record start to pick up commentaries and then memoirs by students as participant-observers, whether in student newspapers or in diaries and other accounts. That distinction in perspectives is crucial because even a founding president who was visionary and caring, who urged students to consider new courses and subjects, generally wanted to maintain control of his or her hothouse academic plots. Founders often were surprised, even disappointed and angry, when the student subcultures veered in directions the founders did not favor or foresee. Another fascinating part of the experimental college story is the role of serendipity in determining who· gets the opportunity and resources to create and then try to lead a new model college. Did the president of a university system grant a favor to a former graduate school roommate who had long harbored a hankering to start a new college? Was the president-elect of a proposed new state campus receiving a political payback from an admiring legislature? When a founding president finally got funding and permission to hire professors, there was a strong emphasis on loyalty and allegiance to the president.

Starting in 1958 the established colleges and universities in western Massachusetts's Pioneer Valley collaborated to anticipate future demand for more colleges—and for a new design for undergraduate education. Amherst College, Mount Holyoke College, Smith College, and the University of Massachusetts at Amherst worked together to plan a new institution, Hampshire College. In 1966 the founding president and vice president explained their vision's blueprint in their book *The Making of a College*.[13] They noted, "Central to the new institution was the conviction that the curriculum of Hampshire College relies minimally on course work, instead emphasizing seminars, field studies, contract studies and other approaches to inquiry through which students prepare for comprehensive examinations at three stages to qualify for a degree."[14] Deliberate planning over several years meant that Hampshire College missed the 1960s but carried the decade's spirit into the 1970s. Its rustic setting, small-scale buildings, and location in western Massachusetts kindled keen anticipation among liberal high school students. It was unconventional and creative in its grading, social atmosphere, and curriculum. In its first two years Hampshire College attracted eleven applicants per admissions slot, but by 1974 its luster had dimmed. It probably would have been more attractive and enduring had it opened around 1965 instead of in 1970. Hampshire College's founding academic reflected that he failed to realize, when Hampshire first opened, that few undergraduates, even at a new and experimental college, knew how to design a coherent course of study.

New Public Colleges in New Jersey

New Jersey was a chronically underbuilt state for colleges and universities, especially for public higher education. To supplement its existing flagship state university, Rutgers, and six teachers' colleges, the state authorized founding and funding for two new innovative undergraduate campuses: Ramapo College and Richard Stockton State College. Planning and tooling up took place in the mid- and late 1960s, and in 1969 and 1971, respectively, the two colleges admitted their first cohort of undergraduates. Ken Tompkins, who had joined the Stockton faculty at the start as a literature professor and dean, collaborated with Rob Gregg to edit and contribute to an anthology published as part of the college's fortieth anniversary.[15] This included Political Science Professor William Daly's extended commentary on "The Stockton Idea" that guided the founding and first years. Professor Daly explained the college's raison d'être—and its potential limitations:

> The Stockton Idea proposed to make available to state college students at state college prices the kind of interdisciplinary and individualized liberal arts instruction initially developed in America for the children of the ruling elite and, in the contemporary world, usually reserved for students at the most exclusive and expensive private liberal arts colleges. In other words, what was arguably the best and most expensive undergraduate education in the country was to be delivered to the students who most needed it but who also could least afford it and (as a number of early critics argued) might also be the least prepared for it and the least interested in it.
>
> State college students were known to range from very well-prepared to very poorly prepared, but the average level of academic preparation was likely to be a good deal lower than that which could be assured by rigorous admissions standards for entering students at exclusive liberal arts colleges.

And the economic situation of many state college students and their parents was likely to place them generally in the career-oriented camp. They were unlikely to be attracted to a college that preached the civilizing impact of liberal arts education unless it could be demonstrated that such an education would also contribute directly to career success and economic gain.[16]

The Stockton State College hopes and dreams seemed to echo the Lovin' Spoonful's 1965 rock 'n' roll hit song "Do You Believe in Magic?" Tompkins elaborated, "This attempt to combine what was in the early days virtually open admission access with high-powered education once admitted, to combine working-class career education with upper-class liberal arts education, was exquisite 1960s stuff—noble to the core in concept but also audacious and likely to prove difficult in the implementation phase—as we and a few other like-minded colleges of the Sixties were soon to discover."

Strategies to make the new college different included avoiding traditional academic department structures along with implementing the scattered office system, in which faculty members of markedly diverse fields deliberately were placed next to one another. William Daly, a professor of political science, recalled, "It was my distinct impression, as the first-year faculty assembled in the Fall of 1971, that those of us who had packed our bags and come running to serve the Stockton Idea were attracted both by the nobility of Stockton's educational goals and by the near impossibility of achieving them. We were overwhelmingly young. It was the end of the '60s. And we could still hear the ringing words of John Kennedy, speaking of the quest to put men on the moon, 'We choose to do these things, not because they are easy but because they are ha-a-a-ard' (New England for 'hard')."[17]

Members of the original faculty cohort recalled:

We arrived at the College (temporarily housed in the collapsing boardwalk Mayflower Hotel) to discover that the administrative planning team, which had spent the previous year constructing an initial plan for Stockton, had anticipated many of the difficulties associated with Stockton's declared and very ambitious mission and had built distinctive structures into the College plan designed to give us a fighting chance of actually making elite liberal arts education work for a career-oriented state college student body. All of those distinctive structures were compelled by hard realities to evolve during the first ten years of the College. But they are all still here and are all still central to what makes Stockton different, and arguably better, than most other undergraduate institutions.[18]

The four pillars of the Stockton Idea were as follows: the general studies program and the traditional degree programs; the skills program; the preceptorial advising program; and finally, college-wide faculty involvement in all of the above.

Established colleges of the decade also ventured into internal reforms. Another reform model was to create new living and learning units at an established university. Innovations at the University of the Pacific in Stockton, California, represented this approach. Three new cluster colleges were established at Pacific in the 1960s, in the model of British universities such as Oxford and Cambridge. These colleges integrated faculty and students into distinct living and learning communities. Raymond College, established in 1962, was an accelerated interdisciplinary liberal arts program where students shaped their own courses of study. Elbert Covell College, established in 1963, was a unique inter-American college. Half the students were from the United States and half from Latin America, with classes taught in Spanish. Callison College, established in 1967, focused on non-Western studies with a year of study in an Asian culture. The cluster colleges were absorbed into the rest of the university in 1982. Their values, including a close-knit learning community, accelerated and interdisciplinary programs, and self-designed majors, have left a lasting impact on the University of the Pacific. Their emphasis on global education continued in the School of International Studies, founded in 1987 as the first university-based undergraduate school of international studies in California. In 2012, the School of International Studies, while retaining its autonomy as a school, became part of the College of the Pacific.

A problem that proponents of creating new colleges faced had two dimensions. First were the unexpected consequences of their academic visions and realities held by the original academic (adult) leaders. The second dimension involved the students. Having opted to be academic pioneers, students found dealing with all the details of establishing new programs and activities to be exhausting and potentially never-ending. They might devote more of their time and pursuits to structure than to the substance of undergraduate education. Furthermore, a new institution unfettered by tradition was not always a good thing. Many, perhaps most, students went to college to be part of traditions and heritage, ranging from activities to academics.

Faculty at UC Santa Cruz faced at least one unpleasant surprise: their tenure and promotion process was subject to review by the entire University of California system. It was not clear that commitment to the kind of intensive teaching and advising embraced by their home campus would be compelling in evaluations that ultimately were system-wide, where scholarly expertise and advanced research were the coin of the UC realm. Beyond its impact on individual professors, this dilemma compounded into a structural and institutional one—a gradual but persistent tendency for a college that started out daring and different to move, over time, toward the mean of being more or less a typical college or university.

The excitement of innovation, especially in full-time residential liberal arts education, which characterized most of the new colleges, eventually met complications. The first dean of Hampshire College mused that many deans and professors had failed to realize that most eighteen-year-olds did not want to take responsibility for planning a rigorous, coherent, individualized curriculum and course of study.[19] A larger consideration was that since adults—founding president, donors, and faculty—took the lead in planning everything from the mission statement to the curriculum and construction of a new campus, they carried a notion, deliberately or not, of how things should work out and end up. If their aim was to allow students to be active and full participants (as was the case with experimental colleges), there usually was either a conflict or an avoidance between academic officials and students. Would faculty and deans, for example, stand by and acquiesce if student initiatives went in a direction markedly different from what the faculty or president had hoped or planned?

Experimental Colleges: If You Build It They Will Come

Many of the proposed experimental colleges did not get off the ground until the early 1970s, and many had deflated from their original initiative by about 1975. Students, faculty, and administrators all appreciated the liberal academic programs and lifestyles they encountered while at the same time coping with unexpected and sometimes insurmountable problems. The result was that college reform was thoughtful yet more restrained than the student exhilaration of 1967 and 1968.

STUDENTS AS ACADEMIC PIONEERS

Students were neither the founders nor planners of the host of innovative colleges that opened in the late 1960s and early 1970s. They were, however, the academic pioneers who quickly brought their own priorities and values to teaching and learning along with the round of campus life into which they had been cast. This meant that they negotiated with faculty and administration the boundaries and terms of the hidden curriculum. Primary sources for tracing their entrance into campus life are, predictably, student newspapers and yearbooks. Numerous oral histories and memoirs are now available, in college and university archives and in published anthologies and accounts. Yet it remains difficult to assemble and refine a comprehensive, detailed profile of this subset of American college students within the broad contours of all college students within the decade.

The new experimental colleges had some capacity to attract a self-selected group of freshmen who were adventurous. Most of the students who chose to enroll appear to have been well behaved and thoughtful, and simultaneously unclear as to what their new college stood for—and how much or how little they embraced its distinctive mission. A historian's windfall of student accounts belongs to a group of twelve students at UC Santa Cruz. For their senior seminar project, they compiled, reconstructed, and wrote a self-conscious history of Cowell College. In fall 1968, at the start of the cohort's senior year, Cowell's provost, Page Smith, and a prominent professor, Jasper Rose, "began rounding up Cowell students who would be interested in writing a short history of the first four years of their college, the first college of the University of California, Santa Cruz campus." The object of the resulting history workshop was "to study the practical problems involved in writing contemporary history and to produce a narrative of the first four years of Cowell College's existence."[20]

The members of the history workshop were members of the very first group to enter the new UC Santa Cruz in 1965. Furthermore, within the university they were members of Cowell College. The two affiliations are important for understanding experimental colleges and cluster colleges. UCSC was indeed new and different. One of the distinguishing differences was that UCSC was planned as a honeycomb of residential colleges, each of which had an identity and finite size. Each residential college was to be both an architectural setting within the campus and the home of particular academic emphases, with its own residential faculty and families. This was an American hybrid that brought to mind the historic English universities Oxford and Cambridge—where, for example, although a student entered the university, she or he also had a close, lifelong affiliation with one of its member colleges. UCSC students were not typical of all college students; harder to say is whether they were representative of fellow experimental college freshmen, circa 1965–70.

At Santa Cruz and many of the other new colleges, one unexpected determinant was that the campus was unfinished. At Santa Cruz, a concentration of trailers served as residences and a few common buildings— a natural sciences building that was the central academic facility, along with a field house that provided dining commons and other meeting spaces. Adjusting to trailers, including self-determination of rules of conduct, courtesy, etiquette, generated a freshman year that was comparable to a summer camp in the business of daily rustic living, combined with negotiating the terms of academic life. Without established college activities, ranging from varsity athletic teams to clubs or a Greek system, students were somewhat like the lost boys in *Peter Pan* or Golding's *Lord of the Flies*.

The unfinished campus, combined with Santa Cruz's beautiful, largely undeveloped setting in the forests and by the Pacific Ocean, made the university an isolated, island community. Cowell College students good-naturedly picked up on journalistic images of their campus and referred to the lure of "groovin' in the redwoods."[21] A 1969 commentary by one student made a special point of noting that when the class entered, in 1965, they were in the "pre-hippy era." That was an important historical distinction, especially since Santa Cruz would be known within the state and nationwide as perhaps the most extreme manifestation of the permissiveness of the counterculture. This at the time was largely unexplored territory. Yet what student memoirs indicate is that even a nontraditionalist student group devoted a great deal of time to a search for order— often an unconventional order, but order nonetheless. Students were high achievers academically as measured by course grades and SAT scores, but many students were wary of what they considered to be conventional student government and class offices that many had encountered in public high schools. So, they developed their own norms as to what constituted Cowell College governance. Foremost it centered on the civility and courtesies associated with living in the cramped quarters of the trailers that constituted daily life. One of the dilemmas faced at Santa Cruz and at all new experimental colleges was the demand to create statutes and structures, because few of them were in place.

Students who were part of the first entering cohort also faced a problem that, unlike at established colleges, at Cowell there were no sophomores, juniors, or seniors on campus. The opportunity to create new organizations according to your own specifications might have been exhilarating. It also could be disorienting and tiring. Navigating a new curriculum took patience and skill for even the most able students.

Absence of letter grades, reliance on portfolios for assessment, and a large measure of freedom in shaping a course of study was tied to an overriding emphasis, at Cowell, on the history of Western civilization. Illustrative of the trade-offs of a new curriculum was that Santa Cruz welcomed students who wanted an alternative to frequent exams, graded quizzes, and semester grades. In return, however, students took a high-stakes series of essay examinations in the spring, in which 20% of them were deemed unsatisfactory by the faculty. Twenty percent was a high and harsh standard, given that the admitted students were carefully recruited and selected and were considered to be among the best within the entire UC system.

The history seminar project, published as a book in 1970 with the title *Solomon's House,* describes intense, highly personal relations between students and their residential college, their classmates, and the faculty and academic administrators. The provost, an established historian who had come from the UCLA faculty, was known not only for his peculiar teaching topics (for example, the importance of chickens in civilization) but for his habit of riding a bicycle on the steep campus hills—and often challenging students to a bike race down the hill (but, according to student lore, only if he thought he could win). Since students worked closely with faculty in studies and a range of other campus and college activities, a familiarity and candor emerges in the seminar project. Student assessments of the faculty were keen, often intense and critical. The embryonic campus culture tended to cast students into sharp polarities. After four years, some of the charismatic professors and academic leaders gained praise and respect, but some students saw them as dubious and opportunistic. By this standard the campus approximated an academic commune edging toward evolving into a community.

Students eventually became aware of the gains and losses of having opted for an alternative, protean college. For academically strong students who consciously rejected the high-pressure academic demands of a Stanford or a Princeton where emphasis on performance and grades was pervasive, Santa Cruz provided academic excellence in terms of students and faculty, within a less competitive classroom scene. Students had freedom without stigma to devote themselves to personal development. Yet there were large numbers of students who planned and prepared to go to graduate school, law school, or medical school. If in an innovative college courses did not have conventional letter grades, how would a student fare when applying to professional schools or graduate schools? One compromise resolution was to allow letter grades in selected courses, usually in the sciences.

Students' social values at a campus such as Santa Cruz were extreme, but even so, the student culture at these schools was markedly different from the subculture of student radicals at nearby UC Berkeley. Most Santa Cruz students and their student groups were beyond or outside politics and viewed their campus as a home and as a refuge and retreat. The general impression across several experimental colleges was that the pioneering students had favorable recollections of their education and experiences.[22] A decade later, however, it was less clear that these same colleges had remained experimental in character.

LESSONS AND LEGACIES

Students and professors both discovered that in this utopian campus there still could be trouble in paradise. Indeed, students discovered that the often-maligned elective system at large universities did, indeed, offer opportunities for a lot of courses and majors. Small size brought coherence and interaction, but students could find it stifling and limiting, as well.

Elsewhere, especially in the new liberal arts colleges in New Jersey, when students were given the option of self-determination, some of their preferences leaned toward establishment courses and programs. Professors may have presumed that the students' orientation was toward self-discovery and experimental topics, but for some students, college also meant the freedom to take more predictable paths.

Although many educators and students had high expectations for the experimental colleges, many of the enduring innovations in the established college course of study were accomplished by accretion—in skirmishes at many institutions and over several years. In assessing the relative success of the experimental colleges, it is necessary to distinguish between the institution itself and its influence as a model whose practices were watched and even adopted elsewhere. The experimental colleges, both public and private, did remain true to their commitment to small size, as an alternative to the large multiversity. In some cases, this achievement was problematic in that size was too small, signaling a lack of sufficient applicants and enrollments, but most of the experimental colleges reached enrollment levels of about one to five thousand students and persisted in showing that a small to medium-sized liberal arts campus could thrive within the public sector, making a significant contribution to the diversity of American higher education.

Students Reforming Higher Education from within and on the Margins

In contrast to academic leaders' efforts to create a new campus from the top down, there were numerous examples where groups—students and faculty—responded to what they saw as gaps or flaws in established higher education and worked on the margins of and in nooks and crannies within institutions to create alternatives. Less grandiose than founding colleges, many of these student initiatives were probably also more effective and enduring than chartering a new institution.

Undergraduate discontent with the lecture system of instruction was widespread. Why were lectures maligned? Photographs of large auditoriums with the "sage on the stage" were often associated with passive pedagogy and impersonality of instruction. Ironically, the introduction of the lecture course format in the late nineteenth and early twentieth centuries was a dramatic innovation whose aim was to end dreary recitation classroom teaching. Some universities made a decision to recruit outstanding professors, based on the logic that students were better served by having a lecturer who was well known as a scholarly expert than having instructors who were not distinguished.[23] And often this resolution worked well. In some departments, it was an honor to be the senior professor selected to teach the large introductory undergraduate course. Furthermore, the large communal lecture twice per week was to be supplemented with "sections" for class discussion in small groups, often led by an advanced graduate student in the field. Most likely the lecture system became a source of disdain for students because it was overused by deans and provosts. If it were leavened with a reasonable number of classes with small enrollments and a teaching and learning style that emphasized discussion, most likely the outrage over large, impersonal lectures would have been reduced substantially.

Perhaps the real culprit in the neglect of undergraduate education was impersonality and indifference by the faculty and academic departments toward undergraduates. Illustrative of mean-spirited faculty indifference to undergraduates was the infamous sign a professor posted on his office door with the message: "If you have to ask, you won't understand!" Historian Larry Cuban documented how since 1890 scholars trumped teachers, producing what he called "change without reform" in university curriculum.[24] Prime factors in this drift were the priority given to sponsored research and the emphasis on PhD programs.

The piecemeal reforms and innovations in questioning the lecture system and some early attempts to demonstrate student consumerism were prelude to attempts at wholesale curricular reforms by undergraduates. One of the most successful examples of student activism in transforming the course of study came about at Brown University in 1968–69. Brown undergraduates had shown moderate interest and participation in civil rights demonstrations, protests against military recruiters, and establishment guest speakers. Yet Brown was characterized as a quiet campus. Within the undergraduate culture, student writers and editors continually chided the administration over Brown's split personality in balancing selective admissions, medium size, and aspirations for research excellence. A memorable student parody written and published in 1968 by the editors of the campus humor magazine, *The Brown Jug*, was a replica of the official catalogue, but with the title *Bulletin of Brown Semiversity*.[25] The humorous lampoon indicated that Brown students took the educational mission seriously and subjected their alma mater to critical discussion and dissection. It also brought attention to the dilemma of an institution that tried to steer between the polarities of a large research university and the mission, character, and size of a liberal arts college.

Where Brown differed from academically selective and visible campus counterparts was that over several years an accumulation of curricular initiatives culminated in a quiet revolution that put undergraduates in control over academic processes and programs. These areas were usually the exclusive territory of faculty and academic senates. According to historian Luther Spoehr, a handful of committed, highly organized student leaders started by establishing a new course format, the GISP (Group Independent Study Project), as the module in which students could create and shape courses. Using this building block, combined with working papers and manifestoes on curriculum and college mission, the leaders pushed to redefine the purpose of undergraduate education as self-discovery and fulfillment. Ironically, student dissatisfaction with the established curriculum gained momentum even though Brown University presidents had used generous Ford Foundation funding over the preceding decade to revamp course offerings and degree requirements to be fairly flexible. Students had access to modes of thought seminars with senior professors. However, for the student reformers around 1965, these efforts were seen as unsatisfactory and too restrained.

Student rallies at Brown dealt with curricular reforms. In May 1969, a large percentage of the student body, along with faculty and staff, settled down on the campus green as loudspeakers broadcast a three-day-long faculty meeting. Student representatives who had campaigned and lobbied for a new curriculum, including pass–no pass options, creation of new majors, eliminating elective requirements, and making foreign language study optional, overwhelmingly prevailed in the final faculty vote. As Luther Spoehr observed, student activists at Harvard, Columbia, and Yale, along with the national media, acknowledged that the Brown student reformers had, indeed, pulled off an academic coup.[26] Without violence or extremism, the student curriculum reformers were effective in large part because they were organized and persistent, and because they succeeded in persuading large numbers of fellow undergraduates to participate in the campaigns and to enroll in the new courses—much to the surprise of the faculty and deans and the university president. The new curriculum was officially implemented in fall 1969 and changed the academic culture while also attracting an increasing number of applicants for admission.

A more subtle approach operating at many colleges was what sociologists and psychologists called the hidden curriculum. Benson Snyder noted that at the Massachusetts Institute of Technology students and faculty were involved in a battle of wits as to what the course of study was about. At MIT, the particular compact was that of intense academic pressure, with the tone and standards set by the faulty. But at other colleges and universities, the game and goals were different.[27]

The tunneling around in the established campus and curriculum in the 1960s was manifest in a cornucopia of innovations by and for undergraduates. Long before ratemyprofessors.com, students took initiative outside faculty approval to conduct student course evaluations that combined statistical profiles with student narrative reviews. Whether or not such publications had official approval did not matter, as students were both respondents and readers. This grassroots innovation in student consumerism was far in advance of official academic policies and practices, as deans and provosts did not start to adopt the practice of relying on official course evaluations until about 1978, when they developed their own versions of surveys that were similar to those pioneered by student groups years earlier.

Student consumerism became increasingly comprehensive and sophisticated. Starting in 1968, editors of the *Yale Daily News* regularly compiled and published *The Insider's Guide to the Colleges,* which relied on student correspondents at over one hundred colleges across the nation. The aim was not to compete with standard college guides, but rather to provide readers with "a candid and factual report by those in the best position to know, the students themselves." The anthology gained a following far beyond Yale, as it was published by G. P. Putnam and enjoyed brisk sales. It collated information directed at students applying to college and then added snapshots and student comments about courses, departments, and campus culture. This kind of information was unlikely to be covered in official college publications. Many of the campus profiles were provocative and controversial, infused with regional stereotypes and biases—a mix of subjective observations and reliable data—but they kindled student interest in what was going on in their own campus and at campuses nationally. Most important, *The Insider's Guide* was a student project beyond the control of institutional officials.

A variation on the theme of the Yale national guide was the 1971 anthology compiled by Susan Berman, *The Underground Guide to the College of Your Choice.* Its format superficially followed that of the Yale guidebook, but it also was opportunistic in its contrived attempt to fuse itself with the jargon and slogans of the student counterculture. Its promotional blurbs touted it as a "book from the hip to the hip. Use it well. And Peace." The profile for each college surveyed included the categories "Sergeant Pepper," "Academic Bullshit," "Bread," "Brothers and Sisters," "Survival," and "Environment." The publishers proclaimed that it was "the one guide that gets you into the campus life-style before you're there. . . . THE UNDERGROUND GUIDE lays it on the line. The bread you'll need and your chances of getting it through scholarships and campus gigs. The admission standards. The ratio of chicks to cats and how the school stands on drugs, sex, political activism, and general life-style. There's necessary data on everything from the local pigs to the best courses and most popular teachers. You'll learn where the local hangouts are, what the physical environment is like, and all the other vital data the catalogs don't give you."

Enhanced student consumerism meant that by the mid-1960s students at many campuses were learning to navigate the official curriculum and regulations to create interesting, original academic projects, even creating a new major or concentration. At most universities, faculty had created interdisciplinary programs in such fields as American studies in which traditional departmental walls between history, English, and political science were eased. Important to keep in mind is the timeline of these innovations taking place on the margins of established colleges and universities. Most of them were in place and flourishing before many of the showcased new experimental colleges had admitted their first group of entering freshmen. Many established campuses, for example, saw a rise in applications to enroll in independent study courses. Universities, sensitive to the indictments about large lecture classes, provided a growing number of seminar courses in which instructors proposed special topics, with class size limited to fifteen to twenty students. Opponents of the war in Vietnam and US policies in Southeast Asia organized teach-ins. Outside the formal curriculum, at some institutions student groups created their own free university, complete with courses, catalogues, and instructors.

The appeal of curricular reforms initiated by students and faculty extended beyond high-profile, selective colleges to relatively young commuter campuses. A good example was at Cal State Long Beach, where two sociology professors challenged the conventional catalogue of courses by attempting to make their courses more relevant. They changed classroom furniture and seating arrangements, introduced discussion sections, and selected new, unorthodox readings for the syllabus. In 1969 they broadcast the message of their innovations by publishing a paperback book, *The Halls of Yearning: An Indictment of Formal Education, a Manifesto of Student Liberation*. One of the professors was fired for what the administration considered outrageous, inappropriate courses and conduct. The course innovations and book hardly transformed the mainstream of undergraduate education at Long Beach State or elsewhere, but they did signal that the diffusion of educational reform had spread across the American higher education landscape.[28]

Course catalogues did not tell the full story of teaching and learning at a college, but they did provide some clues about change. According to a 2016 feature story by NPR, "In the late 1960s, Amherst and other liberal arts colleges responded to faculty demands for flexibility and switched from a core curriculum, where students pretty much all took the same courses, like English, math and the history of western civilization, to an open curriculum." In 2016 Catherine Epstein, dean of Amherst College, told NPR reporters that the 1966 course catalogue was concise by the standards of the twenty-first century, at 223 pages, compared to about 500 pages today. Innovative courses of the mid- and late 1960s included titles such as Birth of the Avant-Garde: Modern

Poetry and Culture in France and Russia, 1870 to 1930.[29] New courses also dealt with American popular culture, including the serious reading and analysis of comic books, or a course on the history of movies (mostly black-and-white and silent films).

The formal established curriculum showed signs of being responsive to student initiatives for innovations. Good examples were the slow but persistent legitimacy being conferred by university academic senates to such fields as Black studies, women's studies, Hispanic studies, and numerous other interdisciplinary approaches to themes and groups that students and faculty believed had been understudied and overlooked. The demand for such new courses and programs came in part from student groups, such as the African American Student Association, along with interest and support from graduate students and scholars who had the requisite research background and academic experience to increase legitimacy of the demands. The machinery for consideration and approval, however, was slow. Usually the burden of proof was on the innovators to persuade deans and department chairs and provosts that new fields were substantive and enduring. Interdisciplinary courses and programs took years of negotiation and application to gain approval as formal academic departments. The first approved program in women's studies was established at Cornell University in 1969.

The academic pioneers who started these initiatives in the 1960s eventually gained widespread inclusion, acknowledgment, and even legitimacy from the faculty senate. Important to note, however, is that these strands emphasizing scholarly fields shaped by diversity and social justice coexisted alongside new initiatives to create new departments such as computer science and, at professional schools, joint JD/MBA programs geared toward future corporate executives. The relativism of the American university cafeteria curriculum meant that the liberation of broadening the course of study could go in any number of directions, to the right as well as to the left, in support of socially conservative as well as liberal or progressive agendas.

By 1970 the teaching styles, course offerings, and fields of concentration were larger and more diverse than they had been in 1960. At the same time, most of the additions and innovations fit into the familiar academic structures and machinery of the established university. A sobering fact was that the liberation and reform of college curricula took place primarily in what was considered the liberal arts undergraduate curriculum, especially in the humanities and social and behavioral sciences.

In contrast, traditional PhD programs were the site of some new ventures in advanced scholarship which coexisted with the typically conservative control of the faculty guild. A frequent result was a departmental faculty divided into ideological factions, leading to intense curricular wars. Meanwhile, professional schools such as business, engineering, agriculture, pharmacy, law, nursing, and medicine, along with the natural and physical sciences departments, ascended in relative appeal and power within the university structure—marked by a large number of applicants, academic selectivity, and the ability to obtain research grant funding. These prestigious fields remained relatively impervious to a decade of criticism and attempts to bring substantive change to the courses of study.[30] Course catalogues for major universities in 1970 describe curricula that reflect a spirit of accommodation, providing something for all constituencies. Courses of study were diverse and sprawling, but often with little overarching coherence among the multitude of choices in degree programs.

Although the four-year colleges and universities received the most attention and visibility, a substantive change in public two-year junior colleges had taken place by 1970: enrollment growth and expanded faculty hiring were most pronounced in this sector, with a large number of new colleges being constructed nationwide. Furthermore, this institutional category underwent a major mission transformation reflected in the name change from junior college to community college.[31] The new branding meant a declining role as an academic transfer institution that sent students on to four-year colleges to complete the bachelor's degree. This mission of providing a path toward a bachelor's degree continued after 1970 but increasingly shared resources and enrollments with nondegree programs and courses dealing with a range of vocational, recreational, and social service functions. These were commuter institutions whose tuition charges were usually low and which had diminishing articulation arrangements with the bachelor's degree–granting institutions of both the public and private sectors.

In the 1960s the public junior colleges granting associate's degrees in academic subjects were hailed as an effective source of education for the freshman and sophomore years of college, leading to smooth transfer of students to the flagship state university, but in the 1970s this was no longer the case. Two developments changed this confident solution: first, fewer high school seniors opted for the transfer track and, second, four-year universities noted that junior college transfer students were no longer showing strong academic records in their upper-division work and bachelor's degree completion.[32] One legacy of the events of the 1960s was a dilution in the academic role in the new model of the open-door colleges as a central component in the emergence of the broad umbrella network known as postsecondary education.

6

College Sports
Big Games and Big Problems

Starting Point: Students and Athletics in the Early 1960s

Between August 26 and September 11, 1960, Chris von Saltza stood on the victory podium at the Olympic Games in Rome four times to receive swimming medals, a total of three gold and one silver. Later she entered Stanford University, graduating in 1965 with a bachelor's degree in Asian history, and then gained prominence over a long career as a computer scientist. After the 1960 Olympics, when von Saltza was at her peak, she never had an opportunity to swim competitively for a team again. Stanford, after all, did not offer varsity athletic teams for women.[1] What was a young woman to do? There was no recourse or appeal, as Stanford's practice was accepted by all as standard. For better or worse, in American sports this was the way things were. Von Saltza's competitive sports career had a perplexing ending, and so it is fitting that her story open this chapter about changes in intercollegiate athletics in the sixties.

Over half a century later another American high school senior, swimmer Katie Ledecky, won five medals at the 2016 Olympics held in Rio de Janeiro. Like Chris von Saltza at the time of her Olympic wins, Ledecky was about to graduate from high school and would enroll at Stanford as a freshman. But when Ledecky entered, in fall 2016, she did so with a full athletic grant-in-aid plus a year-round national and international schedule of training and competition along with prospects for substantial income from endorsements and a professional athletics career. Connecting the dots of issues and events to explain the contrasts surrounding these two Olympic champion women swimmers who also were students at Stanford requires thoughtfully reconstructing the condition of college sports for students in the decade 1960 to 1969.

About the time that von Saltza returned to the United States from her successful Olympic competition, many of the nation's sports fans turned

Women as athletes in the early 1960s: Olympic swimming champion and
Stanford student Chris von Saltza. (Photo by Harry Pot 1961)

their attention to the college football season. The championship climax
took place on Monday, January 2, 1961, with the annual Rose Bowl as the
New Year's celebration capstone event. A stadium crowd of over ninety-
seven thousand spectators joined with thirty million Americans who
watched the game broadcast by NBC on national television. At halftime,
with the University of Washington Huskies leading the Minnesota Golden
Gophers 17 to 0, fans settled back for the traditional festivities of marching bands and other events before the two college teams returned to the
field for the second half. As was the custom, students in the flip-card
cheering section entertained the crowd with a succession of flip-card

Caltech hoax at the 1961 Rose Bowl. (Courtesy of the Archives, California Institute of Technology)

displays. The first eleven displays went as planned. After that, the card show unraveled—first spelling HUSKIES backward as SEIKSUH, then featuring a stylized beaver (the Caltech mascot), and closing with CALTECH displayed on flip cards for all the nation to see.[2]

The elaborate, clandestine flip-card project was masterminded by a small group of Caltech students dubbed "the Fiendish Fourteen." They were quiet rebels who wanted to lampoon big-time college football, and they accomplished their deed apart from the approval or cooperation of Caltech's administration or any adult supervision. Over several weeks around Thanksgiving break, they sneaked into the files where the University of Washington halftime activities folders were stored, and one by one altered 2,232 individualized instruction sheets for the University of Washington students who were part of the card cheering section. This is considered by many to be one of the greatest college student pranks of all time: NBC broadcasters, Rose Bowl pageant officials, and university athletic administrators were caught by surprise. Such a characterization was high praise for a tradition of good-natured rebellious imagination that ran deep and dear in American campus life. At least for the sake of appearances, Caltech had gone to the Rose Bowl.

What both stories from the early 1960s—the Rose Bowl story and von Saltza's story—showed is that college sports had great potential both to include students and to exclude them. Students were at the heart of college sports, participating in a variety of roles. No activity had a stronger link to the undergraduate experience, and college sports represented a distinctively American tradition. No other nation looked to higher education to provide highly competitive sports performances and related pageantry played before large crowds. This was true in 1960 and only escalated over the decade.

College Sports in American Life

The 1960s was a decade in which college sports enjoyed great public appeal as a reassuring celebration of national conformity. This popular role accelerated, but by the end of the decade college sports had to confront new elements of conflict and controversy. This latter development made college sports of the late 1960s part of what journalist Jack Scott called "the athletic revolution."[3] The result was that college sports, once guaranteed as a source of national consensus, became increasingly divisive along lines of polarized national and campus politics.

Throughout the decade college sports connected the American campus to the American public with ceremonies and ritualized events that were highly publicized. For example, each year in late November the entire nation watched traditional rivalries at the end of the regular football season. The slate included Indiana versus Purdue playing for the Old Oaken Bucket, Texas versus Texas A&M, Tennessee versus Kentucky, Harvard against Yale, the Army-Navy football game held in Philadelphia, Alabama versus Auburn, and Oklahoma against Oklahoma State. On the Pacific Coast, the traditional Big Game pitted Stanford against Berkeley, with the governor of California sitting on one side of the field for the first half, the other side for the second. On the same day, the University of Southern California played against UCLA for bragging rights in Los Angeles. Harmony and continuity shaped institutional rivalries into good-natured events whose pageantry symbolically reaffirmed civic virtues and American values. These big games could also reflect a collegiate response to a national crisis.

Nowhere was this more evident than the day after Friday, November 22, 1963, in recognition of and deference to the assassination of President John F. Kennedy. Nationwide, college games scheduled for that Saturday were promptly cancelled or rescheduled. A nation at mourning might inspire administrators and bosses to cancel classes or the workday. But to stop big-time college spectator sporting events that had been planned well in advance was another matter. It was difficult to do—and therefore prominently conveyed respect for a grieving nation and the death of a president. That the National Football League (NFL) commissioner opted *not* to cancel the professional games scheduled for Sunday, November 24, endeared college football even more to the American public.

Despite its popularity there were persistent signs that intercollegiate athletics as public spectator events perpetuated rather than reduced inequities in American life. Numerous college stadiums had racially segregated seating. Some major college football teams in the South did not allow Blacks to buy tickets or even attend games. When bowl games such as the Cotton Bowl featured, for example, a team from the Midwest, such as Notre Dame, against a team from the South, such as the University of Texas, there were bitter tensions over race as well as regionalism.

The Character and Condition of College Sports in the 1960s

For college students who wanted to watch intercollegiate athletics, the 1960s was a good decade. For college students who sought to play varsity sports, it was a great decade if you were a White male. All other students encountered a peculiar mix of opportunities and exclusions. In some cases, college sports programs exploited students, especially women and racial minorities. Most colleges offered numerous varsity teams for men. The slate of major sports was football, basketball, baseball, and track and field. Other popular varsity Olympic-style sports included swimming, tennis, cross country, wrestling, and gymnastics. A few additions might be regional favorites, such as ice hockey in New England or lacrosse in upstate New York, soccer in St. Louis, or water polo in California. An example of extraordinary local dedication to a particular sport was soccer played by the St. Louis University Billikens. Drawing almost all their players from Catholic high schools in their home city of St. Louis, they won seven National Collegiate Athletic Association (NCAA) championships between 1960 and 1970.

If a talented young man liked to play sports, college coaches were glad to oblige, and it was not unusual to find on each campus a student athlete who played two or three sports each year. Furthermore, the National Collegiate Athletic Association did not place limits on the number of players on a team roster. Most colleges and their coaches encouraged walk-on candidates to try out for a squad if they had not been recruited. Even at big-time campuses, participation was a labor of love for students, as few colleges or universities offered athletic scholarships outside varsity football and basketball.

By the standards of 2018, college sports seasons of the 1960s were significantly shorter on the calendar and in the number of games or matches played by a team in a season. Many college football teams did not play their first game until mid-September, and most seasons concluded by Thanksgiving. There were few postseason football bowl games, with about five major bowl games played around New Year's Day. Some universities, such as Notre Dame and the eight members of the Ivy League, prohibited their football teams from playing in postseason competition. Participation in the NCAA postseason tournaments was uneven in other sports, as schedules often were uncoordinated. In individual sports such as wrestling, there were few formal requirements for participation in the national tournament other than an institutional agreement to participate, travel money, and scheduling. In basketball, only one team per conference was allowed to enter the NCAA tournament—a marked contrast to March Madness and the sixty-four college teams that will qualify for tournament play today. The NCAA did not make great formal divisions among teams, although in some sports there was a college division and a university division. The result was a fluid and sometimes vague landscape of national tournaments and championships.

In the 1960s the college student athlete held an honored place on campus and in American life. In addition to applauding those who were named All-Americans for accomplishments on the court or field, there was a special place of honor for those who also excelled in the classroom. One of the most prestigious honors, personifying the combination of excellence in academics and athletics, was for a graduating senior to be named a Rhodes Scholar. Bill Bradley, class of 1965 at Princeton University, truly was all-American. In high school near St. Louis, he did well academically and was an all-county and all-state basketball player. He was offered seventy-five college scholarships but declined them all to attend Princeton University. He earned a gold medal as a member of the 1964 Olympic basketball team and was named the NCAA Player of the Year in 1965, when Princeton finished third in the NCAA Tournament. After graduating in 1965, he attended Oxford on a Rhodes Scholarship, delaying a decision for two years on whether to play in the National

Basketball Association. While at Oxford, Bradley played one season of professional basketball in Europe; he eventually decided to join the New York Knicks in the 1967–68 season, after serving six months in the air force reserve. He spent his entire ten-year professional basketball career playing for the Knicks, winning two championship titles. Retiring in 1977, he was elected to a seat in the US Senate the following year, from his adopted home state of New Jersey. He was reelected in 1984 and 1990, left the Senate in 1997, and was an unsuccessful candidate for the 2000 Democratic presidential nomination. Bradley affirmed amateurism in college sports. The Ivy League, including Princeton, did not offer athletic scholarships, and Bradley's parents' annual income was sufficiently high that Bradley did not qualify for need-based financial aid.

Except in a handful of big-time football and basketball programs, college athletic recruiting was limited by lack of information and reliance on mail, and so was primarily local and regional in scope. In some sports, a typical strategy was for the coach to be on the lookout for raw talent. In crew, for example, coaches scouted tall freshmen who had been cut from the basketball squad and had never been in a crew shell in the water but had the attributes associated with good rowing.

Freshmen were not eligible for varsity competition at colleges belonging to the NCAA.[4] The logic of the NCAA was that a new student needed time to become acclimated to studies and other aspects of college life without the time demands and pressures of trying to make a varsity squad against seasoned athletes who were sophomores, juniors, and seniors. Most colleges, even small colleges, offered a full slate of freshman teams in each sport, along with the varsity squads for sophomores, juniors, and seniors. Each conference and its member institutions determined standards of academic eligibility. The NCAA handbook was little more than a pamphlet of suggestions and vague guidelines. Colleges tended to their autonomy in determining student-athlete eligibility. Indeed, when the NCAA attempted to impose a 1.6 grade-point-average standard on member institutions in 1966, foremost resistance came from academically select universities, led by members of the Ivy League who resented the notion that the NCAA would supersede an academic dean in ruling whether a player, even one with low grades, could play varsity sports.[5] Most important, our notions of students' rights and organizational accountability were alien sixty years ago. The paradox of college sports in the 1960s is that it was a student activity that was not run by or for students.

Creating the Commercial College Cartel:
The National Collegiate Athletic Association

By 1960 big-time college sports had weathered scandals involving player recruitment and had solved numerous serious financial problems that had threatened the well-being of athletic departments nationwide in the preceding decade. Television broadcasts of live games to large audiences threatened college game ticket sales by keeping fans in front of a television set and away from the stadium. At the same time there was the increasing spectator appeal of professional sports and the declining attendance at small college games. These developments were areas of grave concern that created schisms among institutions and led some to project that many colleges would no longer be able to afford to field teams. Several Catholic universities in metropolitan areas had dropped varsity football due in part to their inability to compete for ticket sales and fans where NFL teams played. The NCAA also battled with the long-established Amateur Athletic Union for governance and control of intercollegiate athletics.

How did athletic directors and their colleges and universities address these assorted threats? First, they granted the NCAA the right to be the collective representative on policies and programs for televising all college games. Member institutions and conferences were not allowed to negotiate their own television broadcast packages. The NCAA approach was to limit football broadcasts to a total of eight per week. On a given Saturday, the nationwide television market would be divided into four regions. The NCAA then selected for each region two games: one starting at noon, a second around three in the afternoon as the NCAA Game of the Week. The NCAA signed a contract of $6.5 million with NBC in 1965 for exclusive rights to broadcast twenty-nine selected college games. Each subsequent year the contract increased substantially, to the benefit of the NCAA. By 1970, for example, the NCAA had ended ties with NBC, and its new television football contract, with ABC, had risen to $12 million for a single season, almost double the amount in the agreements for 1965 and 1966.[6] This cartel arrangement remained in place until overturned in 1984 in a case where the US Supreme Court ruled in favor of plaintiffs the University of Oklahoma and the University of Georgia. For the 1960s, it meant that the NCAA, not a campus or a conference, controlled broadcasts, advertisements, revenues, revenue sharing, and, above all, selection of the teams and games to be showcased. Limiting the number of television broadcasts was intended in part to halt or at least slow down the decline in fans buying tickets and attending games at their nearby colleges. The NCAA became, in fact, a cartel.[7]

Having turned television into a source of revenue (for the NCAA and to a lesser extent for the colleges and universities fielding the teams), the NCAA also succeeded in holding at bay the threat posed by the increasing popularity of professional games, especially NFL games. The deal struck was that Friday night was reserved for high school games, Saturday for college games, and Sunday for professional games. The NFL and the NCAA also defused potential conflict when the NFL adopted its own regulations to prohibit drafting a college player until his class was scheduled to graduate. This truce allowed all segments to prosper and was mutually beneficial, since each level of sports team depended on the others. The football negotiation was in marked contrast to that in baseball, where most high school players with outstanding professional promise signed contracts with major league teams immediately following high school graduation. As a result, intercollegiate baseball was not a revenue-producing spectator sport. Since many big-time football teams were at universities located in small towns and in rural areas, the NFL teams and games posed little threat in competition for ticket sales and fans. Towns such as Baton Rouge, Tuscaloosa, Columbus, Knoxville, and Lincoln relied on a local fan base of alumni, students, and local residents to fill their stadiums (which have now grown to over one hundred thousand seats filled every week).

Commercial broadcast contracts signed by the NCAA and NBC ensured that for college sports, football would be the goose that laid the golden egg. The NCAA oversaw a revenue-sharing program in which some broadcast monies were shared, albeit unevenly, across all member institutions. This income was crucial to most small and medium-sized college sports programs, which had trouble balancing their budget based on ticket sales or media broadcasts. It also caused resentment among a relatively small number of big-time programs that did not like being thwarted in their own broadcasts, with the added insult of having to share income with what they considered to be marginal spectator teams. Radio station contracts, which were not controlled by the NCAA, provided some institutional autonomy and funding. To balance the budget, most athletic departments relied on mandatory student fees as a substantial and guaranteed revenue stream.

Campus Power and the College Coach as Cultural Hero

Coaching staffs were small. King Football might command a staff of one head coach and four assistant coaches along with a training staff, while most other sports had a single coach. Furthermore, many coaches had assignments for more than one sport, stretched over three seasons. The wrestling coach might serve as assistant coach for track and field in the spring. The assistant football coach probably helped out with lacrosse. Many coaches, and almost all assistant coaches, held off-season jobs such as selling real estate or working at local stores. Many coaches also taught activity classes or worked with the intramural programs. One trainer was usually assigned to several minor sports teams. At Berkeley, the national championship rugby team was a club sport coached by an alumnus and former rugby star who was a dentist in nearby Oakland. At many small colleges it was not unusual to have a faculty member find time to help out as an assistant coach or keep statistics and help with team organization.

Basketball, a moneymaker in the twenty-first century, might attract enthusiastic home crowds, but most campus field houses could hold only one to two thousand spectators. UCLA's cramped, rustic gym was known as the B.O. Barn—replaced in 1966 by the larger Pauley Center. Major network television coverage for basketball was miniscule, even in the national tournaments up until the final championship game. For postseason play, there was no road to the Final Four with numerous rounds of televised games over several weeks.

An irony of American higher education was that college sports were described and invoked as a student activity, whether in viewbooks or in regional accreditation reports. Yet students seldom had much voice in the operation of college sports programs. At most colleges, students paid a mandatory annual student athletics fee of about twenty dollars but had little say in how and where those monies were spent. Adding insult to injury for some students, possibly, was that the 1960s was a decade in which a winning college coach could be a campus hero.[8]

Since football was paramount in terms of prestige and ticket sales, many colleges had the football coach also serve as athletic director. A successful coach in a major sport acquired both power and prestige on his home campus. It was not unusual for a coach to have more public visibility than the university president. And in many cases, presidents deferred to a powerful coach. One anecdote about Darrell Royal, head football coach at the University of Texas, described an alumni booster exclaiming, after a big victory, "Why, you could be governor!" To which the coach allegedly replied, "Why would I want to do that? I would take a loss in pay and prestige." In many states, the college football coach is still the highest paid public employee of the state. Paul "Bear" Bryant at the University of Alabama, Frank Broyles at Arkansas, and numerous other football coaches served as their own athletic directors, leading to a curiously uncontrolled supervisory situation. Annual athletic department budgets at the largest programs in the nation consumed between two and three million dollars each year.

How did a student activity come to be outside the control of students and student organizations? One route at state universities was the creation of separately incorporated athletic associations, typically called SUAAs, state university athletic associations. They received 501(c)(3) status from the Internal Revenue Service as nonprofit tax-exempt organizations, because their purpose ostensibly was to raise money and provide resources for student financial aid. This they did. But the SUAAs' efforts often were disingenuous, because whatever monies went for athletic grants-in-aid could be matched or surpassed by departmental expenses such as salaries for coaches and administrative personnel, utility bills, construction, travel—all of which, expenditures too, were counted as tax exempt. A closely related ploy was to create a private fund-raising umbrella, usually with a colorful name such as the Wolfpack Fund. Alumni and boosters then could donate directly to the athletic program. Donors received a tax deduction for this educational gift and the incorporated fund paid no income taxes on gift revenue. All of these activities were justified officially as assisting students via services and financial aid.[9]

In the 1960s as part of this expanded focus on athletics, many universities approved the funding and construction of elaborate dormitories reserved exclusively for student athletes, usually football players. The NCAA exerted no restrictions or oversight. A chorus of critical analysts pointed out that these amenities tended to exploit student athletes by indulging them in luxuries without giving much concern to their academic success—as long as they remained eligible to play for the season. Football coaches at big-time programs created new staff positions such as the academic athletic advisor, sometimes known as the brain coach. In addition to providing tutors for student athletes, the academic advisor worked as a liaison between the head football coach, the academic deans, and the faculty. The culmination of these staffing measures and services was that toward the end of his career, Coach Bear Bryant conceded that the term *student athlete* really was misleading, that *athlete student* was more accurate. Between 1960 and 1970 athletic directors succeeded in creating and refining what Murray Sperber would call "College Sports, Inc."[10] The athletic department was a part of, but apart from, college and university operating procedures and accountability. These allowances meant that big-time college sports enjoyed an era of consolidation and confidence with prosperity and autonomy.

Women's Collegiate Athletics

Stanford's Chris von Saltza was not alone in her experience of women's collegiate athletics. Indeed, since World War II, American women had triumphed in the Olympic Games every four years—but had little standing in high school or college sports. At the 1964 Olympic Games in Tokyo the star of women's swimming was Donna de Varona, who won two gold medals. In 1964, she was featured on the covers of both *Time* and *Life* magazines and was selected as the most outstanding woman athlete of the year. Despite her talent and achievement and youth, her competitive swimming career was over, as there were few, if any, options for formal training and participation in competitions in higher education or elsewhere.

In the sixties, Wilma Rudolph was one of the few women Olympic medalists championed in college for her athletic excellence. Rudolph won three gold medals in track and field at the 1960 Olympics in Rome. She had benefited from one of the rare college track and field programs for women in the United States, at historically Black Tennessee State University. Most of TSU's competition was at Amateur Athletic Union meets, with no conference or national college championship meets available. Furthermore, funding and facilities were lean.

Many women competed in collegiate athletics, yet the attention and numbers attracted by women's sports were small compared to the situation for male college athletes. Furthermore, seldom did the women's athletic teams enjoy the formal status or funding of "varsity" sports. The character and status of women's sports is partially revealed in the college yearbooks of the era. Whether at universities or at colleges, a co-educational campus yearbook devoted about fifty pages to the men's sports, especially the major sports of football and basketball, while women's athletics typically received two to three pages of coverage. In team pictures women athletes wore gym suits as uniforms. The play format was for one college to sponsor a play day in which five to ten colleges within driving distance gathered to sponsor tournaments in several sports at once. Softball, field hockey, basketball, and lacrosse were integral.

Coaches, almost always women, usually held faculty or staff appointments, often in physical education, where they taught activity classes. The women's gym had only a few bleachers. Coaches of the women's teams usually lined the playing fields with chalk, mopped and swept up the gymnasium floors, and gathered soiled towels to send to the laundry. One indispensable piece of equipment for a woman coach was a station wagon, as players and coaches piled in with equipment to drive to nearby colleges for games and tournaments. The women's athletic activities often had their own director—yet another example of separate but unequal in the organization of intercollegiate athletics as of all student activities. There was one perverse equality, however: women students were required to pay the same mandatory athletic fee as men, even though the bulk of it went to provide a subsidy for the men's varsity teams (there were no varsity teams for women).

Despite the relative lack of intercollegiate sports options for women in the 1960s, there were some signs of life. One was the creation of alliances and formal associations which eventually led to the chartering of the national organization the Association for Intercollegiate Athletics for Women (AIAW) in 1971, with over 280 colleges as members. The Division for Girls and Women in Sports (DGWS), established in 1941, created the Commission on Intercollegiate Athletics for Women (CIAW) in 1967 to assume responsibility for designing, sponsoring, and sanctioning women's intercollegiate sports and championships. The purposes of the CIAW were to provide the framework and organization for women's intercollegiate athletic opportunities and to sponsor national championships for college women under the authority of the DGWS. The AIAW developed from the CIAW in recognition of the need for institutional membership and elected representation. The AIAW officially dissolved into the NCAA (men's and women's divisions) in 1982.

One heroic figure associated with women's sports to emerge in the decade was Donna Lopiano, who graduated with a degree in physical education from Southern Connecticut State University in 1968. She excelled in several sports as a youth and was the top player picked in the Stamford, Connecticut, Little League local draft. She was forbidden to play baseball with the boys, however, due to specific language about gender restrictions in Little League's bylaws. Lopiano started playing women's softball at the age of sixteen. After graduating college she was an assistant athletic director at Brooklyn College, coached basketball, volleyball, and softball, and then took on leadership roles in national women's sports associations. Eventually she was named director of women's athletics at the University of Texas along with receiving a succession of honors and appointments in sports policies and programs. She also was one of the most honored athletes of her era. Her experiences, including being excluded from teams, shaped her dynamic leadership over several decades.

The highs and lows in the experiences of women athletes such as Donna Lopiano, Chris von Saltza, and Donna de Varona demonstrate decisively that although the 1960s have been celebrated as a period of concern for equity and social justice, there is slim to no evidence that colleges showed much concern for women as student athletes. Conventional analyses portray passage of Title IX in 1972 as ushering in a new era for women and scholastic and college sports. These analyses were true in a sense but must carry the asterisked note that in the formative and plenary discussions in Congress and other forums between 1970 and passage in 1972, college sports for women were seldom if ever mentioned by either advocates or opponents of Title IX. All sides were taken by surprise when the issue unexpectedly surfaced in 1972.[11]

Black Male Student Athletes

The ideal of the outstanding White student athlete long occupied a prominent place in American colleges and culture, as noted earlier, in the profile of Princeton's Bill Bradley. Often overlooked is that in the early 1960s some of the most celebrated collegiate achievements came from young Black men who excelled in both studies and sports. The following profiles are illustrative, not exhaustive. But recognizing even a representative group provides a sharp contrast to a prevalent caricature of Black college athletes of the 1960s and beyond—namely, that of the dumb jock. These men were pioneers in desegregating their athletic conferences, and they did it while enduring insults and threats. Indeed, the theme that would surface and then gain momentum starting around 1968 was that the college sports machinery often exploited Black athletes—suggesting all the more reason why it is important for the historical record to note those who defied the stereotypes.

In 1962 and 1963 African Americans John Edgar Wideman, University of Pennsylvania class of '62, and J. Stanley Sanders, Whittier College class of '63, were selected as Rhodes Scholars. Wideman, who played basketball, earned his MA at Oxford and was a distinguished author, literary critic, and professor of English at Brown University. Stan Sanders graduated in 1959 from Jordan High School in Los Angeles (located on 103rd Street, later well known as the epicenter of the August 1965 Watts Riots). As an undergraduate at Whittier College from 1959 to 1963 he was an all-conference athlete in football and in track, won Little All-American honors as a football receiver, and concentrated in history. In 1963 he set off to Oxford University as a Rhodes Scholar. Two years later he entered Yale Law School and received his JD in 1968. In addition to practicing law in Los Angeles, he was active in civic affairs, including as a candidate for mayor.

Other exemplary Black student athletes from early in the sixties include Rafer Johnson, UCLA class of '60, who was both NCAA and Olympic decathlon champion. Arthur Ashe, UCLA class of '66, was an honor student and a member of naval ROTC, won the NCAA tennis singles championship, and led his UCLA squad to the team title. He was the first African American member of the US Davis Cup team, won the Championships, Wimbledon, and was ranked the most outstanding tennis player in the world. Ashe had grown up in segregated Richmond, Virginia, where he was not allowed to play on the premier tennis courts. He graduated first in his high school class. Ernie Davis excelled as a student and athlete at Syracuse University and was the first African American to be awarded football's Heisman Trophy, in 1961 of his senior year.

Another outstanding and often overlooked Black student athlete of the era was William (Bill) Wood, Jr., Brown University class of 1962. Wood graduated summa cum laude, concentrating in history, was a three-year varsity letterman in wrestling who had two undefeated dual meet seasons, and placed second in the heavyweight division of the EIWA before going on to the NCAA tournament. One bit of campus lore was that early one afternoon he won the William Gaston Prize for Excellence in Oratory, then excused himself from the awards ceremony podium, took a taxi to the gym located a mile from the main campus, and donned his wrestling uniform just in time to win by fall over his opponent. After graduation, he continued his studies at Yale Law School, receiving a JD in 1965.

In 1967 Perry Wallace, an undergraduate at Vanderbilt University, was the first Black student athlete to receive an athletic scholarship in the Southeastern Conference. Wallace excelled for three years in basketball and graduated with a degree in electrical engineering. He then received his JD from Columbia University Law School and had a long career as professor of law at American University in Washington, DC.

The dumb jock image that numerous sociologists, historians, and psychologists have documented came about because athletic departments often recruited student athletes whose high school record and preparation did not predict academic success at the college level. The devious strategy was to keep such outstanding athletes barely academically eligible for two or three seasons by providing them with help in writing term papers and in other academic areas. Then, when they completed their senior year of varsity competition, the props were withdrawn and student athletes were allowed to drop out or flunk out, leaving college without a bachelor's degree.

Although the major trends in college sports in the 1960s had been characterized by consolidation and confidence, there were signs of dissatisfaction on the margins which brought standard practices and customs into question by students and assorted student groups. Foremost was what was called the "revolt of the Black athlete."[12]

One enduring question the athletics revolution raised was whether sports, especially intercollegiate athletics, was a source of upward mobility. Closely related was the "truism" that college sports represented a level playing field. Systematic studies increasingly cast doubt on such traditional claims. One obvious dissent in the national liturgy was that at colleges and universities in numerous states, intercollegiate athletics remained racially segregated. Another perplexing and surprising pattern was that even though most colleges and universities were racially desegregated by 1962, there was no imperative or pressure for athletic directors and coaches to allow Black student athletes on varsity rosters. The University of Kentucky did not have a Black player on its basketball team until 1971. The Southeastern Conference had its first Black basketball player in 1966; in the Southwestern Conference, the Atlantic Coast Conference, and the Southeastern Conference, nominal racial desegregation of varsity rosters took place between 1964 and 1968, although several member universities waited additional years.[13] When racial desegregation of a college's teams did take place, coaches in basketball and football monitored the racial composition of the team on the field. For a basketball coach to send a majority of Black players on to the court was to run the risk of angering the fans.

For Black students who wished to play college sports, especially for those students from the seventeen or so southern states, most opportunities were in the Historically Black Colleges and Universities. Grambling

State University and Southern University, along with many of their conference members, played in segregated conferences. This was a feature that did not go unnoticed by professional sports scouts and coaches.

Athletic directors and coaches of racially exclusive sports programs attempted to extend their institutional racism to other teams. This meant, for example, refusing to play college teams whose rosters included Black players. Or, another variation, to either request or demand that a visiting college team that was racially integrated agree not to bring or allow to play their African American players. Response was mixed to these demands or requests. By the mid-1960s most coaches refused to comply with them. In 1963 the head basketball coach and players at Mississippi State University defied a Mississippi law prohibiting mixed-race college sports games, as the coach had his all-White basketball squad play in the NCAA tournament at East Lansing, Michigan, against a racially integrated team from Loyola University of Chicago. The Loyola team won in a game that marked a victory for good sportsmanship, as the captain of the Loyola team met before tip-off at center court to shake hands with the captain of the Mississippi State team (the two became lifelong friends). After this game the Loyola team went on to play what has been called the Game of Change, in which its squad featured four Black players in the starting lineup (from a university whose students were overwhelmingly White) and scored numerous upsets, eventually defeating the top-ranked and defending champion University of Cincinnati team in the championship game. In so doing they had to transcend spitting and racial slurs and other insults from hostile fans.[14]

Racial change and opportunities for Black student athletes often took place foremost at racially desegregated colleges that did not have the reputation or resources of the established big-time programs of the Big Ten, the Southeastern Conference, the Southwestern Conference, the Pacific Coast Conference, and the Atlantic Coast Conference. A conspicuous example is decisions made by the coach at Texas Western University, later known as the University of Texas El Paso, whose 1967 team featured five Black starters. The team won the 1967 National Collegiate Championship by defeating perennial power Duke University in the semifinals and then the University of Kentucky in the final game. Neither of those opponents had yet included a Black player on its squad, so the 1967 championship game eventually was elevated into symbolic importance for race relations and college sports history.

College sports had fallen short in fulfilling its own rhetoric of providing social mobility and opportunity. It may have done so in some cases and at some institutions. Yet equally strong was a record of resistance and reluctance by coaches and athletic directors, with presidents and boards of trustees acquiescing to their athletic administrators. The result was that the racial strife of 1969 was, as Michael Oriard expressed it, "college football's season of discontent."[15] Even when Black student athletes finally did gain the right to play on varsity teams, coaches unofficially but effectively slotted players, with few Black athletes allowed to play in such skill positions as quarterback. According to Michael Oriard and James Michener, Black football players at the University of Wyoming and a number of other major programs felt isolated when enrolled at campuses whose students were overwhelmingly White and affluent. Social life was limited because coaches and other college officials discouraged them from dating White women. The Black players were reluctant to protest various mistreatments, but as the percentage of Black players on team rosters rose to a relatively high level, the result was a combustible list of complaints.

From Consensus to Conflict

An accumulation of questions, sometimes turning into complaints and criticisms, pushed student reform groups away from athletic directors and college sports programs. Athletic directors and powerful coaches added to this dissonance when they chose to align themselves as "patriots" with the larger political ideology of national politics. By 1968 there was an escalation of symbolism and rhetoric. Coaches got a lot of mileage out of annual rituals such as the president of the United States hosting the championship college football team at the White House. The only dissent was when a disgruntled coach thought his team was Number One and should have been invited. But this hardly signaled a political disagreement with President Richard Nixon between 1968 and 1972.

Furthermore, the most successful big-time coaches and their athletic directors frequently seized the opportunity to speak for their players, emphasizing that they were clean-cut, law abiding, and patriotic—in other words, the embodiment of established national values. Student athletes were restricted in their right to speak to the press. The ideal image of the student athlete was shored up by policies on deportment and hair length. Coaches reinforced this message within their teams by dismissing from the squad players who refused to shave off moustaches or cut their hair. Little by little, however, there were signs that the coaches were not necessarily expressing the attitudes of the student athletes, but rather were proselytizing to advance their own agenda. In a flow of autobiographical articles and books, present and former student athletes have written at length about the excesses of coaches and team regulations, often using provocative titles such as *Out of Their League.* One former student athlete, Gary Shaw, published an exposé of the hidden world of Texas football in the late 1960s. The jacket copy for his book *Meat on the Hoof* reads:

> They raise cattle and football players in Texas. The cattle are treated better. *Meat on the Hoof* is a startling look at big-time college football. The University of Texas Longhorns under Coach Darrell Royal have long been a major football power. How did they get there? Gary Shaw says by juggling the approved limit of athletic scholarships. By placing the players in psychological bondage through a complex series of physical and mental maneuvers. And by running off all the "meat" which had "quitter" in it or couldn't take it. And by setting up an elaborate caste system that had the surviving players clawing to get to the top. *Meat on the Hoof* is a weekday look at Saturday's heroes in which Gary Shaw debunks the myth of American college football's Super-male. He examines in detail the real motivations behind these machismo efforts at glory. Gary Shaw was a high-school football star in Denton, Texas, recruited by Darrell Royal as a lineman. He was one of the few who made the team. But all along the line he had a vague uneasy feeling that something was wrong. Now he tells what the transformation from high-school star to "just another body" at Texas was like for him and his teammates. He tells of the "education" coach whose job it was to help athletes get the most out of their Texas days but in fact did little more than steer mighty Longhorns into gut course after gut course.[16]

Former college track stars also influenced a new generation of student athletes with such highly visible protests against racism as raised fists and bowed heads on the awards stand at the 1968 Olympic Games held in Mexico City. When students, and student athletes, expressed their dissent with incumbent athletic policies as well as national politics, the polarization of college sports continued.

In a few instances, some universities started to offer new courses on sports and society, most of which had a critical and politically left–leaning bias. Athletic directors adopted a defensive attitude about the courses, trying to brush away such scholarship and teaching, along with student-athlete exposés about college sports, as constituting either a lunatic fringe or the whining of disgruntled former players who now were aligned with radical professors.

Commercialism and College Sports as an American Civil Religion

By 1970 the athletics establishment of the NCAA, conference commissioners, athletic directors, and celebrity coaches had consolidated their position to increase the commercialization and spectator appeal of big-time college sports. Students, whether as athletes or as a campus constituency, lost ground in the governance of intercollegiate athletics, as accountability and revenues spiraled into autonomous departments, many of which had their own boards of directors drawn from alumni booster clubs and major donors. In other words, the threads of discontent that were intended to lead to wholesale reform in intercollegiate athletics made a dent in student awareness and had some public shock value. But they were defused by coaches and athletic directors who responded with increased public relations campaigns and promotions of championship teams and big games. Most university presidents stood outside the fray and acquiesced in this backlash. Presidents, for example, had little formal or informal influence on the policies and initiatives advanced by the executive director of the NCAA.

Big-time college sports enjoyed a halo effect of praise as their metaphors and jargon worked their way into speeches by governors, congressmen, and even the US president. Although national politics, especially issues and politicians with a conservative tilt, might have been a source of attraction to the college sports establishment, their most important consideration was on campus matters.[17] The main concern was that athletic directors and coaches considered demands for rights for student athletes to represent a threat to administrative control, to be squelched as if they were comparable to demands made in a peasants' revolt. This response is illustrated in some measures taken by the NCAA in the early 1970s. First, varsity eligibility was extended to freshmen, who had five years in which to play four seasons. Second, athletic grants-in-aid were changed from a four-year award to a one-year award, subject to review and renewal each year. This latter measure was crucial, because it meant that problematic players who questioned coaching authority and regulations could be summarily dismissed or financially abandoned. The result was that student athletes, especially those who were recruited to play in the high-profile sports at big-time programs, were lavished with perks and privileges but did not gain rights. To the contrary, signing acceptance of an athletic grant-in-aid meant signing away and forfeiting many rights held by students who were not varsity athletes.

As for extending athletic opportunities for women, the NCAA took no interest in the 1960s and mounted an active opposition to the proposed Title IX legislation in 1971. Not until 1978 did the NCAA change its priorities. To attract women's athletic programs from colleges to join the NCAA, it sponsored championships for women in selected sports. This concession was less a commitment to Title IX and more a strategy to undermine its rival, the AIAW, which it succeeded in doing, as the AIAW was absorbed into the NCAA only a few years later.

College students along with concerned parents and faculty had gained increased information about the conduct of intercollegiate athletics—a balance sheet that established a critical lens and continued scrutiny. Students who were dismayed with the conduct and condition of established varsity sports programs gained a measure of energy and justification to create their own sports clubs and teams. As college sports entered the 1970s, these innovations did little to impede the growing commercial success and spectator appeal of big-time college sports for fans who bought tickets at the stadium, for television viewers, or for sponsoring advertisers. The powerful intercollegiate athletics association pulled off a coup as the established programs and athletic directors had effectively countered the counterculture.

Conclusion

The New City of Intellect

B Y THE MIDDLE of 1970 many American colleges were exhausted from student demonstrations. They had been forced to cancel commencement ceremonies and had suffered other disruptions to the customary round of academic life. The sense of the campus as a beleaguered village was amplified as students deserted campus for home or travels as part of summer break. In contrast to the optimism that pervaded higher education in 1960, uncertainty and loss of confidence now characterized the American campus mood. Sinking morale can be tracked in the numerous task force studies conducted at the time, to gauge the present and future of higher education. Between 1967 and 1974 a blend of soul-searching, forecasting, explanation, and puzzlement emanated from blue-ribbon commissions, panel discussions, foundations, scholarly associations, and magazine editors. Numerous distinguished, official groups published reports with titles such as *The Report of the President's Commission on Campus Unrest*, "American Higher Education: Toward an Uncertain Future," "What Went Wrong in the '60s?," *Institutions in Transition*, and *Campus 1980: The Shape of the Future of American Higher Education.*[1]

Even during the optimistic periods earlier in the decade there were scattered alerts cautioning that, despite the growth and prosperity then in progress, American higher education would face a new set of challenges by about 1970. Clark Kerr, for example, concluded his 1963 book, *The Uses of the University,* with a chapter on the "Future of the City of Intellect." Projecting from early 1960s data and observations, he posited reasonable predictions and concern, some of which are reflected in the various blue-ribbon commission reports noted above. It seemed probable, for example, that generous support from state governments, private donors, and federal agencies would not shield colleges and universities from growing pains and problems associated with what sociologist

Martin Trow had described as the extended transition from elite to mass and then toward universal access to higher education.[2] Analyzing these trends and making projections about the American campus has persisted, as suggested by sociologist Steven Brint's 2002 anthology *The Future of the City of Intellect*.[3] Taking stock from the perspective of the early 1970s, what had Clark Kerr foreseen a decade earlier, and how did his predictions turn out?

The Legacies of Campus Unrest and Political Activism

By 1970 academic leaders were beginning to see incidents of campus unrest and student activism substantially differently from how they saw them in 1960. Early in the decade, the tendency was to either underestimate or ignore the gravity of the political activism. In contrast, between 1967 and 1971, presidents and trustees overcorrected their earlier denial by reacting strongly and tending to regard student movements and rallies as perpetually occurring and possibly permanently impacting American higher education. For historians and other readers today it is useful to heed the questions posed by sociologist Kenneth Andrews: How did the campus protests and social movements matter? Did they really bring about change? How did protests work?[4]

Andrews's scholarship has included studies of the civil rights movements across the 1950s and 1960s. The concern here is narrower and the time frame is advanced, with a focus on the distinct phenomenon of the student activism and campus movements between 1960 and 1970. At the time the movements' conspicuous and often violent character brought the government and the public's attention to universities, but the movements did not necessarily bring about deep or lasting change. An example of this mixed balance sheet is how the increased campus protests against the Vietnam War sufficiently unnerved President Lyndon B. Johnson to influence his decision in 1968 not to seek reelection, compared to the failure of student movements to transform national public opinion enough to substantially alter nationwide voting patterns.[5] Election of Richard M. Nixon as president of the United States in 1968 and his reelection in 1972 hardly signaled a ballot-box victory for anti-war groups. Furthermore, during these same years Governor Ronald Reagan of California effectively used public resentment of campus protestors as a tool for his own reelection and subsequent rise on the national political stage.

Campus demonstrations were meteoric, in that their illumination of issues and policies was followed by a rapid descent and dissolution. It was difficult to sustain the intensity and energy. The violent campus demonstrations may have been dysfunctional in cases where they elicited strong countermovements characterized by opposition that galvanized public opinion against the student demonstrators. These strong reactions have been documented with the recent rediscovery and review of photographs and other records from police surveillance units taken in the 1960s suggesting that the activism of the so-called revolution led to equally strong counterrevolutions, leaving the United States as a nation divided.[6]

Dissecting the historical impact of the campus activism in this decade is complicated by its diffusion beyond colleges and universities with varying degrees of absorption into other large-scale initiatives. By 1967, for example, Washington, DC, and New York City held annual massive marches, some focusing on civil rights and others on opposition to the Vietnam War. How much and how little these public events were indebted to, or extensions of, campus activism is unclear. Although colleges and universities were an integral source of protest and reform, student groups hardly had a monopoly on either the idea or the implementation of mass demonstrations in American political life. October 2017, for example, marked the fiftieth anniversary of the March on the Pentagon, an event that attracted an estimated seventy thousand protesters and then gained publicity from Norman Mailer's account of the event, titled *The Armies of the Night*. Students were participants in but did not lead or dominate this memorable event.[7] Less spectacular than campus marches was a strategy of dissent against established policies and programs at the federal and state level that relied on sub-strategies of systematic research to counter and even derail government programs that claimed certain results and effectiveness. Environmental impact studies or economic analyses of government spending represented the kinds of applied policy research well suited to college and university activists who formed new think tanks and research institutes, and whose reports could be used in lobbying state legislatures and Congress.

Town and Gown

Major changes in the presence of universities within metropolitan areas had taken place starting around 1955 in Chicago, Berkeley, Boston, and Cambridge, where federal urban renewal programs allowed city governments and campus administrations to raze what were considered deteriorating neighborhoods adjacent to university borders. The result was that by 1960 such universities as the University of Chicago, the University of California, Berkeley, Harvard University, and the Massachusetts Institute of Technology had expanded their real estate holdings and embarked on construction of massive high-rise office towers and dormitories.[8] Juxtaposed against these new buildings, the archetypal college town adjacent to a campus featured a distinctive but limited array of shops and businesses that catered to a traditional undergraduate elite. It might be a Brooks Brothers, Ralph Lauren, or J. Press store, but more often it was a variant of a local college clothier's shop probably run by a few guys who were alums of the adjacent college. In some college towns a boutique existed to cater to "college women," offering dresses, slacks, and favored footwear in prestigious brands. The restaurants and pubs featured local fare consumed while surrounded, in most places, by photographs of the local college's athletic triumphs, winning coaches, and all-conference athletic stars. Gourmet cooking it was not.

By 1970, as described in chapter 4, a new slate of businesses set up shop in the college town. Coffee shops, restaurants featuring ethnic cuisines, grocers or farmers' markets offering organic foods, shops for new media such as photocopying and offset printing—along with newsstands featuring alternative publications, "head shops" for drug paraphernalia, art galleries, movie theaters showing innovative and classic cinema, vinyl record stores, and other services and products loosely associated with the counterculture—flourished. Many towns included such aggressive franchises as Tower Records and the clothing chain The Gap.

Meanwhile, waning student demand for penny loafers, wool sports coats, and neckties gave way to adoption of bellbottoms and polyester. Fashion changes rendered many fixtures of the campus community archaic and obsolete. On Bancroft Avenue, across from Sproul Plaza in Berkeley, one traditional men's clothier that had been in business since the 1920s retooled to adjust to the new student vocabulary and taste by diversifying stock and advertising itself as representing "fashion evolution, not revolution."[9] But the recasting of images and goods proved futile for many traditional stores, at least until the 1980s when there was a renaissance of demand for preppy styles such as polo shirts, Shetland sweaters, and herringbone sports coats. The generational change of students eventually changed much of the campus community and commercial landscape.

The Campus Condition

The immediate trauma of student demonstrations and campus destruction was followed by the less dramatic yet more enduring problems that many American colleges faced: a decline in morale and a decline in funding. Deterioration of the academic physical plant was one manifestation of budgetary shortfalls that were going to persist and even accelerate after 1970. The 1973–74 OPEC oil embargo skyrocketed the price of oil, a development that was especially problematic for nonprofit organizations, including colleges and universities, in balancing their budgets. One self-destructive result was that colleges and universities tried to save money by deferring campus maintenance, a strategy that was disastrous over the long run. Whereas a decade earlier, state governments and private donors readily provided funding for construction and expansion, colleges and universities were now in a prolonged period that Berkeley economist Earl Cheit called American higher education's "new depression."[10] The bad news got worse as the 1970s wore on. The Carnegie Foundation for the Advancement of Teaching projected that between one-quarter and one-third of American colleges and universities faced daunting financial crises that would cause them to close.[11] At about the same time, Lewis Mayhew, a distinguished Stanford education professor, provided college and university officials with a guide to "surviving the eighties" that presented strategies for resolving higher education crises associated with problems in enrollments and finances.[12]

Perhaps the biggest shock to university presidents came in the area of external relations, including funding from groups outside the campus. The presumption (and expectation) that they acquired in the early and mid-1960s was that the federal government was poised to provide massive, direct funding to deserving campuses. To their surprise, by 1972 a drastic change in congressional mood meant eschewing that approach, opting instead for a large set of programs of student financial aid. In the new arrangement students, especially those with substantial financial need and from modest income families, were to be beneficiaries of direct grants for tuition and some living expenses that were portable. In other words, the student could carry her or his federal financial aid package to the college of her or his choice. This shift in congressional funding practices changed the dynamics of the academic marketplace. American higher education entered an era of student consumerism.[13]

The need-based federal student financial aid programs approved in the 1972 reauthorization of the Higher Education Act of 1964 represented a public policy acknowledgment of social justice combined with a pragmatic fact of political life: members of Congress had come to the realization that serving families of college-bound students carried more votes than giving direct aid to university presidents and their campuses. That presidents were often seen as having lost control of their campuses accelerated this change in program direction. Numerous federal agencies, ranging from the Department of Defense to the Central Intelligence Agency, pulled out of longtime collaboration and funding for campus-based projects.[14]

Students

When in the early 1970s federal funding for higher education shifted to include an emphasis on need-based portable student aid, institutions were given at least some increased incentive to enroll applicants from underrepresented groups. Need-based aid combined with affirmative action increased the diversity of the student profile substantially in contrast to 1960 or 1965. By the late 1970s, however, affirmative action would be contested in the courts with such cases as *DeFunis v. Odegaard* and *Regents of the University of California v. Bakke*. Despite such judicial contests, the gains in social justice were enduring if not complete.

What is the legacy of students who went to college in the 1960s? It is difficult to capture the diverse range of students and their colleges, and sweeping descriptions of generations are not meaningful. One plausible insight is that as alumni they provided the United States with an unprecedented, large critical mass of citizens who were college educated and informed as they moved into adult roles of service and leadership. This large cohort was a result of the earlier shift toward mass higher education. Alumni brought activism to civic participation which was not at all confined to a liberal or left-leaning group. It extended across the political spectrum, left and right, Democrat and Republican. Flamboyant political activists such as Abbie Hoffman and Jerry Rubin were celebrities who dominated headlines in the late 1960s, but they were not typical of the larger, enduring student activism legacy. As *New York Times* columnist David Brooks observed in 2017:

> In the late 1960s along came a group of provocateurs like Abbie Hoffman, Jerry Rubin and the rest of the counterculture to upend the Protestant establishment. People like Hoffman were buffoons, but also masters of political

theater. . . . The late 1960s were a time of intense cultural conflict, which left a lot of wreckage in its wake. But eventually a new establishment came into being, which we will call the meritocratic establishment. These were the tame heirs to Hoffman and Rubin. They were well educated. They cut their moral teeth on the civil rights and feminist movements. They embraced economic, social and moral individualism. They came to dominate the institutions of American society on both left and right.[15]

What Brooks did not mention was that the 1960s was a formative period for leaders and devotees across the entire political spectrum. George W. Bush, Mitt Romney, and Donald Trump, all prominent and successful in business careers and as Republicans in politics, also came of age as college students in the 1960s.

The Organized Campus and the College Experience

The changes in services and official attitudes toward students between 1960 and 1970 were substantial. One enduring legacy was that new concerns about student morale and student retention led colleges and universities to provide offices and services for undergraduates that would have not been recognizable a decade earlier: multicultural groups, disability services, career planning, counseling, living-learning programs, honors programs, along with increased student rights in disciplinary hearings.

STUDENTS AND THE CURRICULUM

Undergraduates at campuses both large and small succeeded in adding numerous options for courses and for degree programs. Seminars and courses with enrollment limits of fifteen, for example, leavened the standard lecture course offerings. As detailed in chapter 5, at some colleges students petitioned to create their own major or to combine fields in new interdisciplinary combinations. Another significant change came in grading, as students after 1970 typically could opt for pass–no pass evaluations as distinguished from letter grades of A through F. These innovations, however, remained on the margins, especially at large campuses where enrollments continued to grow. Large lecture classes, multiple-choice question examinations, and student preference for majoring in fields they considered to lead to entry-level jobs remained at the heart of the college curriculum nationwide.

WOMEN AND THEIR MAJORS AND FIELDS

Women associated with women's rights and the women's movement of the early 1970s, such as Betty Friedan, Kate Millett, and Gloria Steinem, to name just a few, were effective in having their books published and read widely. Their success in turn led to persistent changes in course offerings and, eventually, to new majors and women's studies departments. The most dramatic change came about in the transition from undergraduate to graduate studies, as an increasing number of women enrolled in such advanced studies as professional schools of law and medicine as well as in PhD programs. Women would not fill half the student enrollments in law or medicine for several decades, but their representation was conspicuous. One limit of these gains was that in PhD programs, although women fared about the same as male applicants for admission to programs, women as graduate school applicants significantly skewed toward some fields and were virtually absent in others.[16] Women's self-limited selection of fields would change only after years of initiatives in secondary schools and undergraduate studies to inform and persuade young women to consider such historically alien-to-women fields as physics or engineering. But the roots of change in access were in place by 1970.

COLLEGE SPORTS

As noted in chapter 6, by 1970 intercollegiate athletics had shown few concessions to social justice and the kinds of demands associated with student campus demonstrations. Desegregation ending racial exclusion on varsity teams and for all athletic conferences still was not complete by 1970. Extending opportunities for Black student athletes to play on college teams at times verged on exploitation, with university officials showing little concern for the athletes' academic opportunities. In other words, the colleges and their coaches and fans usually got the better of the deal. The first sign of potential change in college sports and gender inequities came about in 1972 with Title IX. However, this legislation was not championed by college and university presidents and other officials. Furthermore, inclusion of intercollegiate sports in matters of federal oversight was unexpected, and it took all parties by surprise. It also took several decades to show substantial, reluctant gains in allowing women as student athletes.

Most athletic departments increased the number of varsity sports they offered for men, a trend that increased spending with little added revenue from ticket sales. Some costs were lowered when conferences and the National Collegiate Athletics Association allowed freshmen in many sports to compete as members of a varsity team immediately as freshmen. The growing problems in the financing of college sports would not be evident in the early 1970s. By 1978, however, even major conferences acknowledged problems in which they either had to reduce expenses or increase revenues. The latter option gained an unexpected windfall with court cases contesting the NCAA control of television broadcasts. But from the perspective of 1970, neither these problems nor these transformational solutions were part of discussions among athletic directors.

The Faculty

Clark Kerr in the early 1960s noted that there probably would be a surplus of PhDs by 1970.[17] By 1970 the faculty job market nationwide had tapered, and in 1972 it plummeted, with little or no hiring taking place in the traditional liberal arts and sciences fields. Demand for new professors did continue in new fields related to science, technology, and health, such as computer science, electrical engineering, and numerous biomedical syntheses such as biochemistry, biostatistics and bioengineering. The major institutional category for faculty hiring was the two-year public community colleges.

Forecasts in the early 1960s identified a new role, the professor as entrepreneur, a role that increased visibility and prestige and income, as well as consulting gigs and grants. Yet the enterprising professors were a relatively small percentage of the total faculty and tended to be concentrated at prestigious research universities. And whereas in 1967 articles and books made proclamations about mobile professors, by 1972 this movement had stalled and then stopped. Nationwide, the faculty as a profession became constricted and immobile. Since hiring had slowed, faculty were less likely to have job offers that would allow them to move geographically and on to a higher rank elsewhere. As the number and percentage of professors who were granted tenure in the 1960s increased and new faculty vacancies declined, analysts started to discuss the graying of the faculty.

Given the academic job market by 1970, relatively few faculty, especially in traditional liberal arts fields, would be drawn from the ranks of those who had been undergraduates in the 1960s. Professors in the 1960s who were influential in connecting scholarship to campus activism tended to be a conspicuous minority of senior professors in mid-career who were sufficiently confident because they were established and successful in their own research and who extended their critical analyses into the lecture room and then into the public forum. Representative of this cohort were the activist scholars who contributed to the 1968 anthology edited by historian Theodore Roszak, *The Dissenting Academy*, with critical essays by academic stars such as Noam Chomsky, about the teaching of humanities in American universities.[18]

Another good example of the "activist scholar" who emerged in the 1960s was Douglas Dowd, a radical economics professor and author who was in the vanguard of early teach-ins and other demonstrations against the Vietnam War. Dowd earned his PhD at the University of California, Berkeley, in 1949 and taught at Cornell University from 1951 to 1970. According to Sam Roberts, who wrote Dowd's obituary in the *New York Times*, "He repeatedly reminded students that universities were not isolated havens but 'an integral and functioning part of an American socio-economic-military system,' and he argued that some radical groups had failed because they never ventured beyond the college gates to confront the real world. 'You can't fight imperialism on campus, you can't fight racism on campus,' Professor Dowd said. 'You can only fight their manifestations.' The role of the university, he wrote in an Op-Ed article in The *New York Times* in 1971, is to become a place where 're-examination, uncertainty, change and conflict become an integral part of what is studied.'"[19]

Scholars such as Douglas Dowd and those who contributed to *The Dissenting Academy* were memorable and influential because they were exceptional. Considering all institutions and all fields and departments at an American university, it is clear that most professors were *not* radical in their scholarship and teaching.

The Managerial Revolution in Campus Administration

In the aftermath of student dissent and the weakened finances of many colleges and universities that followed, higher education underwent a change in the scope and size of administration that has proven persistent. Instead of an academic revolution, higher education after 1970 underwent a managerial revolution.[20] This shift in administration and decision making at colleges and universities since 1975 toward substantially greater reliance on data and analysis to respond to constituencies—federal agencies, state legislators, students, parents, and donors—was fueled by improved technology, especially information systems and computers that informed decision making. Technology pervaded all offices across a campus and linked a campus to its system-wide information databases. Admissions, financial aid, fund-raising, and other offices whose effectiveness relied on initiative and innovation were central to new strategies and tools. Eventually the managerial revolution took on a new identity and became a source of enterprising evolution within the typical American campus. These innovations took root during an extended problematic period of financial problems from 1970 to 1985 and were instrumental in helping many colleges avoid financial disaster.

Connecting Past to Present

In 1961 the president of the Ford Foundation, John W. Gardner, was chair and primary author of a report on education in the United States. The challenging rhetorical question he and his committee posed for American education, especially its colleges and universities was, "Can we be equal and excellent too?"[21] That is an appropriate question to guide our consideration of the continuity and change, gains and losses, in the American experience of going to college between 1960 and now.

Today, more than half a century after the Ford Foundation report as well as various state master plans, and despite the impressive expansion of higher education, the United States has yet to achieve that goal that was indelibly associated with going to college in the 1960s. Although the disputes and controversies at colleges and universities during the 1960s did not constitute a coherent reform agenda, variations on themes of fair treatment, equity, and social justice surfaced time and again. By this standard, the character and condition of higher education probably would frustrate and puzzle 1960s students, including student reformers, if they were to visit campuses today.

Summary figures on overall expansion of higher education are impressive. By 2010 higher education in the United States was an enterprise that included more than four thousand degree-granting institutions whose total enrollment surpassed twenty million students. It included a substantial number of nontraditional students, students older than the traditional college cohort age of eighteen to twenty-four years old. Disaggregating these gross figures, however, reveals that for all the gains in student financial aid, curricular reform, and extended initiatives for accessibility and affordability in higher education, American colleges of the early twenty-first century represent at best a partial fulfillment of the hopes and ideals associated with the 1960s.

Most conspicuous is the growing bifurcation of American higher education into uneven factions strongly associated with family income and social class. Even as many worked to make college admissions and enrollment equitable across family income categories, the gap has increased, not decreased. The schisms between categories of institutions have been accentuated. A graphic illustration of the accelerated connection between academics and affluence comes from an upscale lifestyle publication, *Town & Country* magazine. The August 2017 issue featured several articles organized around the theme of "The College Anxiety Guide" and "Admissions Insanity: A $1.7M Map to Getting In." According to the magazine's editors, campus life, especially at academically selective colleges, "routinely turns into headline news." Prestige carries a price, as today even affluent families devote a great deal of time to learning "how to navigate cutthroat admissions, skyrocketing costs . . . all while getting a great education." In 2017 the path for a child to go from "birth to B.A." was estimated to cost $1,715,742, an increase from *Town & Country*'s 1973 estimates of a cost of $300,000, indexing for inflation. Expenses for admissions coaches, followed by music and art classes, study abroad, Scholastic Aptitude Test preparation courses, summer internships, volunteer experiences, special sports camps, mentoring, college prep summer camps, and a succession of expensive supplements to regular school courses and activities suggested that both the prestige and the price of going to college had soared since 1960.[22]

The paradox and problem of the changes in going to college between 1960 and 2017 are that higher education overall has at least nominally and superficially achieved or at least approached many of the standards and goals set forth by the master planners of sixty years ago. The number and percentage of high school graduates who enroll in college have increased. They are eligible for federal, state, and institutional financial aid in far greater amounts than were their counterpart students about half a century ago. Celebrations of these achievements, however, are dampened when the overall profile is disaggregated to home in on going to college as being delineated by two variables: first, highly prestigious academic institutions and, second, those institutions meshing with students from affluent or upper income families. The congruence is overwhelming and daunting. Within the cosmos of college, the inequities of academic privilege and family prosperity tend to trump numerous other programs and strategies to expand the combination of access, admission, and affordability in college choice. According to economist Charles T. Clotfelter of Duke University, "affluent families managed to hold their own in this increasingly meritocratic admissions process." Clotfelter concluded, "Just as critics have asserted, therefore, the economic gap between the great mass of students attending the less-selective public institutions and those at the most-selective private colleges has indeed grown. Most of this growing economic disparity does *not* reflect students from the richest families taking the places of those from lower down the income distribution; rather, it reflects the spectacular increases in income enjoyed by those at the top."[23]

Clotfelter's sobering findings confirm the characterization of economics as the "dismal science," at least in their implications for the trends in going to college in America from 1960 to 2017. Furthermore, a 2009 study, *Crossing the Finish Line,* by economists William Bowen, Matthew Chingos, and Michael McPherson, presented detailed data to show that despite sustained efforts to increase undergraduate persistence, students at state universities showed few gains over three decades in their retention and bachelor's degree completion, with most flagship state universities having a persistent graduation rate of about 60%.[24]

Since California's 1960 Master Plan for higher education was a nationally acclaimed model for expanding access and academic achievement, it is a useful, significant document to use in tracking changes from its passage to today. California's higher education system now struggles with budget cuts and an uncertain future. The reasons are many. The percentage of Californians seeking to go to college gradually increased, and so did the overall number of high school graduates. Consequently, the expansion in college enrollments over a little more than half a century was incredibly large. In 1960, for example, the total enrollment for all institutions in the state was 234,000. By 2015 the University of California enrolled 253,000 students at 10 campuses, California State University enrolled 395,000 students at 16 campuses and the community colleges enrolled 1,138,000 at 113 campuses. California has experienced a sevenfold enrollment increase since 1960, the most among all states in the nation.[25]

This overall growth has not meant that equity or affordability have been achieved in California higher education or elsewhere. In contrast to 1960, student fees and tuition increased while state general fund subsidies per student tapered. In 2015, tuition charges at UC were $12,240, a tenfold increase over 1960 when the state took great pride in its no-tuition policy. During the past four decades, California's public colleges and universities have endured lean budgets. This trend was accelerated in 1978, when passage of Proposition 13 placed a ceiling on property taxes—taxes that, among other sources, had helped provide revenues to the state for meeting expenditures for public education. In the twenty-first century there are serious concerns that the public universities, as a result of budget cuts, are soon going to be public no more.[26] Even the preeminent research campus of the UC system, Berkeley, has been hit by budget cuts. Consistent with economist Charles Clotfelter's observation about national trends, UC's cuts happened at the same time that California's outstanding private colleges and universities have soared in terms of academic standards, selective admissions, tuition revenues, new construction, federal research grants, and endowments.[27] The plight of California's public higher education funding and student performance is not an isolated example. An October 2017 article in *The Atlantic* reports that "The Decline of the Midwest's Public Universities Threatens to Wreck Its Most Vibrant Economies."[28] The profile for college students was made even bleaker by reports on growing student indebtedness brought about by a combination of rising college prices and a sustained shift in federal student aid from grants to loans.

In conclusion, we return to John Gardner's 1961 question about higher education: "Can we be equal and excellent too?" The answer is, "Perhaps, but not yet and not quite." Looking back to 1960, this response today is troubling and disappointing. Colleges and universities have overall expanded access. The gains, however, are skewed so that the net result includes severe imbalances. Because of the inordinate prestige and power of a small number of academically and financially strong institutions, combined with a growing concentration of academic preparation in a small percentage of affluent American families, the unexpected development since 1960 is that higher education expands educational opportunity yet increases inequality.[29] This is not what the planners and dreamers of higher education had in mind in 1960. Today, more than half a century later, despite the impressive expansion of higher education, the United States has yet to achieve the goals or fulfilled the hopes that were indelibly associated with the initiatives and optimism that characterized going to college in the 1960s.

Preface

1. Dorothy E. Finnegan, "Distant Memories, Current Implications: Experiencing the '60s Impact on Teaching and Scholarship in Higher Education" (commentary on research symposium and panel session, Association for the Study of Higher Education, Washington, DC, November 21, 2014).

2. Ted Widmer, "The Summer of Love's Dispiriting Fall," *New York Times,* September 2, 2017. See also Robert Love, "Celebrating the 50th Anniversary of the Summer of Love, 1967–2017," *AARP The Magazine,* August/September 2017, 31–33.

3. Patricia Cohen, "The '60s Begin to Fade as Liberal Professors Retire," *New York Times,* July 3, 2008.

Chapter One: Rediscovering the 1960s in American Higher Education

1. Carol Pogash, "At Berkeley, Free (Though Subdued) Speech, 50 Years Later," *New York Times,* October 2, 2014.

2. Adam Nagourney, Carol Pogash, and Tamar Lewin, "It's Not the Old Days, but Berkeley Sees a New Spark of Protest," *New York Times,* December 10, 2014. See also "Campus Unrest and Student Protest: Mario Savio's 'Put Our Bodies upon the Gears' Speech at Sproul Plaza, University of California, Berkeley (1964)," in *Essential Documents in the History of American Higher Education,* ed. John R. Thelin (Baltimore: Johns Hopkins University Press, 2014), 249–252.

3. Sources on college students in the 1960s include Allen Betterton, *Alma Mater: Unusual Stories and Little-Known Facts from America's College Campuses* (Princeton, NJ: Peterson's Guides, 1988); Jeffery L. Lant, ed., *Our Harvard: Reflections on College Life by Twenty-Two Distinguished Graduates* (New York: Taplinger, 1982); Will and Martin Lieberson, eds., *College Parodies: Hilarious Imitations of* Life, Playboy, *the* New Yorker *and Other Favorites by the Top College Humor Magazines* (New York: Ballantine Books, 1961); The Yale Daily News, *The Insiders' Guide to the Colleges* (New York: G. P. Putnam's Sons, 1970); Susan Berman, *The Underground Guide to the College of Your Choice: The Only Handbook That Tells You What's Really Happening at Every Major College and University in the U.S.A.* (New York: Signet, 1971).

4. Thomas Fuller, "A Free Speech Battle at the Birthplace of a Movement," *New York Times,* February 3, 2017.

5. Thomas Fuller and Stephanie Saul, "Latest Battle at Berkeley: Free Speech versus Safety," *New York Times,* April 22, 2017.

6. Helen Lefkowitz Horowitz, "The Sixties," and "Revenge of the Nerds," in *Campus Life: Undergraduate Cultures from the End of the Eighteenth Century to the Present* (New York: Alfred A. Knopf, 1987), 220–244; Arthur Levine, *When Dreams and Heroes Died* (San Francisco: Jossey-Bass, 1980).

7. Owen Johnson, *Stover at Yale* (New York: Frederick Stokes, 1912), 238–239.

8. Brian Cassity and Maxine Levaren, *The '60s for Dummies* (Hoboken: Wiley, 2005).

9. "Dear Reader: Which Decade Do You Want Back?," *New York Times Magazine,* April 9, 2017, 10.

10. Todd Gitlin, *The Sixties: Years of Hope, Days of Rage* (New York: Bantam, 1993); David Farber, *The Age of Great Dreams: America in the 1960s* (New York: Hill and Wang, 1994); G. Kerry Smith, ed., *Agony and Promise: Current Issues in Higher Education 1969* (San Francisco: Jossey-Bass, 1969).

11. Henry Finder, ed., *The 60s: The Story of a Decade* (New York: Random House, 2016).

12. Todd Gitlin, *The Sixties.*

13. Clara Bingham, *Witness to the Revolution: Radicals, Resisters, Vets, Hippies, and the Year America Lost Its Mind and Found Its Soul* (New York: Random House, 2016).

14. Steven Kelman, *Push Comes to Shove: The Escalation of Student Protest* (Boston: Houghton Mifflin, 1970).

15. Buell G. Gallagher, *Campus in Crisis* (New York: Harper and Row, 1974).

16. Sol Stern, "The Free Speech Movement at 50: The Movement Won; Free Speech Lost," *City Journal,* September 25, 2014.

17. Jennifer Schuessler, "Columbia's Uprising: A 50-Year-Old Legacy," *New York Times,* March 22, 2018.

18. J. W. Ralph Eubank "Ole Miss Is Still Torn 24 Years after Meredith," *Washington Post,* September 27, 1982. See also "Racial Desegregation at State Universities: Commemorative Plaque at the University of Mississippi," in Thelin, ed., *Essential Documents,* 244–245.

19. William Grimes, "Kevin Starr, Prolific California Chronicler, Dies at 76," *New York Times,* January 17, 2017.

20. Howard Gillette, Jr., *Class Divide: Yale '64 and the Conflicted Legacy of the Sixties* (Ithaca, NY: Cornell University Press, 2015).

21. Stephanie Coontz, "Beware Social Nostalgia," *New York Times,* May 19, 2013.

22. Linda Eisenmann, *Higher Education for Women in Postwar America, 1945–1965* (Baltimore: Johns Hopkins University Press, 2006); Ruth Rosen,

The World Split Open: How the Modern Women's Movement Changed America (New York: Penguin Books, 2000); Nancy Weiss Malkiel, *"Keep the Damned Women Out": The Struggle for Coeducation* (Princeton, NJ: Princeton University Press, 2016); Linda Greenhouse, "How Smart Women Got the Chance," *New York Review of Books* (April 6, 2017), 21.

23. Ibram H. Rogers, "The Black Campus Movement and the Institutionalization of Black Studies, 1965–1970," *Journal of African American Studies* 16, no. 1 (2012): 21–40.

24. Clark Kerr, *The Gold and the Blue: A Personal Memoir of the University of California, 1949–1967* (Berkeley: University of California Press, 2003); James A. Perkins, *The University in Transition* (Princeton, NJ: Princeton University Press, 1966); Nathan M. Pusey, *The Age of the Scholar: Observations on Education in a Troubled Decade* (Cambridge, MA: Harvard University Press, 1963).

25. See, for example, student histories about a new campus founded in 1965, in Paige Smith and Jasper Rose, eds., *Solomon's House: A Self-Conscious History of Cowell College* (Felton, CA: Big Trees Press, 1970).

26. Norman A. Fedde, *Preparing for College Study: A Handbook of Basic Study Skills for All College Students and Preparatory School Students* (New Haven, CT: Reader's Press, 1961).

27. Burton R. Clark, *The Distinctive College: Antioch, Reed and Swarthmore* (Chicago: Aldine, 1970). See also Katharine Kinkead, *How an Ivy League College Decides on Admissions* (New York: W. W. Norton, 1961).

28. Christopher J. Broadhurst, "'We Didn't Fire a Shot, We Didn't Burn a Building': The Student Reaction at North Carolina State University to the Kent State Shootings, May 1970," *North Carolina Historical Review* 87, no. 3 (2010): 283–309.

29. Nicholas Lemann, *The Big Test: The Secret History of the American Meritocracy* (New York: Farrar, Straus and Giroux, 1999). See also Elizabeth L. and Michael Useem, eds., *The Education Establishment* (Englewood Cliffs, NJ: Prentice-Hall, 1974).

30. John T. Wilson, *Academic Science, Higher Education, and the Federal Government, 1950–1983* (Chicago: University of Chicago Press, 1983); Roger L. Geiger, *Research and Relevant Knowledge: American Research Universities since World War II* (New York: Oxford University Press, 1993); Charles V. Kidd, *American Universities and Federal Research* (Cambridge, MA: Harvard University Press, 1959); John Ernst, *Forging a Fateful Alliance: Michigan State University and the Vietnam War* (East Lansing: Michigan State University Press, 1998).

31. Jennifer Schuessler, "Ken Burns Tackles His Most Ambitious Project Yet: The Vietnam War," *The Lexington Herald-Leader (KY)* (*New York Times* Service), September 16, 2017.

32. Patrick Chura, "The Mythology of Jackson State," *Chronicle of Higher Education,* October 20, 2017.

33. Daniel Horowitz, *On the Cusp: The Yale College Class of 1960 and a World on the Verge of Change* (Amherst: University of Massachusetts Press, 2015).

34. David O. Levine, *The American College and the Culture of Aspiration, 1915–1940* (Ithaca, NY: Cornell University Press, 1986).

35. Calvin B. T. Lee, *The Campus Scene, 1900–1970: Changing Styles in Undergraduate Life* (New York: David McKay, 1970).

36. Philip Roth, "'Joe College': Memories of a Fifties Education," *Atlantic Monthly*, December 1987, 41–61.

37. Larry Cuban, *How Scholars Trumped Teachers: Change without Reform in University Curriculum, Teaching, and Research, 1890–1990* (New York: Teachers College Press, 1999); Luther Spoehr, "Making Brown University's 'New Curriculum' in 1969: The Importance of Context and Contingency," *Rhode Island History* 74, no. 2 (2016): 52–71.

38. Thomas D. Snyder, ed., *One Hundred and Twenty Years of American Education: A Statistical Portrait* (Washington, DC: United States Department of Education, National Center for Educational Statistics, 1993), 75, table 23. Snyder is the source of data that appear in the several paragraphs following this one.

39. Clark Kerr, *The Great Transformation in Higher Education: 1960–1980* (Albany: State University of New York Press, 1991); Martin Trow, "Reflections on the Transition from Elite to Mass to Universal Higher Education," *Daedalus* 99, no. 1 (1970): 1–42.

40. Richard M. Freeland, *Academia's Golden Age: Universities in Massachusetts, 1945–1970* (New York: Oxford University Press, 1992); John R. Thelin, "'Gilt by Association': Higher Education's Golden Age, 1945 to 1970," in *A History of American Higher Education*, 2nd ed. (Baltimore: Johns Hopkins University Press, 2011), 260–316. A recent example of reliance on this twenty-five-year period is Roger L. Geiger, Nathan M. Sorber, and Christian K. Anderson, eds., *American Higher Education in the Postwar Era, 1945–70* (New York: Routledge, 2017).

41. Theodore Roszak, *The Making of a Counter Culture: Reflections on the Technocratic Society and Its Youthful Opposition* (Garden City, NY: Doubleday, 1969).

42. Harry Edwards, *The Revolt of the Black Athlete* (New York: Free Press, 1969); Jack Scott, ed., *The Athletic Revolution* (New York: Free Press, 1971); James Michener, "Colleges and Universities," in *Sports in America* (New York: Random House, 1976), 219–280; John R. Thelin, "Critics and Controversies," in *Games Colleges Play: Scandal and Reform in Intercollegiate Athletics* (Baltimore: Johns Hopkins University Press, 1994), 115–178.

43. Nevitt Sanford, ed., *The American College: A Psychological and Social Interpretation of the Higher Learning* (New York: John Wiley & Sons, 1962).

44. Patricia Baldwin, *Covering the Campus: The History of "The Chronicle of Higher Education," 1966–1993* (Denton: University of North Texas Press,

1995). Jacqueline Adams et al., "An Era of Protests: The Depth and Breadth of Campus Activism Are Apparent in Excerpts from Our Coverage," *Chronicle of Higher Education,* November 5, 2016.

45. Stephanie Saul, "Fiery Speeches on Campuses, Backed by a Conservative Force," *New York Times,* May 21, 2017.

46. "Student Debt's Grip on the Economy," *New York Times,* May 21, 2017.

Chapter Two: College Prep

1. Frank Bruni, "College Admissions Shocker!" *New York Times,* April 16, 2016.

2. Marcia G. Synnott, *The Half-Opened Door: Discrimination and Admissions at Harvard, Yale, and Princeton, 1900–1970* (Westport, CT: Greenwood Press, 1979); Harold S., Wechsler, *The Qualified Student: A History of Selective College Admissions in America* (New York: John Wiley & Sons, 1977).

3. Michael Young, *The Rise of the Meritocracy, 1870–2033* (Harmondsworth, Middlesex, England: Penguin Books, 1961).

4. Claudia Goldin and Lawrence F. Katz, *The Race between Education and Technology* (Cambridge, MA: Harvard University Press, 2008).

5. David B. Tyack, *The One Best System: A History of American Urban Education* (Cambridge, MA: Harvard University Press, 1974).

6. Wayne J. Urban, *More Than Science and Sputnik: The National Defense Education Act of 1958* (Tuscaloosa: University of Alabama Press, 2010).

7. Steven Kelman, "Memoir of Steven Kelman '70," in *Our Harvard: Reflections on College Life by Twenty-Two Distinguished Graduates,* ed. Jeffrey L. Lant (New York: Taplinger, 1982), 287–304. See also "Student Memoir: Steven Kelman on Political Activism at Harvard, from 1966 to 1970," in *Essential Documents in the History of American Higher Education,* ed. John R. Thelin (Baltimore: Johns Hopkins University Press, 2014), 253–264.

8. Norman A. Fedde, *Preparing for College Study: A Handbook of Basic Study Skills for All College Students and Preparatory School Students* (New Haven, CT: Reader's Press, 1961).

9. Ralph H. Turner, "Sponsored and Contest Mobility and the School System," *American Sociological Review* 25, no. 6 (1960), 855–867. The nationwide Boys State summer program has been sponsored by the American Legion since 1937 to develop civic, state, and national leadership via mock elections and campaigns. Each high school's principal picked one (male) student who was going to be a senior and who was a leader. Within the ranks of all delegates to the Boys State summer program, two were selected to attend, later in the summer, the Boys Nation workshops and programs. Girls State and Girls Nation were parallel programs.

10. Nicholas Lemann, *The Big Test: The Secret History of the American Meritocracy* (New York: Farrar, Straus and Giroux, 1999).

11. For example, Valerie Strauss, "Answer Sheet: What Does the SAT Measure? Aptitude? Achievement? Anything?," *Washington Post,* April 22, 2014.

12. See, for example, https://www.insidehighered.com/news/2010/06/21/sat.

13. David Boroff, *Campus U.S.A.: Portraits of American Colleges in Action* (New York: Harper, 1961).

14. Bruce J. Friedman, *A Mother's Kisses: A Novel* (Chicago: University of Chicago Press, 1965), 9–12.

15. Daniel J. Boorstin, *The Image: A Guide to Pseudo-Events in America* (New York: Harper Colophon, 1963).

16. "The University's Image and Its Projection," *Report of the President's Committee on the Educational Future of Columbia University* (New York: Columbia University, 1957), 17.

17. "The Public Images of Harvard," *Admissions to Harvard College: A Special Report by the Committee on College Admissions Policy* (Cambridge, MA: Harvard University, February 1960), 14.

18. *Information about Harvard College for Prospective Students: Official Register of Harvard University* 60, no. 22 (1963): 76–77.

19. William C. Fels, "Modern College Usage," *Columbia Forum,* Spring 1959, 41.

20. *Preface to Pomona* (Claremont, CA: Pomona College, 1961).

21. Dorothy E. Finnegan, "A Small Campus on the Hill: A Cultural Ecology of Students and Institution" (paper presentation, Association for the Study of Higher Education, Washington, DC, November 2014).

22. Dorothy E. Finnegan, "Segmentation in the Academic Labor Market: Hiring Cohorts in Comprehensive Universities," *Journal of Higher Education* 64, no. 6 (1993): 621–656.

23. Finnegan, "Small Campus on the Hill," 2–3.

24. Paul Wiseman, "Kids Today: They Don't Work Summer Jobs the Way They Used To," *Lexington Herald-Leader (KY),* June 23, 2017. See also K. J. Dell'Antonia, "The End of the Summer Job," *New York Times,* June 13, 2012.

25. John R. Thelin, "Higher Education's Student Financial Aid Enterprise in Historical Perspective," in *Footing the Tuition Bill: The New Student Loan Sector,* ed. Frederick M. Hess (Washington, DC: American Enterprise Institute, 2007), 19–41.

26. Richard W. Trollinger, memoir and personal correspondence with the author, July 5, 2017.

27. Sam Roberts, "Irving Fradkin, 95: Founded Dollars for Scholars Program," *New York Times,* December 4, 2016.

28. Calvin Trillin, "An Education in Georgia," in *The 60s: The Story of a Decade/The New Yorker,* ed. Henry Finder (New York: Random House, 2016), 124–146 (originally published as "Integrating a Public University," *New Yorker,* July 13, 1963).

29. Peter Wallenstein, "Black Southerners and Non-Black Universities: Desegregating Higher Education, 1936–1967," *History of Higher Education Annual* 19 (1999): 121–148.

30. Melissa J. Kean, *Desegregating Private Higher Education in the South: Duke, Emory, Rice, Tulane, and Vanderbilt* (Baton Rouge: Louisiana State University Press, 2008).

31. Nancy Weiss Malkiel, *"Keep the Damned Women Out": The Struggle for Coeducation* (Princeton, NJ: Princeton University Press, 2016); Linda Greenhouse, "How Smart Women Got the Chance," *New York Review of Books* (April 6, 2017), 21.

32. Steven Brint and Jerome Karabel, *The Diverted Dream: Community Colleges and the Promise of Equal Educational Opportunity, 1900–1985* (New York: Oxford University Press, 1989).

33. *Missions and Functions of the California Community Colleges* (Sacramento: California Postsecondary Education Commission, May 1981).

34. Charles McArthur, "Subculture and Personality during the College Years," *Journal of Educational Sociology* 33, no. 6 (1960): 260–268. See also Charles McArthur, "Personalities of Public and Private School Boys," *Harvard Educational Review* (1954): 256–262.

35. Katherine Kinkead, *How an Ivy League College Decides Admissions* (New York: W. W. Norton, 1961).

36. *Admissions to Harvard College: A Special Report by the Committee on College Admissions Policy* (Cambridge, MA: Harvard University, February 1960).

37. Alexander Astin and Calvin B. T. Lee for the Carnegie Commission on Higher Education, *The Invisible Colleges: A Profile of Small, Private Colleges with Limited Resources* (New York: McGraw-Hill, 1972).

38. Alden B. Dunham for the Carnegie Commission on Higher Education, *Colleges of the Forgotten Americans: A Profile of State Colleges and Regional Universities* (New York: McGraw-Hill, 1969).

39. "Brown Grows the Ivy," *Newsweek*, October 12, 1964; Astin and Lee, *The Invisible Colleges.*

40. "Is the Ivy League Still the Best?," *Newsweek*, November 23, 1964, 66.

41. Christopher Tudico, "Beyond Black and White: Researching the History of Latinos in American Higher Education," in *The History of U.S. Higher Education: Methods for Understanding the Past*, ed. Marybeth Gasman (New York: Routledge, 2010), 163–171; Sharon S. Lee, "Where Is Your Home? Writing the History of Asian Americans in Higher Education," in Gasman, ed., *History of U.S. Higher Education*, 150–162.

42. Synnott, *Half-Opened Door.*

Chapter Three: The Knowledge Industry

1. Ellen Condliffe Lagemann, *Private Power for the Public Good: A History of the Carnegie Foundation for the Advancement of Teaching* (Middletown, CT: Wesleyan University Press, 1983).

2. Clark Kerr, *The Uses of the University*, 5th ed. (Cambridge, MA: Harvard University Press, 2001).

3. "Education: Master Planner," *Time*, October 17, 1960, 60–68.

4. "Education: Master Planner."

5. "The Land: The Man with a Plan," *Time*, September 6, 1963, 82–86.

6. LaDale C. Winling, *Building the Ivory Tower: Universities and Metropolitan Development in the Twentieth Century* (Philadelphia: University of Pennsylvania Press, 2018).

7. W. Bruce Leslie and Kenneth P. O'Brien, *Sixty-Four Campuses—One University: The Story of SUNY* (Albany: State University of New York Press, 2017). See also W. Bruce Leslie, Kenneth P. O'Brien, and John B. Clark, eds., *SUNY at Sixty* (New York: Acumen Press, 2010).

8. Richard M. Freeland, *Academia's Golden Age: Universities in Massachusetts, 1945–1970* (Oxford: Oxford University Press, 1992).

9. Robert O. Berdahl, *Statewide Coordination of Higher Education* (Washington, DC: American Council on Education, 1971).

10. *Donahoe Report: California Master Plan for Postsecondary Education* (1960), California State Senate Bill 33, section 1, division 16.5 of the Education Code, Higher Education Chapter 1, General Provisions. See also "The 1960 California Master Plan for Higher Education," in *Essential Documents in the History of American Higher Education*, ed. John R. Thelin (Baltimore: Johns Hopkins University Press, 2014), 237–243.

11. "Education: Master Planner."

12. David W. Breneman and Chester E. Finn, Jr., eds., *Public Policy and Private Higher Education* (Washington, DC: Brookings Institution, 1978).

13. Higher Education Act of 1965, Pub. L. No. 89-329 (November 8, 1965).

14. "Higher Education's Student Financial Aid Enterprise in Historical Perspective," in *Footing the Tuition Bill: The New Student Loan Sector*, ed. Frederick M. Hess (Washington, DC: American Enterprise Institute, 2007), 19–41.

15. Chester E. Finn, Jr., *Scholars, Dollars and Bureaucrats* (Washington, DC: Brookings Institution, 1978).

16. Hugh Davis Graham and Nancy Diamond, "Comparing Universities in the Golden Age of the 1960s," in *The Rise of American Research Universities: Elites and Challengers in the Postwar Era* (Baltimore: Johns Hopkins University Press, 1997), 51–83.

17. Clark Kerr, "The Frantic Race to Remain Contemporary," in *The Contemporary University: U.S.A.: A Timely Appraisal*, ed. Robert S. Morison (Boston: Beacon Press, 1968), 19–38.

18. Daniel Golden, "The CIA's Favorite College President: How the CIA Secretly Exploits Higher Education," *Chronicle of Higher Education*, October 20, 2017.

19. David Halberstam, *The Best and the Brightest* (New York: Random House, 1972).

20. Kai Bird, *The Color of Truth: McGeorge and William Bundy, Brothers in Arms: A Biography* (New York: Simon and Schuster, 1998). See also Mark

Danner, "Members of the Club," review of *The Color of Truth: McGeorge Bundy and William Bundy: Brothers in Arms*, by Kai Bird, *New York Times*, April 4, 1999.

21. John Ernst, *Forging a Fateful Alliance: Michigan State University and the Vietnam War* (East Lansing: Michigan State University Press, 1998).

22. Robert Arnove, ed., *Philanthropy and Cultural Imperialism: The Foundations at Home and Abroad* (Bloomington: Indiana University Press, 1982).

23. Homer T. Babbidge and Robert M. Rosenzweig, *The Federal Interest in Higher Education* (New York: McGraw-Hill, 1962). See also Finn, *Scholars, Dollars and Bureaucrats*.

24. Michael Schudson, "Organizing the Meritocracy: A History of the College Entrance Examination Board," *Harvard Educational Review* 42, no. 1 (1972): 34–69. See also Nicholas Lemann, *The Big Test: The Secret History of the American Meritocracy* (New York: Farrar, Straus and Giroux, 1999).

25. Rodney T. Hartnett, *College and University Trustees: Their Backgrounds, Roles, and Educational Attitudes* (Princeton, NJ: Educational Testing Service, 1969), 19–40; Elizabeth L. and Michael Useem, eds., *The Education Establishment* (Englewood Cliffs, NJ: Prentice-Hall, 1974).

26. As quoted in W. J. Rorabaugh, *Berkeley at War: The Sixties* (New York: Oxford University Press, 1989), 11.

27. James A. Perkins, *The University in Transition* (Princeton, NJ: Princeton University Press, 1966).

28. Perkins, *University in Transition*, 57.

29. Howard R. Bowen, "The Goal of Individuality at Iowa" (inaugural address), *Des Moines Sunday Register*, December 13, 1964.

30. See, for example, Howard R. Bowen, *Investment in Learning: The Individual and Social Value of American Higher Education* (San Francisco: Jossey-Bass, 1977).

31. Earl F. Cheit, ed., *The Business Establishment* (New York: John Wiley & Sons, 1964).

32. Charles E. Davidson, ed., "William and Mary as a Prototype of a Miniversity," in *Report of the Self-Study Committee of The College of William and Mary* (Williamsburg, VA: The College of William and Mary, 1974), 5–20.

33. Christopher Jencks and David Riesman, *The Academic Revolution* (Garden City, NY: Doubleday Anchor, 1968).

34. "Deukmejian Argues for UC Student Tuition Plan," *The Daily News* [Whittier, CA], October 14, 1967.

35. Dorothy E. Finnegan, "Segmentation in the Academic Labor Market: Hiring Cohorts in Comprehensive Universities," *Journal of Higher Education* 64, no. 6 (Nov–Dec 1993): 621–656. See also Hugh Davis Graham and Nancy Diamond, "Comparing Universities in the Golden Age of the 1960s," in *The Rise of American Research Universities: Elites and Challengers in the Postwar Era* (Baltimore: Johns Hopkins University Press, 1997).

36. Quoted in obituary release, UC Berkeley Public Affairs, "Former UC President Clark Kerr, a National Leader in Higher Education, Dies at 92," *UC Berkeley News*, December 2, 2003.

37. Gray Brechin, "Classical Dreams and Concrete Realities," *California Monthly*, March 1978, 12–15; John R. Thelin and James Yankovich, "Bricks and Mortar: Architecture and the Study of Higher Education," in *Higher Education: Handbook of Theory and Research*, ed. John C. Smart (New York: Agathon Press, 1986), 57–83. See also Thomas R. Gaines, *The Campus as a Work of Art* (New York: Praeger, 1991).

Chapter Four: Student Activities and Activism

1. Robert Schwartz, *Deans of Men and the Shaping of Modern College Culture* (New York: Palgrave Macmillan, 2010).

2. Roger G. Baldwin and John R. Thelin, "Thanks for the Memories: The Fusion of Quantitative and Qualitative Research on College Students and the College Experience," in *Higher Education: Handbook of Theory and Research*, ed. John C. Smart (New York: Agathon Press, 1986), 337–360.

3. See "Vassar Myths and Legends," at the online *Vassar Encyclopedia*. This episode has been attributed to Jane Fonda, http://vcencyclopedia.vassar.edu /vassar-myths-legends/.

4. Dean of Students at the University of California, Berkeley, as quoted in "Education: Master Planner," *Time*, October 17, 1960, 60–68.

5. See "Town and Gown: Anthony Wood's Riot at Oxford," in *Essential Documents in the History of American Higher Education*, ed. John R. Thelin (Baltimore: Johns Hopkins University Press, 2014), 2–6.

6. J. A. Latham and T. G. Plate, *Where the Boys Are* (Amherst, MA: Amherst Publishing, 1966).

7. Dorothy E. Finnegan, "A Small Campus on the Hill: A Cultural Ecology of Students and Institution" (paper presentation, Association for the Study of Higher Education, Washington, DC, November 2014).

8. "Morals, Sex & The Pembroke Girl," *Time*, October 8, 1965. See also Richard Blumenthal, "Doctor at Brown Upheld in Giving Girls Birth Pills," *Harvard Crimson*, September 29, 1965.

9. Katy Abbott, "Free Speech Movement Issue 2014: For Women in the Movement, a Dual Struggle," *Daily Californian*, October 10, 2014. See also Ruth Rosen, *The World Split Open: How the Modern Women's Movement Changed America* (New York: Penguin Books, 2000); Linda Eisenmann, *Higher Education for Women in Post-War America, 1945–1970* (Baltimore: Johns Hopkins University Press, 2009).

10. Linda Greenhouse, "How Smart Women Got the Chance," *New York Review of Books* (April 6, 2017). See also Nancy Weiss Malkiel, *"Keep the Damned Women Out": The Struggle for Coeducation* (Princeton, NJ: Princeton University Press, 2016).

11. Weiss Malkiel, *"Keep the Damned Women Out."*

12. See, for example, the summary and case study data in P. J. Bickel, E. A. Hammel, and J. W. O'Connell, "Sex Bias in Graduate Admissions: Data from Berkeley," *Science* 187, no. 4175 (1975): 398–404.

13. Barbara Solomon Miller, *In the Company of Educated Women: A History of Women and Higher Education in America* (New Haven, CT: Yale University Press, 1989). For a critical account of the women's colleges, see Liva Baker's *I'm Radcliffe! Fly Me! The Seven Sisters and the Failure of Women's Education* (New York: Macmillan, 1976).

14. Frank Newman, "Chapter Eleven: Barriers to Women," in *Report on Higher Education* (Washington, DC: US Department of Health, Education and Welfare, March 1971), 51–56. See also the policy analyses and implications as discussed in Eisenmann, *Higher Education for Women in Post-War America*.

15. Pennsylvania State University, *Years of Crises: The 1960s* (University Park: Pennsylvania State University Archives).

16. Greg and Lindy Lyndon Boeck, "1964 All Over Again," *Centre Piece: The Alumni Magazine of Centre College*, Winter 2016, 6–11.

17. Finnegan, "Small Campus on the Hill," 11.

18. *The Campus Unrest Collections* (California State University Northridge Oviatt Library, April 29, 2014).

19. Bob Baker, "BSU, SDS Join in Occupation of Administration Building," *Daily Sundial,* November 5, 1968.

20. Steven Lubar, "'Do Not Fold, Spindle or Mutilate': A Cultural History of the Punch Card," *Journal of American Culture* 15 (1992), 40–53.

21. Clark Kerr, "The Knowledge Factory" speech of 1964, in *Berkeley in the Sixties*, directed by Mark Kitchell (New York: First Run Features, 1990).

22. William J. McGill, *The Year of the Monkey: Revolt on Campus, 1968–69* (New York: McGraw-Hill, 1982).

23. Jeffrey A. Turner, *Sitting In and Speaking Out: Student Movements in the American South, 1960–1970* (Athens: University of Georgia Press, 2010). See also Christopher J. Broadhurst, "'We Didn't Fire a Shot, We Didn't Burn a Building:' The Student Reaction at North Carolina State University to the Kent State Shootings, May 1970," *North Carolina Historical Review* 87, no. 3 (July 2010): 283–309; William C. Hine, "Civil Rights and Campus Wrongs: South Carolina State College Students Protest, 1955–1968," *South Carolina Historical Magazine* 97, no. 4 (1996): 310–331.

24. Broadhurst, "'We Didn't Fire a Shot, We Didn't Burn a Building.'"

25. Ibram H. Rogers, "The Black Campus Movement and the Institutionalization of Black Studies, 1965–1970," *Journal of African American Studies* 16, no. 1 (2012): 21–40. See also Quintard Taylor, "The Civil Rights Movement in the American West: Black Protest in Seattle, 1960–1970," *Journal of Negro History* 80, no. 1 (1995): 1–14; Clyde Z. Nunn, "Support of Civil Liberties among College Students," *Social Problems* 20, no. 3 (1973): 300–310.

26. George Lowery, "A Campus Takeover That Symbolized an Era of Change," *Cornell Chronicle*, April 2009.

27. David Streitfeld, "Father-Son Revolutionaries," *New York Times*, July 23, 2017.

28. John R. Thelin, "Horizontal History and Higher Education," in *The History of U.S. Higher Education: Methods for Understanding the Past*, ed. Marybeth Gasman (New York: Routledge, 2010), 71–83.

29. Steven Kelman, "The New Left Takes Control of Our Mass Media," in *Push Comes to Shove: The Escalation of Student Protest* (Boston: Houghton Mifflin, 1970), 202–219.

30. Kelman, *Push Comes to Shove*, 169.

31. Theodore Roszak, *The Making of a Counter Culture: Reflections on the Technocratic Society and Its Youthful Opposition* (Garden City, NY: Doubleday Anchor, 1969).

32. Charles A. Reich, *The Greening of America* (New York: Random House, 1970).

33. Streitfeld, "Father-Son Revolutionaries."

34. See, for example, Alexander Astin, *Four Critical Years: Effects of College on Beliefs, Values, and Knowledge* (San Francisco: Jossey-Bass, 1977).

35. Steven Brint and Jerome Karabel, *The Diverted Dream: Community Colleges and the Promise of Educational Opportunity in America, 1900–1985* (New York: Oxford University Press, 1989). See also Thomas Diener, *Growth of an American Invention: A Documentary History of the Junior and Community College Movement* (Westport, CT: Greenwood Press, 1986).

36. Burton R. Clark, "The 'Cooling-Out' Function in Higher Education," *American Journal of Sociology* 65, no. 6 (1960): 569–571.

37. Alexander Astin, "Implications for Policy and Practice," in *Four Critical Years*, 242–262. See also foreword to Alexander Astin, *What Matters Most in College? "Four Critical Years" Revisited* (San Francisco: Jossey-Bass, 1993).

38. Earl F. Cheit, *The New Depression in Higher Education: A Study of Financial Conditions at Forty-One Colleges and Universities* (New York: McGraw-Hill, 1971).

Chapter Five: Colleges and Curriculum

1. Larry Cuban, "Teaching and Learning at the Research University," *Peer Review* 2, no. 4 (2000): 15–19.

2. John R. Thelin, "A Legacy of Lethargy? Curricular Change in Historical Perspective," *Peer Review* 2, no. 4 (2000): 9–14. See also Frederick Rudolph, "The Last Fifty Years," in *Curriculum: A History of the American Undergraduate Course of Study since 1636* (San Francisco: Jossey-Bass, 1966), 245–289. The quote about the curriculum and moving a graveyard has been attributed to numerous public figures, including Calvin Coolidge and Woodrow Wilson;

·

Daniel Bell, *The Reforming of General Education: The Columbia College Experience in Its National Setting* (New York: Columbia University Press, 1965).

3. Susan Berman, *The Underground Guide to the College of Your Choice* (New York: Signet Books, 1971).

4. Gerald Grant and David Riesman, *The Perpetual Dream: Reform and Experiment in the American College* (Chicago: University of Chicago Press, 1978).

5. Burton R. Clark, *The Distinctive College: Antioch, Reed and Swarthmore* (Chicago: Aldine, 1970).

6. Arthur Levine, *Handbook on Undergraduate Curriculum* (San Francisco: Jossey-Bass for the Carnegie Council Series, 1978).

7. Christopher Jencks and David Riesman, *The Academic Revolution* (Garden City, NY: Doubleday Anchor, 1968).

8. John R. Thelin, "Gilt by Association: Higher Education's 'Golden Age,' 1945 to 1970," in *A History of American Higher Education*, 2nd ed. (Baltimore: Johns Hopkins University Press, 2011), 296. See also Verne A. Stadtman, *The University of California, 1868–1968* (New York: McGraw-Hill, 1970), 254.

9. Gerald Grant and David Riesman, *The Perpetual Dream: Reform and Experiment in the American College* (Chicago: University of Chicago Press, 1978).

10. Frank Newman, "The Lockstep," in *Report on Higher Education* (Washington, DC: US Department of Health, Education, and Welfare, 1971), 4–7.

11. James Axtell, *The School upon a Hill: Education and Society in Colonial New England* (New Haven, CT: Yale University Press, 1976).

12. Gerald Grant and David Riesman, "New College," in *The Perpetual Dream*, 218–252.

13. Franklin D. Patterson and Charles R. Longsworth, *The Making of a College* (Cambridge: Massachusetts Institute of Technology Press, 1966).

14. Robert C. Birney, "Hampshire College," *New Directions for Higher Education* 82 (1993): 9–22.

15. Ken Tompkins and Rob Gregg, eds., *Reaching 40: The Richard Stockton College of New Jersey* (Galloway: Richard Stockton College of New Jersey, 2011).

16. William T. Daly, "Inside the Stockton Idea: Elite Education for State College Students," presented on the college's website http://intraweb.stockton.edu/eyos/reaching40/stockton_idea.html, drawing from Tompkins and Gregg, *Reaching 40*.

17. Quoted in Tompkins and Gregg, *Reaching 40*.

18. Quoted in Tompkins and Greg, *Reaching 40*. See also "Stockton Celebrates Its 40th Anniversary," *Stockton Times: Our Community News*, September 23, 2011.

19. Robert C. Birney, conversation with the author, Williamsburg, VA, March 4, 1986.

20. Pat Berdge et al., *Solomon's House: A Self-Conscious History of Cowell College* (Felton, CA: Big Tree Press, 1970).

21. Author's interview with Wolfgang Tatsch, class of 1969, February 8, 1974.

22. Author's interview with Alan J. DeYoung, alumnus of Cowell College, University of California Santa Cruz, class of 1969, September 5, 2017.

23. Thelin, "Gilt by Association," 287. See also "The University of California: The Biggest University in the World Is a Show Place for Mass Education," *Life,* October 25, 1948, 88–112.

24. Larry Cuban, *How Scholars Trumped Teachers: Change without Reform in University Curriculum, Teaching, and Research, 1890–1990* (New York: Columbia University Teachers College Press, 1999).

25. Peter C. Sprague and Peter Ujlaki, eds., *Bulletin of Brown Semiversity* (Providence, RI, *The Brown Jug,* 1968).

26. Luther Spoehr, "Making Brown University's 'New Curriculum' in 1969: The Importance of Context and Contingency," *Rhode Island History* 74, no. 2 (2016): 52–71.

27. Benson Snyder, *The Hidden Curriculum* (New York: Alfred A. Knopf, 1971).

28. Don Robertson, *The Halls of Yearning: An Indictment of Formal Education, A Manifesto of Student Liberation* (Long Beach, CA: Andrew Printing, 1969).

29. Kirk Carapezza, "Zombies, Garbage and Vampires? It's Not a Nightmare, It's Your College Course Catalogue," *National Public Radio Morning Edition,* August 18, 2016.

30. Earl F. Cheit, *The Useful Arts and the Liberal Tradition* (New York: McGraw-Hill, 1974).

31. The Carnegie Commission on Higher Education, *The Open-Door Colleges: Policies for Community Colleges* (New York: McGraw-Hill, June 1970).

32. *Missions and Functions of the California Community Colleges* (Sacramento: California Postsecondary Education Commission, 1981).

Chapter Six: College Sports

1. Karen Crouse, "A Bond between Champions: How Two Teenage Stars, Decades Apart, Struck up a Friendship and Found Insight," *New York Times,* July 9, 2017. See also about high school tennis player Claire Liu, "Decision Time: Go to College or Turn Pro?," *New York Times,* August 16, 2017.

2. John R. Thelin, "California and the Colleges: Part 2," *California Historical Quarterly* 56, no. 3 (1977): 245–246.

3. Jack Scott, ed., *The Athletic Revolution* (New York: Free Press, 1971).

4. The National Association of Intercollegiate Athletics (NAIA), however, did allow freshmen to play varsity sports and also allowed four years of eligibility.

5. John R. Thelin, "Critics and Controversies, 1960 to 1980," in *Games Colleges Play: Scandal and Reform in Intercollegiate Athletics* (Baltimore: Johns Hopkins University Press, 1997), 157.

6. Ronald Smith, *Play by Play: Radio, Television, and Big-Time College Sports* (Baltimore: Johns Hopkins University Press, 2001), 106–108.

7. Arthur A. Fleisher, III, Brian L. Goff, and Robert D. Tollison, *The National Collegiate Athletic Association: A Study in Cartel Behavior* (Chicago: University of Chicago Press, 1992). See also Paul R. Lawrence, *Unsportsmanlike Conduct: The National Collegiate Athletic Association and the Business of College Football* (New York: Praeger, 1987).

8. James Michener, "Colleges and Universities," *Sports in America* (New York: McGraw-Hill, 1976).

9. Thelin, "Critics and Controversies," 154–178.

10. Murray Sperber, *College Sports, Inc.: The Athletic Department vs. the University* (New York: Henry Holt, 1990).

11. John R. Thelin, "Good Sports? Historical Perspectives on the Political Economy of Intercollegiate Athletics in the Era of Title IX, 1972 to 1997," *Journal of Higher Education* 7, no. 4 (2000): 391–410. See also Welch Suggs, *A Place on the Team: The Triumph and Tragedy of Title IX* (Princeton, NJ: Princeton University Press, 2006).

12. Harry Edwards, *The Revolt of the Black Athlete* (New York: Free Press, 1969).

13. Charles H. Martin, "Hold That (Color) Line! Black Exclusion and Southeastern Conference Football," in *Higher Education and the Civil Rights Movement: White Supremacy, Black Southerners, and College Campuses*, ed. Peter Wallenstein (Gainesville: University Press of Florida, 2008). See also John R. Thelin, "World War II: Essay Review," *History of Education Quarterly* 51, no. 3 (2011): 389–396.

14. Mike Lopresti, "Loyola's 'Game of Change' an Afterthought," *USA Today Sports*, March 12, 2013.

15. Michael Oriard, "College Football's Season of Discontent," *Slate*, September 3, 2009. See also Michael Oriard, *Bowled Over: Big-Time College Football from the Sixties to the BCS Era* (Chapel Hill: University of North Carolina Press, 2009).

16. Dave Meggyesy, *Out of Their League* (Berkeley, CA: Ramparts Press, 1970); Gary Shaw, *Meat on the Hoof: The Hidden World of Texas Football* (New York: St. Martin's Press, 1972).

17. Ike Balbus, "Politics as Sports: The Political Ascendency of the Sports Metaphor in America," *Monthly Review* 26, no. 10 (1975): 27–39.

Conclusion: The New City of Intellect

1. William W. Scranton, *The Report of the President's Commission on Campus Unrest* (Washington, DC: US Government Printing Office, 1970). See also Alvin C. Eurich, *Campus 1980: The Shape of the Future of American Higher Education* (New York: Dell, 1968); Stephen R. Graubard, "University Cities in the Year 2000," in *Toward the Year 2000: Works in Progress*, ed. Daniel Bell (Boston: Houghton Mifflin, 1968); Harold L. Hodgkinson, *Institutions in Transition: A Profile of Change in Higher Education* (New York: McGraw-Hill, 1971); Stephen R. Graubard, ed., "American Higher Education: Toward an Uncertain Future," *Daedalus* 103, no. 4; and 104, no. 1; "What Went Wrong in the '60s? Ford Foundation Turns Retrospective Eyes on Educational Funding, Improvement Programs," *The Ford Foundation Guidepost Newsletter*, January 26, 1973.

2. Trow, "Reflections on the Transition from Elite to Mass to Universal Higher Education," 1–42.

3. Steven Brint, ed., *The Future of the City of Intellect: The Changing American University* (Stanford, CA: Stanford University Press, 2002).

4. Kenneth T. Andrews, "When Movements Stall: How Protest Works," *New York Times*, October 21, 2017.

5. "Behind L.B.J.'s Decision Not to Run in '68," *New York Times*, April 16, 1988.

6. Colin Moynihan, "How Police Surveillance Units Became Unlikely Historians," *New York Times*, October 10, 2017.

7. David Greenberg, "The March on the Pentagon: An Oral History," *New York Times*, October 22, 2017.

8. LaDale C. Winling, *Building the Ivory Tower: Universities and Metropolitan Development in the Twentieth Century* (Philadelphia: University of Pennsylvania Press, 2018).

9. "Men's Fashion: A Return to Elegance," *New York Times*, May 2, 1972; Veronica Manlow, *Designing Clothes: Culture and Organization of the Fashion Industry* (New Brunswick, NJ: Transaction Publishers, 2011).

10. Earl F. Cheit, *The New Depression in Higher Education: A Study of the Financial Conditions at Forty-One Colleges and Universities* (New York: McGraw-Hill, 1971).

11. The Carnegie Foundation for the Advancement of Teaching, *Three Thousand Futures: The Next Twenty Years for Higher Education* (San Francisco: Jossey-Bass, 1980).

12. Lewis B. Mayhew, *Surviving the Eighties: Strategies and Procedures for Solving Fiscal and Enrollment Problems* (San Francisco: Jossey-Bass, 1980).

13. Chester E. Finn, *Scholars, Dollars and Bureaucrats* (Washington, DC: Brookings Institution, 1978).

14. Golden, "The CIA's Favorite College President," 1.

15. David Brooks, "The Abbie Hoffman of the Right," *New York Times*, September 26, 2017.

16. Bickel et al., "Sex Bias in Graduate Admissions," 393–404.

17. Clark Kerr, "The Future of the City of Intellect," in *The Uses of the University*, 5th ed. (Cambridge, MA: Harvard University Press, 2001).

18. Theodore Roszak, ed., *The Dissenting Academy: Essays Criticizing the Teaching of Humanities in American Universities* (New York: Pantheon Books, 1968).

19. Sam Roberts, "Douglas Dowd, 97, Activist and a Critic of Capitalism," *New York Times*, September 16, 2017.

20. John R. Thelin, "Institutional History in Our Own Time: Higher Education's Shift from Managerial Revolution to Enterprising Evolution," *CASE International Journal of Educational Advancement* 1, no. 1 (2000): 9–23.

21. John W. Gardner, *Excellence: Can We Be Equal and Excellent Too?* (New York: W. W. Norton, 1961).

22. "The T&C Guide to College: Admissions Anxiety," *Town & Country* (August 2017), 88–97; Yishai Schwartz, "Admissions Anxiety," *Town & Country* (August 2017), 89–91.

23. Charles T. Clotfelter, "The College Chasm: How Market Forces Have Made American Higher Education Radically Unequal," *Harvard Magazine*, November–December 2017.

24. William G. Bowen, Matthew M. Chingos, and Michael S. McPherson, *Crossing the Finish Line: Completing College at America's Public Universities* (Princeton, NJ: Princeton University Press, 2009).

25. Legislative Analyst's Office, *Overview of Higher Education in California* (Sacramento: Assembly Select Committee on the Master Plan for Higher Education in California, August 31, 2017). See also John R. Thelin, "California's Higher Education: From American Dream to Dilemma," *The Conversation*, November 1, 2017, https://theconversation.com/californias-higher-education -from-american-dream-to-dilemma-84557.

26. Gary C. Fethke and Andrew J. Policano, *Public No More: A New Path to Excellence for America's Public Universities* (Stanford, CA: Stanford University Press, 2012).

27. "Higher Education in California: One State, Two Systems," *The Economist*, August 11, 2012.

28. Jon Marcus, "The Decline of the Midwest's Public Universities Threatens to Wreck Its Most Vibrant Economies," *The Atlantic*, October 15, 2017.

29. John R. Thelin, *American Higher Education: Issues and Institutions* (New York: Routledge, 2017).

ABOUT THE AUTHOR

John R. Thelin is the University Research Professor of Higher Education and Public Policy at the University of Kentucky, where he has received the Provost's Award for Outstanding Teaching and the Sturgill Award for Outstanding Faculty Contribution to Graduate Studies. He graduated from Sierra High School in Whittier, California, in 1965 and attended Brown University, where he concentrated in history, was elected to Phi Beta Kappa, worked as a student waiter, and was a varsity letterman in wrestling. John was a graduate student at the University of California, Berkeley, from 1969 to 1973, after which he was a lecturer there. At the Claremont Colleges, John was Assistant Dean of Admissions at Pomona College and Visiting Professor at Claremont Graduate School. He has been Research Director for the Association of Independent California Colleges and Universities. John was Chancellor Professor at The College of William and Mary in Virginia, where he received the Phi Beta Kappa Award for Outstanding Faculty Scholarship, served as faculty liaison to the Board of Visitors and was president of the Faculty Assembly. Before joining the University of Kentucky faculty in 1996 he was Professor of Higher Education and Philanthropy at Indiana University.

John's books include *A History of American Higher Education, Games Colleges Play: Scandal and Reform in Intercollegiate Sports*, and *Essential Documents in the History of American Higher Education*, all published by Johns Hopkins University Press. He has been president of the Association for the Study of Higher Education (ASHE) and received the association's award for outstanding research. John has received two major research grants from the Spencer Foundation. In 2006 he was selected for the Ivy League's fiftieth anniversary Hall of Fame for outstanding alumni student-athletes.